jMonkeyEngine 3.0 Cookbook

Over 80 practical recipes to expand and enrich
your jMonkeyEngine skill set with a close focus
on game development

Rickard Edén

[PACKT] open source ✲
PUBLISHING   community experience distilled

BIRMINGHAM - MUMBAI

jMonkeyEngine 3.0 Cookbook

First published: August 2014

Production reference: 1060814

Published by Packt Publishing Ltd.
Livery Place
35 Livery Street
Birmingham B3 2PB, UK.

ISBN 978-1-78328-647-8

www.packtpub.com

Cover image by Aniket Sawant (aniket_sawant_photography@hotmail.com)

Credits

Author

Rickard Edén

Reviewers

Abner Coimbre

Benjamin Jakobus

Nicolas Legeay

Nicholas Mamo

Glauco Márdano

Commissioning Editor

Rebecca Youé

Acquisition Editor

Rebecca Youé

Content Development Editor

Manasi Pandire

Technical Editors

Manal Pednekar

Anand Singh

Ankita Thakur

Copy Editors

Gladson Monteiro

Adithi Shetty

Stuti Srivastava

Laxmi Subramanian

Project Coordinator

Aaron. S. Lazar

Proofreaders

Simran Bhogal

Ameesha Green

Paul Hindle

Indexer

Priya Subramani

Graphics

Abhinash Sahu

Production Coordinator

Aparna Bhagat

Cover Work

Aparna Bhagat

Sushma Redkar

About the Author

Rickard Edén is a Java and Android development consultant, game developer, and lifelong game enthusiast, based in Gothenburg, Sweden. Having worked in the past as a designer in the gaming industry, Rickard has worked on a number of different genres and picked up tricks of the trade from many disciplines. He has a pragmatic approach to programming and has developed games for many years using jMonkeyEngine.

It is now his intention to help other developers by sharing what he's learned so far with this book.

> Writing this book has been a tremendous experience, and it certainly could not have been possible without other people clearing the way.
>
> If I have been the storyteller, the heroes of the book are the people who have created jMonkeyEngine. From its first incarnation until now, the third, when it's a fully fledged game development environment.

About the Reviewers

Abner Coimbre, before becoming a technical reviewer for this book, was a lead developer for an educational game funded by the National Science Foundation (NSF Award No. 0835990) where he used jMonkeyEngine to achieve most of the technical milestones that were required for the project. At the time of this writing, he is a system software engineer at NASA, working with a Command and Control System. His home page is `abnercoimbre.com`.

> Sending out warm regards to some of the principal investigators while I was working for the National Science Foundation: Dr. Agustin Rullán, Dr. Bienvenido Vélez, Dr. Cristina Pomales, and Dr. Félix Zapata. It was awesome working with you guys. I appreciate the guidance and scoldings of Linda Crawford, an amazing mentor and human being. I thank all the staff involved in the making of this book, particularly Aaron. S. Lazar for putting up with my erratic work schedule. And, of course, I thank the author many times over for having written a book that will truly help people leverage the interesting features that jMonkeyEngine provides.

Benjamin Jakobus graduated with a BSc in Computer Science from University College Cork, after which he cofounded an Irish start-up. He returned to the university one year later and obtained an MSc in Advanced Computing from Imperial College, London, after which he took up a position as a software engineer in IBM, Ireland. He currently lives in Brazil where he is pursuing a PhD at PUC-Rio.

Nicolas Legeay discovered jMonkeyEngine in 2004, during his studies, when he had to choose an environment to elaborate on and develop a 3D online game project that he had to execute on his own.

It has been really exciting for him to be here at the start of this wonderful engine, and Nicolas then developed several projects with it, to explore all the possibilities that JME allowed then.

Originally a software developer, Nicolas had the opportunity to discover quality assurance in the industrial sector of the rail in 2006.

Over the QA activity, he especially appreciates test automation. His professional experience helped him acquire a proven expertise in this practice. Indeed, in charge of elaborating test strategies in various contexts, test automation always proved a relevant choice; also, he knew when to use the most adapted tools.

Being tech-savvy, Nicolas succeeded in elaborating innovative ways to build automata, such as image recognition and CAPTCHA hacking, making him a very well-appreciated resource regarding his highly sought skills.

Nicolas has had the privilege to work with various and prestigious companies, such as National Opera of Paris, France and PMU, France, on big and crucial projects.

Nicholas Mamo, born in Malta in 1996, is a full-time student and a freelance writer. He is a self-taught game developer and has been developing games at Nyphoon Games since 2008, regularly blogging about his projects on `nyphoon.com`. His articles have been published on Eye For Games, IGDA, and Tuts+, among others. Nicholas is also passionate about football and his opinion pieces have appeared on a number of websites.

Glauco Márdano is 23 years old, and graduated in Systems Analysis. He works as a Java programmer in a private company in Brazil. He has studied a lot about game programming just for fun, and he dreams of building his own business someday.

He was also the technical reviewer for *jMonkeyEngine 3.0 Beginners Guide* and *Augmented Reality for Android Application Development* for Packt Publishing.

> Well, I'd like to thank everybody from jMonkeyEngine's forum, because I've learned a lot from them; the forum is very active. I'd also like to thank Aaron. S. Lazar from Packt Publishing for his help while reviewing this book.

www.PacktPub.com

Support files, eBooks, discount offers, and more

You might want to visit www.PacktPub.com for support files and downloads related to your book.

Did you know that Packt offers eBook versions of every book published, with PDF and ePub files available? You can upgrade to the eBook version at www.PacktPub.com and as a print book customer, you are entitled to a discount on the eBook copy. Get in touch with us at service@packtpub.com for more details.

At www.PacktPub.com, you can also read a collection of free technical articles, sign up for a range of free newsletters and receive exclusive discounts and offers on Packt books and eBooks.

http://PacktLib.PacktPub.com

Do you need instant solutions to your IT questions? PacktLib is Packt's online digital book library. Here, you can access, read and search across Packt's entire library of books.

Why Subscribe?

- ▸ Fully searchable across every book published by Packt
- ▸ Copy and paste, print and bookmark content
- ▸ On demand and accessible via web browser

Free Access for Packt account holders

If you have an account with Packt at www.PacktPub.com, you can use this to access PacktLib today and view nine entirely free books. Simply use your login credentials for immediate access.

Table of Contents

Preface

The overall goal of this book is to provide you with an extensive toolbox of hands-on development tips for jMonkeyEngine that will help you be well prepared for a wide range of projects.

The recipes are written from a practical point of view, and I strived to make sure that each recipe has an outcome that can be used directly in a game. An exception to this is *Chapter 7, Networking with SpiderMonkey*, where we will start from the absolute ground level and work ourselves upwards. *Chapter 1, SDK Game Development Hub*, also stands out as it contains a few more general tips applicable to development in general.

Due to the variation in game projects, another principle has been used to create recipes that have a wide usage potential. Some of the more advanced recipes are exceptions to this rule. They have a more narrow use but contain techniques that can be applied to other implementations. FPS, RTS, and RPG games will be explored in many of the recipes. Naturally, within these genres, games differ widely as well, but hopefully you will find that the examples can be used in your game project with a minimum amount of modification.

In general, I hope that this book will provide you with many tips on how to overcome common hurdles in game projects so that you can focus on the creative parts that make your game stand out.

Common development concepts in jMonkeyEngine

Some common development concepts in jMonkeyEngine are as follows:

- ▶ **Spatial**: Central to all things in the scene graph is the Spatial. In jMonkeyEngine, it's an abstract class, defining translation (location), rotation, and scale of an object. Imagine it as a purely logical object without a physical body. A Spatial is extended into either a Geometry or Node.

- **Geometry**: This extends Spatial. This class is what gives a Spatial its physical presence in the world. It has a Mesh defining its form and shape, and a Material, telling us what the surface of the Mesh looks like.

- **Node**: This extends Spatial. It can have several children attached, and can in turn be attached to a parent. Since it's a Spatial, it has a translation, rotation, and scale, which it will propagate to its children. Unlike a Geometry, it can't have a Mesh. It doesn't have a visible presence in itself.

- **Transforms**: Translation, rotation, and scale are commonly referred to as a Spatial's transforms. A Spatial has both local and world transforms. The local transform is always in relation to its parent (if any). The world transform is the absolute transform with all possible parent transforms propagated together. As an example, imagine your own local translation being the position you have on Earth. Your world translation could be your local translation added to the Earth's local translation in its orbit around the Sun. Normally, you will only work with local transforms. World transforms are handled by the engine.

- **Mesh**: This is made up of triangles. In a Mesh, you will find long lists called buffers detailing the points of these triangles (vertices), how the surfaces of these triangles are made (indices), their colors, normal, and other data. Normally, you will load a model from disk, not having to care about what it looks like on this level, but some recipes will create meshes from scratch, and I recommend having a basic understanding of meshes when you do 3D game development.

- **Material**: This defines the surface of the Mesh. It's backed by a **Material Definition** (**MatDef**), usually containing a vertex shader and a fragment shader. The complexity stretches from simply setting a color or texture for a mesh, to ones that alter the shape of the Mesh. You will get far by using jMonkeyEngine's predefined MatDef.

These are some of the basic *must-know* concepts of the engine. The following concepts can be considered *nice-to-know*. I know from experience that these are the ones you wish you had known when your applications were in the process of being developed. They will also be used quite frequently throughout the chapters of this book:

- **AppState**: This is an object that affects the behavior of the whole application, and you can, for example, use them to specify logic for different parts of the application. An example could be if you have a game that is played out both on a campaign map and on the ground, both player input and game logic would probably differ quite a lot. By using the AppState class, you can manage the code more easily and avoid monstrous classes.

- **Control**: Like AppState, this is a good way to manage your code. The Control affects the Spatial it's attached to, and is commonly used to give Spatials special functionalities. You will see several examples of Control behavior in many of the chapters, so if you prefer learning-by-doing, you're in for a treat.

What this book covers

Chapter 1, *SDK Game Development Hub*, will take a tour around the SDK, always with the game in mind. Learn about built-in functions and plugins that make your life easier.

Chapter 2, *Cameras and Game Controls*, contains a number of concrete ways to use cameras and control avatars for a variety of game types.

Chapter 3, *World Building*, explores different methods you can use to create and modify environments for games.

Chapter 4, *Mastering Character Animations*, enables you to learn all you need to know about controlling character animations.

Chapter 5, *Artificial Intelligence*, contains a look at the basics and common challenges of AI for games.

Chapter 6, *GUI with Nifty GUI*, contains techniques to develop a lot of the common user interfaces a game needs.

Chapter 7, *Networking with SpiderMonkey*, is an introduction to UDP/TCP networking for games in jMonkeyEngine.

Chapter 8, *Physics with Bullet*, will teach you the Bullet implementation and how to apply it to your games.

Chapter 9, *Taking Our Game to the Next Level*, will tell you what to do when your game mechanics are in and the game is playable. Still, you will feel the game lacks something. This chapter shows different methods to advance your game further in quality.

Appendix, *Information Fragments*, contains some generic pieces of code and instructions that can be used across chapters. It also has some full-code segments for recipes that are too long to include in the chapters themselves.

What you need for this book

This book will assume that you already have some experience with either jMonkeyEngine or similar scene-graph-based engines. If you're completely new to this, we'll go through some common concepts in the following pages to give you a basic introduction to 3D game development. If you'd like more in-depth descriptions of these (and other) concepts, I recommend reading and performing the tutorials found at hub.jmonkeyengine.org.

Who this book is for

This book is ideal for intermediate to advanced users of the jMonkeyEngine 3.0 game development engine.

Conventions

In this book, you will find a number of styles of text that distinguish between different kinds of information. Here are some examples of these styles, and an explanation of their meaning.

Code words in text, database table names, folder names, filenames, file extensions, pathnames, dummy URLs, user input, and Twitter handles are shown as follows: "Start by creating a new class called `GameCharacterControl`, which extends `BetterCharacterControl`."

A block of code is set as follows:

```
public void update(float tpf) {
    super.update(tpf);
    Vector3f modelForwardDir =
      spatial.getWorldRotation().mult(Vector3f.UNIT_Z);
    Vector3f modelLeftDir =
      spatial.getWorldRotation().mult(Vector3f.UNIT_X);
    walkDirection.set(0, 0, 0);
```

When we wish to draw your attention to a particular part of a code block, the relevant lines or items are set in bold:

```
camLocation.setY(checkHeight() + camDistance);
cam.setLocation(camLocation);
```

New terms and **important words** are shown in bold. Words that you see on the screen, in menus or dialog boxes for example, appear in the text like this: "Go to the **File** menu and select **Import Model**."

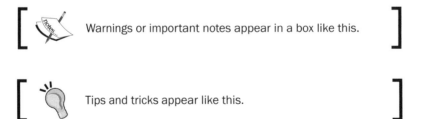

Warnings or important notes appear in a box like this.

Tips and tricks appear like this.

Reader feedback

Feedback from our readers is always welcome. Let us know what you think about this book—what you liked or may have disliked. Reader feedback is important for us to develop titles that you really get the most out of.

To send us general feedback, simply send an e-mail to `feedback@packtpub.com`, and mention the book title through the subject of your message.

If there is a topic that you have expertise in and you are interested in either writing or contributing to a book, see our author guide on `www.packtpub.com/authors`.

Customer support

Now that you are the proud owner of a Packt book, we have a number of things to help you to get the most from your purchase.

Downloading the example code

You can download the example code files for all Packt books you have purchased from your account at `http://www.packtpub.com`. If you purchased this book elsewhere, you can visit `http://www.packtpub.com/support` and register to have the files e-mailed directly to you.

Downloading the color images of this book

We also provide you a PDF file that has color images of the screenshots/diagrams used in this book. The color images will help you better understand the changes in the output. You can download this file from `https://www.packtpub.com/sites/default/files/downloads/6478OS_ColoredImages.pdf`.

Errata

Although we have taken every care to ensure the accuracy of our content, mistakes do happen. If you find a mistake in one of our books—maybe a mistake in the text or the code—we would be grateful if you would report this to us. By doing so, you can save other readers from frustration and help us improve subsequent versions of this book. If you find any errata, please report them by visiting `http://www.packtpub.com/support`, selecting your book, clicking on the **errata submission form** link, and entering the details of your errata. Once your errata are verified, your submission will be accepted and the errata will be uploaded to our website, or added to any list of existing errata, under the Errata section of that title.

Piracy

Piracy of copyright material on the Internet is an ongoing problem across all media. At Packt, we take the protection of our copyright and licenses very seriously. If you come across any illegal copies of our works, in any form, on the Internet, please provide us with the location address or website name immediately so that we can pursue a remedy.

Please contact us at `copyright@packtpub.com` with a link to the suspected pirated material.

We appreciate your help in protecting our authors, and our ability to bring you valuable content.

Questions

You can contact us at `questions@packtpub.com` if you are having a problem with any aspect of the book, and we will do our best to address it.

1

SDK Game Development Hub

This chapter contains the following recipes:

- ▸ Setting up a project
- ▸ Importing a model
- ▸ Using the Scene Composer
- ▸ Modifying heightmaps with Terrain Editor
- ▸ Adding a sky box and lighting
- ▸ Adding water using a filter
- ▸ Adding some ambient audio
- ▸ Creating bitmap fonts with Font Creator
- ▸ Retrieving an attachment node
- ▸ Using ParticleEmitter—Soaring Birds
- ▸ An advanced ParticleEmitter class

Introduction

Welcome to the first chapter of this book! In this chapter, we'll go through various functions of the SDK. These are the features that make the development process accessible to people other than programmers. You can also, in many cases, get quick visual results by just tweaking values and without having to launch an application. In short, it's a development hub because you will return and use these functions from time to time in your project. On the difficulty scale, these recipes lean towards the easy side, with little or no programming. The exception is the last part of the chapter where modifying the core packages is necessary to achieve the results we want.

Setting up a project

The jMonkeyEngine SDK is based around the NetBeans environment. Users familiar with the NetBeans environment will probably have little trouble finding their way around the jMonkeyEngine SDK. For those with no previous experience, some pointers on how to get started might be in place. In this recipe, we'll create a project that can access the jMonkeyEngine test-data library. By doing so, we will have some assets available from the start that can be used to try out many of the recipes.

Getting ready

Before setting up a project, we need to download the SDK. Doing so is as easy as going to `http://hub.jmonkeyengine.org/downloads/` and selecting a suitable package for your operating system.

After downloading and installing the package, we're ready to go!

How to do it...

We can set up a project by performing the following steps:

1. First of all, find the **Projects** window.

2. Right-click somewhere inside it and select **New Project**.

3. In the window that appears, select **JME3** from **Categories** and **BasicGame** from **Projects**.

4. On the next screen, choose a suitable name for the project and click on **Finish** to create it.

5. The project should now appear in the **Projects** window. Right-click on it and select **Properties** from the menu.

6. Select the **Libraries** option, click on the **Add Library...** button, and find the `jme3-test-data` library from the list.

How it works...

When the project is created, it sets up the basic necessities for a jMonkeyEngine project. You will get a **Project Assets** folder where any content can be placed in its subfolders. It also creates the `Main.java` file based on the `SimpleApplication` class. This is the starting point for your application.

Importing a model

Let's start off with a pretty basic scenario. We have this model, which we've exported from a 3D modeling package, and we would like to use it for our game. The first thing we need to do is convert it to the format that jMonkeyEngine 3 uses internally (`.j3o`). The recommended format to use is `.blend` coming from the open source modeling package Blender for which the SDK has extensive support. Another common format is `.obj` for static models and Ogre-mesh XML files.

How to do it...

We can import a model by performing the following steps:

1. Go to the **File** menu and select **Import Model**.
2. Next, we need to choose the project we would like to import.
3. After selecting the actual model to be imported, we get to preview the model and can make sure that all the assets are properly used.
4. Finally, we select where to place it in the **Project Assets** folder structure.

How it works...

The importer converts the model to the internal `.j3o` format. This is a binary format, which means it becomes nonreadable (compare it with a `.obj` file, which can be edited in Notepad). The compactness of a binary file is necessary to keep memory consumption low. It becomes impossible to edit externally, though, so keeping the original files organized is a good idea!

Using Scene Composer

Here, we'll go through the basics of using Scene Composer in the SDK. Scene Composer is a place where we can preview objects, prepare them for in-game usage, and combine them to form scenes. Further usage includes viewing a model's skeleton and bones setup or playing animations. You can also apply materials, lighting, and set some basic geometry data.

Getting ready

Having some models to play around with will be useful if you want to create an interesting scene. We will use the Jaime model from the test-data library. You can find it in the **Jaime** folder inside **Models** and copy it to your project.

How to do it...

Let's start by creating a scene we can use to test our recipes later.

1. Right-click on the **Scenes** folder inside **Project Assets**, select **New**, and then select **Empty jME3 Scene**. The scene will open automatically in the **SceneComposer** window.

2. A scene is just an empty node, and needs to be populated to be useful. To have something to look at, let's add the Jaime model to the scene. Find it in the folder structure, right-click on **Jaime.j3o**, and select **Link in SceneComposer**. The **SceneComposer** window looks as follows:

3. Now, most likely, all we can see is a blue, wire-frame box. This is because there are no lights in the scene. At the top-left part of the screen, there is a button with a light bulb on it.

4. By clicking on it, we should get **PointLight** following the camera; it is not part of the scene, however.

Linking versus adding

Adding means you add an instance of the object itself to the scene. This can then be modified separately to the original object.

Linking means you add a reference to the object in the scene. Apart from making the scene smaller, any modifications to the original object will also affect the objects in the scene.

5. Basic camera orientation in the scene includes dragging with the left mouse button to rotate the camera. Dragging with the right mouse button pressed moves the camera sideways, up, and down. The mouse wheel zooms in and out.

6. The second icon in the top bar of the **SceneComposer** window is the Move icon. By clicking on it, you will see three different colored planes by Jaime. These will be highlighted as you move your mouse over them. If you press the left mouse button while they're highlighted, you will move the object in the dimensions of that plane.

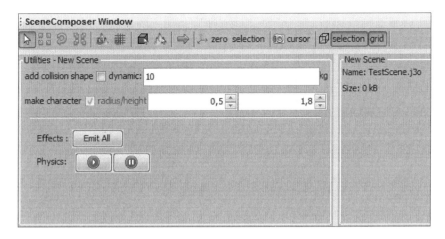

7. The same rules apply to the next icon, Rotation. Note, though, that scaling is uniform across all the axes.

> If you want to have total control over your transformations, you can use the **Properties** window to set the exact values for translation, rotation, and scale.
>
> If you'd like to have an in-depth knowledge of the SDK, have a look at the videos on http://hub.jmonkeyengine.org.

How it works...

Scene Composer runs an instance of a jME application and what you see is very much what you will get when watching the scene in the game (minus the camera light). Use it to preview and tweak your assets before bringing them inside your application.

There's more...

Now that we have a scene, what's needed to load it into an application? Just the following lines of code are needed, really:

```
Spatial scene = assetManager.loadModel("Scenes/TestScene.j3o");
rootNode.attachChild(scene);
```

Add the preceding code in the `simpleInitApp()` method of `Main.java`.

Modifying heightmaps with Terrain Editor

In Terrain Editor, we find a number of functions that let us modify a heightmap-based terrain, something which is used in many games.

A heightmap, in its simplest form, is a 2D array (the dimensions representing x and y coordinates) usually storing floats that represent height values. These can be saved as grayscale images where brighter areas correspond to higher ground and, reversibly, darker areas correspond to lower ground.

The terrain fields of jMonkeyEngine have much more information to help you create a visually appealing terrain. Things like vertex normal data and color and texture data are available for modification through the API, for daring programmers.

A heightmap

How to do it...

We will begin by creating a terrain for the scene before exploring how to modify it. To do this, perform the following steps:

1. First, we either create a new scene or load a scene we've worked with previously.

2. In the **SceneExplorer** window, right-click on the main scene node and select **Add Spatial** and then **Terrain...**.

3. To edit the terrain, we have to find the scene j3o file in the **Projects** window. It should be present in the **Scenes** folder inside **Project Assets**. Right-click on the scene file and select **Edit Terrain**.

4. Now, we have a flat and nice terrain. While it's perfectly functional, let's explore the functions in the **TerrainEditor** window. These functions are shown in the following screenshot:

5. Next to the Add Terrain icon, you have the raise/lower terrain icon. This icon uses the values of **Radius** and **Height/Weight** sliders to modify the terrain. Try it out and see how it can be used to create hills and valleys. The Level terrain icon can be used to create flat areas in the terrain. It works by right-clicking on an area, the height of which you would like to have as a reference, and then holding the left mouse button and flattening out the terrain at the selected height, creating plateaus.

 If you're going to use this as a test bed for the other chapters, try to keep the area just around Jaime at the default height, for now. This is because we don't have any logic to keep it at the actual ground level, and we would like to see what is going on in the recipes.

6. While the terrain comes with basic texturing, we might want to do something more interesting. First of all, we need to add another texture layer. This is done with the icon that looks like a plane with a plus sign on top (the Add another texture layer icon).

7. After clicking on it, there should be another row in the **Painting** window, below it. Clicking on the **Texture** field will bring up a selector with all the textures available to the project. Select a suitable texture among the available ones.

8. Now, to paint, click on the button with a spray can on it. You can now paint by holding the left mouse button over the terrain, and erase by pressing the right mouse button. Like most of the other functions in the **TerrainEditor** window, it uses the **Radius** and **Height/Weight** values.

 When painting a terrain by hand, it is a good idea to have a reference image of the terrain type at hand. That way we can, for example, see how grass grows on slopes, or snow gathers on mountains, and produce more realistic results. Always start by painting in broad strokes, gradually painting with smaller and smaller brushes.

How it works...

The function of most of the buttons is pretty self-explanatory, but let's look at what happens when either of them are applied.

A little bit of smoothing is something that might be needed after generating a heightmap using an automated tool. In such a case, you most likely won't use a brush, though, but rather a filter that will apply it evenly across the whole of the heightmap. The brush might instead be used to smooth out an area where a game character is supposed to move to make it a better game experience. It might also be that the ground of an area is of a type that would most likely be smoother than the surroundings, like a beach among rocky cliffs.

Level terrain has similar uses. If we need sufficient space to place a large building for example, it is the best way to ensure that no part of the building ends up floating or submerged beneath the ground.

Adding a sky box and lighting

Sky boxes or sky domes are small pieces of every day magic in games. They're used to create a mood-setting backdrop for scenes and are excellent for making areas seem larger than they are.

Sky boxes consist of six textures, rendered on the inside of a cube, much like wallpapers. Perceived as enclosing the world, they actually don't need to be very big since they are rendered first in the queue. This means everything else will be drawn on top of them.

How to do it...

The recipe will consist of two sections, where the first section will create a sky box from six textures. After this, we will add sun-like light using **Directional Light**.

1. In the **SceneExplorer** window, right-click on your scene and select **Add Spatial..** and then **Skybox...**

2. There are two options here: either we can load six independent textures or one texture with all the six textures prebaked. This particular recipe uses the six `Lagoon` textures from the `test-data/Textures/Sky` folder.

3. After this, we should now see a moody, watery scene surrounding the terrain.

4. The terrain and skybox don't blend together very well. First and foremost the lighting is wrong. The only light in the scene is a white light coming from the camera's origin. To get a more natural light in this outdoor scene, we can add **Directional Light**.

5. Again, right-click on the scene in the **SceneExplorer** window. Now, select **Add Light..** and then select **Directional Light**. Things just got a lot brighter! It doesn't look better, however. We need to adjust the light to suit the scene.

6. We can see the **DirectionalLight** element in the **SceneExplorer** window. Select it and bring up the **Properties** window. There are just two settings: `Color` and `Direction`.

7. By clicking on the box next to the color values, we see several options to set the color. We can use an image editor and the colorpicker function near the sun to get a suitable color. Grab the RGB values and insert them in that tab. This way, we know that we get a color that matches the scene's sun.

8. Turning off the camera light (the light bulb in the top-left corner) will help us see the blue-tinted color from the light we just added.

It's often a good rule of thumb to have a little less tint than what might first seem like a suitable one. It usually feels more natural in the end. Show it to someone else and see if they think it's "too much". As a developer, your judgment can be "tainted", as you get used to a scene, and it's easy to overdo things like lighting.

9. There's one more thing to do to make the scene and sky box blend better together. The shadows on the terrain are at wrong places in relation to the sun in the scene. The default setting for **Directional Light** is to shine in from the southwest direction and about 45 degrees downwards. This particular sky box has the main source of light coming from the northeast direction. Flipping the minus sign on the x and z values in the **Direction** property seems to make the shadows look more natural.

What you see of a sky box can alter the perception of immersion, greatly. Generally, the player should not see anything below the horizon for it to look believable. You will notice this if you zoom in and out of the scene. As you're close to the ground, it will feel much more natural.

How it works...

The reason sky boxes work is because of how the rendering of the scenegraph happens. Objects can be sorted into different lists or buckets, to help the rendered in drawing. A sky box is sorted into the `Bucket.Sky` list, which is drawn first in every rendering cycle. This is why everything else (normally in the `Bucket.Opaque` list) appears to be in front of it. You can achieve the same effect for any object by calling `Geometry.setQueueBucket (Bucket.Sky)`.

You can achieve the same effect on other objects by changing the `QueueBucket` renderers as follows:

```
Geometry.setQueueBucket(Bucket.Sky);
```

There's more...

If you look closely at Jaime (or any other object you added to the scene) with the camera light turned off, you will notice that the side not facing the light will be completely dark. Unless this is a place devoid of atmosphere, radiance, diffusion, and reflection of other surfaces, one should have given all sides some basic lighting. This is emulated in games by using ambient lighting. It lights all the faces evenly and is added by selecting the scene in the **SceneExplorer** window and choosing **Add Light**.

You can select the same color as **Directional Light**, but make it much darker to get something that will look natural. If you're really serious, and have a somewhat uniform ground color, you can try to blend in a little bit of the ground color, as well.

Adding water using a filter

When it comes to bang-for-the-buck visuals in jMonkeyEngine, there is little that trumps using a water filter. It is very impressive and yet easy to do. Having water in the scene will greatly enhance the mood of our test scene. You can view the great looking water with little efforts in the following screenshot:

Getting ready

The scene used should have some height differences (or we will end up with all water or all ground). If no terrain is available or if it needs adjustments, check out the *Modifying heightmaps with Terrain Editor* recipe in this chapter.

If there isn't already an **Effects** folder in your **Projects Assets** folder, add it.

How to do it...

We can add water using a filter by performing the following steps:

1. Right-click on the **Effects** folder under **Project Assets**, select **New**, and then select **Empty FilterPostProcessor file**. You might have to select **New**, **Other...**, and then click on **Filters** to find it.

2. Name it `Water` and click on **Finish**.

3. Right-click on the newly created **Water.j3f** file and open it.

4. We are now moved to the **FilterExplorer** window. From here, we can create, add, and modify scene-wide effects, choosing from a number of premade ones. Right-click on the **Water** filter and select **Add Filter** and then **Water**.

5. To see filters in the **SceneComposer** window, we need to click on the Eye icon shown in the following screenshot. This should give the scene a whole new look. Do it and see the scene transform.

6. A few properties need to be modified in order to make the water appear smoothly. The **Properties** window for the **WaterFilter** element can seem a bit overwhelming. For now, let's change the **Water Height** parameter. The filter will create foam wherever it meets the land and finds a good separation or where the shore height is essential. The sweet spot is dependent on the scene but starts out with -2 units. Changing the following values will affect the appearance along the shoreline:

Shore Hardness	1.0
Use Foam	✔
Foam Intensity	0.3
Foam Hardness	1.0 .
Foam Existence	[0.0, 0.0, 0.0]
Wave Scale	

7. There are also **Light Direction** and **Light Color** properties in there. Let's copy the values from our **Directional Light** element here to make them match. You will find them by moving to the **SceneExplorer** window, selecting the **Directional Light** element, and looking in the **Properties** window.

8. Lastly, we need to add the following lines to the `simpleInit` method of our test application:

```
FilterPostProcessor processor = (FilterPostProcessor)
assetManager.loadAsset("Effects/Water.j3f");
viewPort.addProcessor(processor);
```

How it works...

Post filters are rendered last as a screen effect in the rendering stage and applied to the entire scene. There are many ready-made filter variants made by the jME team and community that you can use to change how a scene appears. Filter Explorer is a great way to set up and test these before applying them to your game.

Adding some ambient audio

Audio is an extremely important moodsetter in games, and any other cross-media product, which is often overlooked. Bad audio can just as easily break immersion as good audio can improve it.

We're going to add some ambient audio to our scene to help set the mood. Since the sky box we use is a rather gloomy and watery scene, we're going to add the sound of ocean waves crashing against the shore.

Ambient sounds can either be sounds you hear throughout a whole scene, such as the buzzing of traffic in a city, or local to a specific place, the sound of a waterfall, and so on. In this case, we can picture our scene as a small island, and thus the waves should be heard wherever you go.

As it happens, there is a suitable `.ogg` file in the **Environments** folder inside `Sound`. If we have added the `jme3-test-data` library to our project, we can access it easily.

The SDK can handle both `.ogg` or uncompressed `.wav` files. The `.ogg` format is open and free, meaning you won't need any license to use it. This is not necessarily the case with other compression types.

How to do it...

If we've made the previous recipes, we might already have seen the audio node. The following steps will help show us how to add one to the scene:

1. We can find the audio node by right-clicking on a spatial, in this case the main scene node, and selecting **Add Spatial** and then **Audio Node**.

2. Next, select it and look at the **Properties** window.

3. The first important thing to look at is the **Audio Data** parameter. In the drop-down menu, the SDK will automatically show the files in the **Sounds** folder under **Project Assets**, so we should see **Ocean Waves.ogg** here. Unchecking the **Positional** checkbox means there will be no falloff in volume as you move around.

4. Also check the **Looping** box to make sure the sound doesn't end when it's finished playing one time.

5. It's currently not possible to hear the sound in the SDK itself, so we need to start an application to do so. Fortunately, only one line of code is needed to start the sound in our `simpleInitApp` method. The only catch here is that we need to cast the `scene` object in an `AudioNode` instance first. After having loaded the scene, add the following lines of code:

```
Node scene = (Node) assetManager.loadModel
("Scenes/TestScene.j3o");
rootNode.attachChild(scene);
((AudioNode)scene.getChild("AudioNode")).play();
```

6. The sound we added is a very powerful sound and may be a bit overwhelming for our scene. Playing with the `Volume` property of the `AudioNode` element can be used to tone down the effect a bit.

Downloading the example code

You can download the example code files for all Packt books you have purchased from your account at `http://www.packtpub.com`. If you purchased this book elsewhere, you can visit `http://www.packtpub.com/support` and register to have the files e-mailed directly to you.

How it works...

The `AudioNode` element has a position in the 3D world since it extends `Spatial` and can hence be made to be heard only from certain places. It can also easily be made to follow objects around. In addition to volume and falloff, audio can also be modified during runtime by area effects such as reverb.

To learn more about how effects can be used to modify audio, check out *Chapter 9, Taking Our Game to the Next Level*.

Creating bitmap fonts with Font Creator

The Font Creator plugin is a really nifty tool for any game creator and is easily overlooked unless mentioned. By using it, you can create a bitmap font using any system font you have available. Refer to the *Downloading the plugins* section in *Appendix, Information Fragments*, to know how to download a plugin.

How to do it...

We can create bitmap fonts with Font Creator by performing the following steps:

1. Right-click on the **Fonts** folder under **Interface** in our **Project Assets** folder. Select **New** and then select **Other.... Font** is located in the GUI folder.

2. Next, we choose the font we would like to use from the available system fonts.

3. In the **Configure Font** part, we can make adjustments before actually creating the bitmap. It's recommended to use a power-of-two number for the size.

 A higher resolution will make the text more detailed, but it will at the same time take up more memory, not only for the bitmap image itself but also for the text generated. Consider the application requirements or do some testing. You can also try to adjust the size of the font to fit the bitmap.

4. Once we have our font, there are a couple of ways we can use it. First of all, if we want to replace the default font used by the application, we have to name the font `Default.fnt` and make sure it's placed inside the **Fonts** folder under **Interface**. This is what the application is looking for during startup.

5. Another way to use the custom font is to load it in the application by using the following code:

```
BitmapFont myFont = assetManager.loadFont ("Interface/Fonts/MyFont.fnt");
```

6. It can then be used to create text that can be placed anywhere on the screen, as shown in the following code:

```
BitmapText text = new BitmapText(myFont, false);
hudText.setText("Text!");
hudText.setColor(ColorRGBA.Red);
guiNode.attachChild(hudText);
```

How it works...

The `BitmapText` class is spatial, and needs to be attached to a node in order to be displayed. The most common node is probably the `guiNode`. Spatials added to the `guiNode` will be positioned according to the screen space and projected without depth. For this reason, using the `guiNode` is suitable for **HUD** items. Setting the `localTranslation` parameter to `(0, 0, 0)` will make the text appear in the bottom-left corner of the screen. Instead of using `(screenWidth, 0, screenHeight)`, we will place it in the top-right corner.

Retrieving an attachment node

In many games, the characters can be customized to carry different equipment or clothes. In these situations, jMonkeyEngine's Attachments node is extremely useful. It lets us choose a bone and creates a node for us that will follow that particular bone's movement and rotation, without any further work from our side.

Getting ready

We'll need a rigged model with `SkeletonControl`. Fortunately, the Jaime model is already rigged and animated. We'll also need something to attach to it. What goes well with monkeys if not bananas?

How to do it...

1. Open the model in the **SceneComposer** window by right-clicking on it in **Projects** and selecting **Edit** in **SceneComposer**.

2. Expand the `SkeletonControl` class. Located under `Root` is a Bone called `IKhand.R`, as shown in the following screenshot:

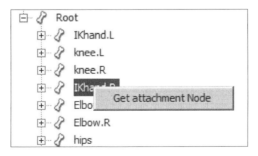

3. Right-click on **IKhand.R** and select **Get attachment Node**.

4. We should now see a node called **IKhand.R_attachnode** created at the top level of the hierarchy. Attach the banana to the node by dragging it into the **SceneExplorer** window. The banana should now appear in Jaime's hand.

> The banana will not fit perfectly in this recipe. To achieve a perfect fit, the best way will be to create an actual bone, just for attachments, in the modeling program of our choice. Since the attached item is attached using the model's center point, we can expect to have to tweak the position of the items as well.

5. To prove that the banana will actually follow the movement of the model, we can play an animation. Select **AnimControl** in the **SceneExplorer** window and look at the **Properties** window. Choose an animation from the drop-down menu.

How it works...

When we first call `getAttachmentsNode` on a `Bone` object, it will create a new node. It will then keep track of it and update its translation, rotation, and scale according to the values of the `Bone` object. It works as a regular node in most regards, with the difference being that it follows the `IKhand.R` bone's movements during animations. It is very handy, isn't it?

There's more...

All this is, of course, possible to do using code as well. Just like in the SDK, we use the following `SkeletonControl` class to achieve this:

```
mySpatial.getControl(SkeletonControl.class).getAttachmentsNode("my
bone");
```

Using ParticleEmitter – Soaring Birds

Particle Emitters, in general, are good in order to create an atmosphere in the games. The most common case is probably for smoke or fire and explosions. Particles can, however, be used for many interesting things. In this recipe, we're going to explore that by tuning a ParticleEmitter to create birds sailing through the sky.

The particles are still sprites, 2D images, so they will work best either far up in the sky, or below us.

The recipe will be divided into two parts. The first one contains setting up the `ParticleEmitter` class in the SDK and writing the `ParticleInfluencer` interface. The second part includes changing the way the `ParticleEmitter` class behaves and extending our `ParticleInfluencer` interface to take advantage of this:

Getting ready

First of all, we need a suitable bird texture. There's one supplied with the project in the **Birds** folder inside **Textures**, which will be fine if the birds are supposed to be far away. Up close, it will not suffice though.

How to do it...

The first section will describe how to set up a material we can use. This consists of the following steps:

1. We're going to start by creating a material to supply to the `ParticleEmitter` class. Create a new material in the **Materials** folder by right-clicking and selecting **New...** and then **Empty Material File**.

2. Rename it to something suitable, for example, `Birds.j3m`.

3. Now, we can open it and are automatically moved to the **Material Editor** window.

4. Here, we set the **Material Definition** value to `Common/Matdefs/Misc/Unshaded. j3md`.

5. The only thing we need to change is the **ColorMap** value, which should be pointed to our birds texture.

Now, we come to the configuration of the `ParticleEmitter` class. This section consists of the following steps:

1. Let's begin by creating a new scene and opening it in the **SceneExplorer** window. Right-click and select **Add Spatial..** and then **Particle Emitter**. A default smoke puffing the `ParticleEmitter` object is created.

2. Now, we can bring up the **Properties** window and start tweaking it.

3. First of all, we set the material to our newly created material for the birds. Don't worry if it looks terrible!

4. Looking at the `Images X` property, we can see that it's set to **15** by default. This is the amount of horizontal "frames" in the texture. If we look at the birds texture, we can see that it's only four frames, so let's change that value. The particles are already looking better.

5. `High Life` and `Low Life` define the maximum or minimum lifespan of a particle. We can assume that the birds should soar across the sky for a while, so let's change it to **30** and **25** respectively.

6. There are an awful lot of birds now. Setting `Num Particles` to **50** will make more sense.

7. `Start Size` and `End Size` affect the size of the particles over time. These should be set to **1** for our birds. They shouldn't inflate.

8. For now, let's increase the radius of the emitter to get a better view. It's a sphere by default and the last value is the radius. Set it to **30**.

9. If we take a look at the birds now, they still just float in space. This is very unbird-like.

10. Let's scroll down a bit to the `ParticleInfluencer` class. The `ParticleInfluencer` class has an opportunity to alter a particle's velocity when it's created, decreasing uniformity. The `DefaultParticleInfluencer` class can set an initial velocity, and a variation, from 0 to 1.

11. Set the `InitialVelocity` parameter to `3.0, 0.0, 0.0` and the `VelocityVariation` to `1.0` to give the particles some individuality.

12. To make the birds look in the direction they're flying, check the **Facing Velocity** box.

New settings won't take effect immediately, but only when a new particle is generated. If you want to speed up the process, click on the "**Emit All**" button to emit all the new particles with the new settings.

How it works...

A ParticleEmitter can be described as a cheap way to draw many identical or near-identical bitmaps. Particle Emitters have a single mesh that stores all its particles. As opposed to drawing each particle individually, it renders them all at once. This is considerably cheaper. The drawback is, of course, that they all look the same.

There's more...

There is another thing we can do to improve the appearance of the generated birds. Since we are expecting to look at them from either above or below, it makes sense to flatten the shape of the emitter to be more of a plane. Let's revisit the `Emitter Shape` property and make a box instead of a sphere, as shown in the following code:

```
[Box, -30.0, -1.0, -30.0, 30.0, 1.0, 30.0]
```

The numbers define the extremes of a box, that is, X^{min}, Y^{min}, Z^{min} and X^{max}, Y^{max}, and Z^{max}. In other words, we have created a box that is 60 units wide and long and only 2 units high.

An advanced ParticleEmitter class

Soaring birds are nice but it's easy to feel that the result of the previous recipe could have been much better if the birds were better animated. If you've worked with the `ParticleEmitter` class before or have been observant of the birds, you will know that particles can actually be animated although they only cycle through every frame once per lifetime. This is much too slow for the birds.

In this recipe, we're going to look at what's needed to make the birds flap their wings. It's not as simple as it sounds and requires modifying the `ParticleEmitter` code and writing our own `ParticleInfluencer` class.

If we have a look at the `ParticleEmitter` class to see what we need to do, we can see that there is an `updateParticle` method that seems like a good place to start. This is called for every particle in each update cycle. One thing that is less obvious at first is that since we have the same `ParticleInfluencer` instance affecting all particles, it also needs to be updated separately for each frame. To achieve the latter, we can use a control.

Getting ready

To be able to modify the `ParticleEmitter` class, we need the source. This means we have to check it out from the repository. If you're not comfortable with this, you can still do the first part and learn more about the `ParticleInfluencer` instance.

After having checked out the source code for jMonkeyEngine from the repository, it should be opened as a project in the SDK.

Build it and then change the reference in the properties for this project to use the `.jar` files from the source code project instead of the supplied `jMonkeyEngine.jar` files.

How to do it...

In the first section, we'll create a new `ParticleInfluencer` instance. This consists of the following steps:

1. The first thing we'll do is create a new class called `BirdParticleInfluencer` and have it extend the `DefaultParticleInfluencer` class. Since the flat particles point in the direction they're flying, it sometimes looks weird when they have a Y-velocity. We're going to fix that by not allowing the particles to have any velocity in the *y* axis. We override the `influenceParticle` method and set the Y-velocity to `0`. After this we need to normalize the velocity, as shown in the following code:

```
public void influenceParticle(Particle particle, EmitterShape
emitterShape) {
  super.influenceParticle(particle, emitterShape);
  particle.velocity.setY(0);
  particle.velocity.normalizeLocal();
}
```

2. We can now replace the `ParticleInfluencer` interface in the `ParticleEmitter` element's **Property** window with our own.

3. That was the easy part, and that's how far we get without modifying the engine. In the next section, we will extend the current `ParticleEmitter` instance to animate particles continuously. This will consist of the following steps:

    1. Let's start by making our `ParticleInfluencer` interface ready to update the particles in every frame. Let's start by making our `ParticleInfluencer` interface ready to update the particles in every frame. We're going to add two methods to it. The first one is for updating the particle, and the second one is for updating the influencer itself, as shown in the following code:

    ```
    public void influenceRealtime(Particle particle, float tpf);
    public void update(float tpf);
    ```

    2. In our `BirdParticleInfluencer` class, we're going to need some new fields. The `maxImages` property keeps track of how many images there are in a cycle. The `animationFps` property defines how fast the animation should run. These two properties should be added to the class's read/write/clone methods as well to ensure that they're saved properly. The `time` and `increaseFrames` are runtime properties only:

    ```
    private int maxImages = 1;
    ```

```
private float animationFps = 10f;
    private float time = 0f;
    private int increaseFrames;
```

3. Now, let's go to our `update` method. This is the method that runs once every frame. We add functionality to check whether it's time to change the frame in the particle or not. The logic goes like this: when the current passed time is larger than the time between frames, increase the frame index by one. Using a `while` loop rather than an `if` statement allows us to compensate for low frame rate, by skipping several frames, if necessary, to keep up with the frames per second:

```java
public void update(float tpf){
  super.update(tpf);
  float timeBetweenFrames = 1f /  animationFps;
  time += tpf;
  increaseFrames = 0;
  while (time > timeBetweenFrames){
    increaseFrames++;
    time -= interval;
  }
}
```

4. In `influenceRealtime`, which is the method that is run once per particle and frame, all we do is tell it to increase the `imageIndex` value if needed, making sure not to exceed the maximum images in the cycle:

```java
public void influenceRealtime(Particle particle, float tpf)
{
  super.influenceRealtime(particle, tpf);
  if(increaseFrames > 0){
    particle.imageIndex = (particle.imageIndex +
increaseFrames) % maxImages;
  }
}
```

5. That's the influencer part. Let's make sure `influenceRealtime` is called from the `ParticleEmitter` class. At the end of the `updateParticle` method, add the following code:

```java
particleInfluencer.influenceRealtime(p, tpf);
```

Unfortunately, we also need to comment out the following line:

```java
//p.imageIndex = (int) (b * imagesX * imagesY);
```

In the last section of the recipe, we will create a control that will update the `ParticleInfluencer` class. This consists of the following steps:

1. We create a new class called `BirdParticleEmitterControl` and make it extend `AbstractControl`. The important bit here is the `controlUpdate` method where we in turn call the `update` method of the `ParticleEmitter` instance:

    ```
    public void controlUpdate(float tpf){
      super.update(tpf);
      if(spatial != null && spatial instanceof ParticleEmitter){
        ((ParticleEmitter)spatial).getParticleInfluencer().
        update(tpf);
      }
    }
    ```

2. Apart from that, we also need to add the following code for it to work properly:

    ```
    public Control cloneForSpatial(Spatial spatial) {
      return new BirdParticleEmitterControl();
    }
    ```

3. To affect the birds by our changes, we need to do a few more things. First, we need to open the birds scene in the **SceneComposer** window.

4. Selecting the **Emitter** element, we need to choose **Add Control..** and then select **Custom Control**. Our newly created control should be available in the list.

5. Now, we need to load the scene inside an application. We just load the scene and move it up into the sky by using the following code:

    ```
    public void simpleInitApp() {
      Node scene = (Node) assetManager.loadModel("Scenes/ParticleTest.
        j3o");
      scene.setLocalTranslation(0, 60, 0);
      rootNode.attachChild(scene);
    }
    ```

How it works...

Particle emitters are normally limited in what control you have over the particles. The `ParticleInfluencer` class gives us some basic control during particle creation.

Since the birds are flat planes, they look best when viewed straight on. This creates a problem when we have said that they should always point in the direction they're flying if they're moving along the *y* axis.

The `influenceParticle` method is a method implemented from the `ParticleInfluencer` interface and it is called upon the creation of every new particle. Since the `DefaultParticleInfluencer` instance is already applying a velocity with variation, we just needed to remove any Y-velocity.

In the `ParticleEmitter` class, we commented out a line in the `update` method. That's the current animation logic that will override our changes every time. A workaround would be to let the `ParticleInfluencer` class keep track of the current frame, but that would make all the birds have the same frame. Another alternative would be to move it to one of the other `ParticleInfluencer` classes.

By using the control pattern to update the `ParticleInfluencer` class, we can offset some code and keep minimum changes in the `ParticleEmitter` class.

Unfortunately, the changes we made to the `ParticleEmitter` class won't be picked up by Scene Composer, as it uses its own compiled classes. So to see it, we had to start an application and load the scene there.

There's more...

The birds now continuously flap their wings like many small birds do when flying. Larger birds tend to glide more, with only an occasional flap. They also fly in straight lines.

The `influenceRealtime` method we created opens up new possibilities to create better looking particles.

An additional touch would be to implement logic to have the birds both soar and flap interchangeably, and circle around a point or change their direction. Are you up for it?

2
Cameras and Game Controls

This chapter contains the following recipes:

- ▶ Creating a reusable character control
- ▶ Attaching an input AppState object
- ▶ Firing in FPS
- ▶ Firing non-instant bullets
- ▶ Creating an RTS camera AppState object
- ▶ Selecting units in RTS
- ▶ Making the camera follow units
- ▶ Following a character with ChaseCamera
- ▶ Adding a game controller and joystick input
- ▶ Leaning around corners
- ▶ Detecting cover automatically in a third-person game

Introduction

This chapter is about controlling avatars and cameras for various game types. Whether your game is a **first person shooter** (**FPS**), **role playing game** (**RPG**), or **real-time strategy** (**RTS**) game, you'll learn some tricks that will help you get past tricky obstacles.

The chapter will rely heavily on the `ActionListener` and `AnalogListener` interfaces. These are essential when listening for the player input in jMonkeyEngine. The `ActionListener` interface will pick up any binary input such as keyboard keys or mouse buttons. The `AnalogListener` interface listens for mouse and joystick movements and other input that is either on or off.

Creating a reusable character control

To start off the chapter, we will create a class that we can use for various character-controlled purposes. The example describes an FPS character, but the method is the same for any player-controlled character.

The `Control` class we'll build will be based on `BetterCharacterControl`. It might be a good idea to have a look at the class or the `TestBetterCharacter` example from the jMonkeyEngine test package if you want to find out how this works. Another good starting point would be the input examples from the same package.

Getting ready

The `BetterCharacterControl` class is based on physics and requires a `BulletAppState` class to be set up in the application. The steps required to do this are described in the *The ImageGenerator class* section in *Appendix, Information Fragments*. To find out more about bullet and physics, refer to *Chapter 8, Physics with Bullet*.

How to do it...

Perform the following set of steps to create a reusable character control:

1. Start by creating a new class called `GameCharacterControl`, which extends `BetterCharacterControl`. This class also needs to implement `ActionListener` and `AnalogListener`. The idea here is to feed this class with actions that it can handle. To control the movement of a character, use a series of Booleans as follows:

   ```
   boolean forward, backward, leftRotate, rightRotate, leftStrafe,
   rightStrafe;
   ```

2. Also, define a float field called `moveSpeed`, which will help you control how much the character will move in each update.

   The control Booleans you added are set in the implemented `onAction` method. Note that a key will always trigger !isPressed when released (note that a key always triggers isPressed == false when released):

   ```
   public void onAction(String action, boolean isPressed, float tpf)
   {
     if (action.equals("StrafeLeft")) {
       leftStrafe = isPressed;
     } else if (action.equals("StrafeRight")) {
         rightStrafe = isPressed;
     } else if (action.equals("MoveForward")) {
         forward = isPressed;
   ```

```
    } else if (action.equals("MoveBackward")) {
        backward = isPressed;

    } else if (action.equals("Jump")) {
        jump();
    } else if (action.equals("Duck")) {
        setDucked(isPressed);


    }
}
```

3. Now that you have handled the key input, put the control Booleans to be used in the `update` method. You might recognize the code if you've looked at `TestBetterCharacter`. The first thing it does is get the current direction the `spatial` object is facing in order to move forward and backwards. It also checks which direction is left for strafing, as follows:

```java
public void update(float tpf) {
    super.update(tpf);
    Vector3f modelForwardDir =
    spatial.getWorldRotation().mult(Vector3f.UNIT_Z);
    Vector3f modelLeftDir = spatial.getWorldRotation().
        mult(Vector3f.UNIT_X);
    walkDirection.set(0, 0, 0);
```

4. Depending on your Booleans, the following code modifies `walkDirection`. Normally, you would multiply the result by `tpf` as well, but this is already handled in the `BetterCharacterControl` class as follows:

```java
if (forward) {
    walkDirection.addLocal(modelForwardDir.mult(moveSpeed));
} else if (backward) {
    walkDirection.addLocal(modelForwardDir.negate().
        multLocal(moveSpeed));
}
if (leftStrafe) {
    walkDirection.addLocal(modelLeftDir.mult(moveSpeed));
} else if (rightStrafe) {
    walkDirection.addLocal(modelLeftDir.negate().
        multLocal(moveSpeed));
}
```

5. Finally, in the `setWalkDirection` method, apply `walkDirection` as follows:

```java
BetterCharacterControl.setWalkDirection(walkDirection);
```

6. The preceding code handles moving forward, backward, and to the side. The turning and looking up and down actions of a character is normally handled by moving the mouse (or game controller), which is instead an analog input. This is handled by the `onAnalog` method. From here, we take the name of the input and apply its value to two new methods, `rotate` and `lookUpDown`, as follows:

```
public void onAnalog(String name, float value, float tpf) {
  if (name.equals("RotateLeft")) {
    rotate(tpf * value * sensitivity);
  } else if (name.equals("RotateRight")) {
  rotate(-tpf * value * sensitivity);
  } else if (name.equals("LookUp")) {
  lookUpDown(value * tpf * sensitivity);
  } else if (name.equals("LookDown")) {
  lookUpDown(-value * tpf * sensitivity);
  }
}
```

7. Now, start by handling the process of turning the character left and right. The `BetterCharacterControl` class already has nice support for turning the character (which, in this case, is the same thing as looking left or right), and you can access its `viewDirection` field directly. You should only modify the *y* axis, which is the axis that goes from head to toe, by a small amount as follows:

```
private void rotate(float value){
  Quaternion rotate = new
    Quaternion().fromAngleAxis(FastMath.PI * value, Vector3f.
    UNIT_Y);
  rotate.multLocal(viewDirection);
  setViewDirection(viewDirection);
}
```

8. In order to handle looking up and down, you have to do some more work. The idea is to let the `spatial` object handle this. For this, you need to step back to the top of the class and add two more fields: a `Node` field called `head` and a float field called `yaw`. The `yaw` field will be the value with which you will control the rotation of the head up and down.

9. In the constructor, set the location of the `head` node. The location is relative to the `spatial` object to an appropriate amount. In a normally scaled world, `1.8f` would correspond to `1.8` m (or about 6 feet):

```
head.setLocalTranslation(0, 1.8f, 0);
```

10. Next, you need to attach the `head` node to `spatial`. You can do this in the `setSpatial` method. When a `spatial` is supplied, first check whether it is a `Node` (or you wouldn't be able to add the head). If it is, attach the head as follows:

```
public void setSpatial(Spatial spatial) {
    super.setSpatial(spatial);
    if(spatial instanceof Node){
        ((Node)spatial).attachChild(head);
    }
}
```

11. Now that you have a head that can rotate freely, you can implement the method that handles looking up and down. Modify the `yaw` field with the supplied value. Then, clamp it so that it can't be rotated more than 90 degrees up or down. Not doing this might lead to weird results. Then, set the rotation for the head around the x axis (think ear-to-ear) as follows:

```
private void lookUpDown(float value){
    yaw += value;
    yaw = FastMath.clamp(yaw, -FastMath.HALF_PI, FastMath.HALF_PI);
    head.setLocalRotation(new Quaternion().fromAngles(yaw, 0, 0));
}
```

12. Now, we have a character that can move and rotate like a standard FPS character. It still doesn't have a camera tied to it. To solve this, we're going to use the `CameraNode` class and hijack the application's camera. `CameraNode` gives you the ability to control the camera as if it were a node. With `setControlDir`, we instruct it to use the location and rotation of `spatial` as follows:

```
public void setCamera(Camera cam){
    CameraNode camNode = new CameraNode("CamNode", cam);
    camNode.setControlDir(CameraControl.ControlDirection.
      SpatialToCamera);
    head.attachChild(camNode);
}
```

Cameras are logical objects and are not part of the scene graph. The `CameraNode` keeps an instance of Camera. It is a `Node` and propagates its own location to the Camera. It can also do the opposite and apply the Camera's location to `CameraNode` (and thus, any other `spatial` object attached to it).

13. To use `GameCharacterControl` in an application, add the following lines of code in the `simpleInit` method of an application. Instantiate a new (invisible) `Node` instance that you can add to the `GameCharacterControl` class. Set the application's camera to be used as a character, and add it to `physicsSpace` as follows:

```
Node playerNode = new Node("Player");
GameCharacterControl charControl = new GameCharacterControl(0.5f,
2.5f, 8f);
charControl.setCamera(cam);
playerNode.addControl(charControl);
charControl.setGravity(normalGravity);

bulletAppState.getPhysicsSpace().add(charControl);
```

How it works...

The `BetterCharacterControl` class of jMonkeyEngine already has a lot of the functionalities to handle the movement of a character. By extending it, we get access to it and we can implement the additional functionality on top of it.

The reason we use Booleans to control movement is that the events in `onAction` and `onAnalog` are not fired continuously; they are fired only when they're changed. So, pressing a key wouldn't generate more than two actions, one on pressing it and one on releasing it. With the Boolean, we ensure that the action will keep getting performed until the player releases the key.

This method waits for an action to happen, and depending on the binding parameter, it will set or unset one of our Booleans. By listening for actions rather than inputs (the actual key strokes), we can reuse this class for **non-player characters** (**NPCs**).

We can't handle looking up and down in the same way as we perform sideways rotations. The reason is that the latter changes the actual direction of the movement. When looking up or down, we just want the camera to look that way. The character is usually locked to the ground (it would be different in a flight simulator, though!).

As we can see, the `BetterCharacterControl` class already has ways to handle jumping and ducking. Nice!

There's more...

Let's say we would rather have a third-person game. How difficult would it be to modify this class to support that? In a later recipe, we will look at jMonkeyEngine's `ChaseCamera` class, but by inserting the following two lines of code at the end of our `setCamera` method, we will get a basic camera that follows the character:

```
camNode.setLocalTranslation(new Vector3f(0, 5, -5));
camNode.lookAt(head.getLocalTranslation(), Vector3f.UNIT_Y);
```

It's all handled by `CamNode`, which offsets the camera's location in relation to its own (which follows the `head` node). After moving `CamNode`, we make sure that the camera also looks at the head (rather than the default forward).

Attaching an input AppState object

In this recipe, we will make an `AppState` object, which will handle the player input for a character. It's a great way to add functionality to the application in a modular way. The `AppState` object we create here could easily be added during the game and removed or disabled during cut scenes or while in the game menu.

Getting ready

We won't require any special assets for this recipe, but it will be beneficial to have a basic understanding of how AppState works and its purpose in jMonkeyEngine. This particular implementation of the recipe will use the character-control class created in the previous example. It can still be used to manipulate a `spatial` object directly without the `GameCharacterControl` class. This recipe will provide pointers on where to do this.

How to do it...

To attach an input `AppState` object, perform the following steps:

1. Start off by creating a class called `InputAppState`, extending `AbstractAppState`, and implementing `ActionListener` and `AnalogListener`.

2. The `InputAppState` class needs a couple of fields to be functional. First of all, we're going to keep a reference to the application's `InputManager` in a field called `inputManager`. We're also adding a `GameCharacterControl` field called `character`. This can be replaced by any `spatial`. Lastly, we're going to have a value that controls the sensitivity of the analog controls. We do this with a float called `sensitivity`. Add getters and setters for character and sensitivity.

3. Next, we'll set up the kinds of input we're going to handle. Strings are used by jMonkeyEngine for the mappings, but enums can be easier to manage across classes. Here, we'll use an `enum` and supply the name of the value as the mapping. We use it to create some basic FPS controls as follows:

    ```
    public enum InputMapping{
        RotateLeft, RotateRight, LookUp, LookDown, StrafeLeft,
        StrafeRight, MoveForward, MoveBackward;
    }
    ```

4. We create a method called `addInputMappings` to add these to `inputManager` and make sure it listens to them. To do this, we supply the name of the `enum` value as the mapping and bind it to a certain input as follows:

```
private void addInputMappings() {
  inputManager.addMapping(InputMapping.RotateLeft.name(), new
    MouseAxisTrigger(MouseInput.AXIS_X, true));
  inputManager.addMapping(InputMapping.RotateRight.name(), new
    MouseAxisTrigger(MouseInput.AXIS_X, false));
  inputManager.addMapping(InputMapping.LookUp.name(), new
    MouseAxisTrigger(MouseInput.AXIS_Y, false));
  inputManager.addMapping(InputMapping.LookDown.name(), new
    MouseAxisTrigger(MouseInput.AXIS_Y, true));
  inputManager.addMapping(InputMapping.StrafeLeft.name(), new
    KeyTrigger(KeyInput.KEY_A), new KeyTrigger(KeyInput.KEY_
    LEFT));
  inputManager.addMapping(InputMapping.StrafeRight.name(), new
    KeyTrigger(KeyInput.KEY_D), new KeyTrigger(KeyInput.KEY_
    RIGHT));
  inputManager.addMapping(InputMapping.MoveForward.name(), new
    KeyTrigger(KeyInput.KEY_W), new KeyTrigger(KeyInput.KEY_UP));
  inputManager.addMapping(InputMapping.MoveBackward.name(), new
    KeyTrigger(KeyInput.KEY_S), new KeyTrigger(KeyInput.KEY_
    DOWN));

}
```

 It's okay to assign several keys to the same mapping. For example, this recipe assigns both the arrow keys and the classical WASD pattern to the movement keys.

5. Finally, in the same method, we tell `InputManager` to listen to the commands, or it won't actually fire on any of the inputs:

```
for (InputMapping i : InputMapping.values()) {
  inputManager.addListener(this, i.name());
}
```

6. Now, once `AppState` is attached, it runs the `initialize` method (in a thread-safe way). Here, we get the reference to the application's `InputManager` object and run the `addMappings` method we just created, as follows:

```
public void initialize(AppStateManager stateManager, Application
app) {
  super.initialize(stateManager, app);
  this.inputManager = app.getInputManager();
  addInputMappings();
}
```

7. Once `InputManager` detects any of the actions and sends them our way, we will just forward them to the `GameCharacterControl` object by applying the sensitivity value to the analog input as follows:

```
public void onAnalog(String name, float value, float tpf) {
  if(character != null){
    character.onAnalog(name, value * sensitivity, tpf);
  }
}


public void onAction(String name, boolean isPressed, float tpf) {
  if(character != null){
    character.onAction(name, isPressed, tpf);
  }
}
```

8. We're actually almost done with this recipe. We just need to make sure that we reset everything when `AppState` is not to be used anymore. We do this by overriding the cleanup method. Here, we remove all the mappings and remove this instance from listeners of `inputManager` as follows:

```
public void cleanup() {
  super.cleanup();
  for (InputMapping i : InputMapping.values()) {
    if (inputManager.hasMapping(i.name())) {
      inputManager.deleteMapping(i.name());
    }
  }
  inputManager.removeListener(this);
}
```

How it works...

The `AppState` object works with the application in a way that is similar to how `Control` works with `spatial`. They give extended functionalities in a modular way. Once it has been attached to `stateManager`, its `update` method will be called every cycle. This gives us access to the application's thread as well. It also has the `stateAttached` and `stateDetached` methods, which can be used to turn functionality on and off easily.

Firing in FPS

There are several ways to perform firing, and the requirements depend heavily on the type of game. This recipe will start off with the basics, which can then be extended to support the different forms of firing. We'll create the necessary functionalities to fire instant bullets; they are performance-friendly and suitable for a fairly close-quarters FPS.

Getting ready

This example will be based on `GameCharacterControl` and `InputAppState` from the *Creating a reusable character control* and *Attaching an input AppState object* recipes of this chapter, respectively. Familiarity with the recipes is beneficial. Further, we'll use the `Ray` class in combination with `CollisionResults` to check whether the bullet has hit anything or not.

Rays can be imagined as infinite lines and are very common in game development. This is a fast way of detecting intersections with game objects and is thus suitable for instant firing. The targets might consist of any kind of `spatial`. In this case, it's a bunch of spheres generated by the recipe's test class.

We will let the `InputAppState` class handle the firing logic, and the `GameCharacterControl` class will keep track of cool down time of the weapon, or how long it takes between each shot. The reason we don't keep everything in `AppState` is that this way, the class can be used for things other than the player's character.

How to do it...

We will start by making some updates to the `GameCharacterControl` class. For the `GameCharacterControl` class, we introduce two new variables, `cooldownTime` and `cooldown`:

1. The first is the time between shots.

2. The second is the current countdown until the character can fire again. We need to add a getter for `cooldown` and the value itself is set in the following `onFire` method:

   ```
   public void onFire(){
     cooldown = cooldownTime;
   }
   ```

3. Lastly, in the update method, we need to subtract `cooldown` by `tpf` if it's more than zero.

In `InputAppState`, we also have to make some changes:

1. We begin by introducing a `List<Geometry>` called `targets`. This is the list of things the fired rays will check for collisions against. In the `addInputMapping` method, add another mapping for `Fire`. A suitable button is the left mouse button. This is implemented as follows:

```
inputManager.addMapping(InputMapping.Fire.name(), new
MouseButtonTrigger(MouseInput.BUTTON_LEFT));
```

2. In the `onAction` method, change the logic slightly. We add a new check for the fire action and we put the existing logic inside the `else` clause. We're telling `character` to handle all actions, except when we fire. This is implemented as follows:

```
if (name.equals("Fire")) {
    if (isPressed && character.getCooldown() == 0f){
      fire();
    }
} else {
    character.onAction(name, isPressed, tpf);
}
```

3. Now, create a new method called `fire`. This is where we're going to add most of the new functionalities. Inside this, we first define a new `Ray` class that we place at the camera's location (if it is an FPS), and we set the direction to be the same as the camera's direction, as shown in the following code:

```
Ray r = new Ray(app.getCamera().getLocation(), app.getCamera().
getDirection());
```

4. Then, create a new `CollisionResults` instance, which we will use to keep track of collisions. We parse through the target list to see whether `Ray` collides with any of them. All collisions are stored in the `CollisionResults` instance as follows:

```
CollisionResults collRes = new CollisionResults();
for(Geometry g: targets) {
    g.collideWith(r, collRes);
}
```

5. Afterwards, check whether there have been any collisions. If so, get the nearest one and display the location as follows:

```
if(collRes.size() > 0){
    System.out.println("hit " + collRes.getClosestCollision().
      getContactPoint());
}
```

6. Finally, call the character's `onFire` method, `character.onFire();`.

How it works...

With this implementation, we handle most of the actual logic that happens when firing inside `InputAppState`. The `GameCharacterControl` class is left to keep control of whether firing is possible or not. Some further work on this could have the character play an animation and keep track of the ammunition.

The `Ray` object we're using is being fired out of the camera. This makes it easy to set both the location and direction. This would be the case for a game in iron sights or sniper mode. If you want to fire from the hip, for example, it would be slightly more complicated.

Rays are normally very fast. Using them can, however, become performance-demanding in large game worlds with complex collision shapes. This is one reason for keeping track of the items to be checked against in a list rather than using the whole `rootNode`. In other cases, it's good to first filter down the list, maybe based on the distance from the player.

The `CollisionResults` class stores collisions between `spatial` or `ray`. It contains a list of `CollisionResult` objects, which in turn has a number of useful methods for determining where a collision has occurred and between what.

Firing non-instant bullets

In the previous recipe, we implemented a basic form of firing that will work for many cases. The exit velocity for a bullet is usually around 300 m/s (or close to 1000 feet/s) and might seem near-instant at close range. For ranges over 30 m (approximately 90 feet), the delay starts to get noticeable though, and more realistic games might need another model. In this recipe, we'll look into a type of bullet that travels in the game world. It's still an invisible bullet, but it can easily be visualized if required.

Getting ready

This recipe can be seen as a more advanced version of the previous recipe and won't require many changes to what we did there but will mainly contain additions. Almost all of the functionalities will be implemented in a new class, called `Bullet` (not to be confused with the physics engine with the same name that we use in a *Chapter 8, Physics with Bullet*).

How to do it...

Perform the following steps to fire non-instant bullets:

1. Let's begin by defining our `Bullet` class. The `worldPosition` and `direction` variables are used by the `Ray` class as a starting position each step it takes. The `RANGE` field is a static field that defines the maximum range, inside which the bullet will be effective. The `distance` variable is the distance the bullet has traveled since it was instanced. It also needs to keep track of whether it's alive or not, for cleanup reasons. It should be said that this particular bullet is rather slow and short lived.

```
private Vector3f worldPosition;
private Vector3f direction;
private float speed = 10;
private Ray ray;
private final static int RANGE = 10;
private float distance;
private boolean alive = true;
```

2. To avoid unnecessary object creation, we instance `Ray` in the constructor as follows, which we'll reuse throughout the lifespan of the bullet:

```
ray = new Ray(origin, direction);
ray.setOrigin(worldPosition);
```

3. It's in the `update` method that most of the work is done. At the beginning, we set the ray's origin to be the current position of the bullet. The direction will stay the same, so no need to change that. We do, however, need to set limit factorized by the time passed for the update (`tpf`). The limit is also the distance the bullet has traveled since the last update, so we use this to update the current position of the bullet:

```
ray.setLimit (speed * tpf);
distance += ray.limit;
worldPosition.addLocal(direction.mult(ray.limit));
```

4. If the total distance is longer than the range, the bullet can be considered beyond its effective range. We set `alive` to `false` as follows so that it can be removed:

```
if(distance >= RANGE){
   alive = false;
}
```

5. The `Bullet` class also has a `checkCollision` method. It takes a list of targets as input and tries a collision between each of them and the ray. If any collision is detected, `alive` will be set to `false` and the closest `CollisionResult` will be returned to the calling method as follows:

```java
public CollisionResult checkCollision(List<Collidable> targets){
  CollisionResults collRes = new CollisionResults();
  for(Collidable g: targets){
    g.collideWith(ray, collRes);
  }
  if(collRes.size() > 0){
    alive = false;
    return collRes.getClosestCollision();
  }
  return null;
}
```

6. Next, we'll add some code to the application class. It needs to keep track of `List<Collidable>`, called `targets` and `List<Bullet>`, called `bullets`.

7. The `simpleUpdate` method updates the movement of all bullets by calling their update method before seeing whether any collisions have occurred or not. Any depleted bullets are removed in a way that avoids `ArrayIndexOutOfBounds` exceptions:

```java
Bullet b = bullets.get(i);
b.update(tpf);
CollisionResult result = b.checkCollision(targets);
if(result != null){
  System.out.println("hit " + result);
}
if(!b.isAlive()){
  bullets.remove(b);
  bulletAmount--;
  if(i > 0){
    i--;
  }
}
```

8. Create a `fire()` method that creates a new bullet by using the camera's location and direction as follows:

```java
bullets.add(new Bullet(cam.getLocation().clone(), cam.
getDirection().clone()));
```

9. The method is called from the InputAppState's `onAction` method, which is similar to how it looked in the previous recipe:

```
if (isPressed && character.getCooldown() == 0f){
  ((CharacterInputTest_Firing_NonInstant) app ).fire();
  character.onFire();
}
```

How it works...

The `Bullet` class can almost be seen as a slow ray. The `Ray` instance we have in `Bullet` is mostly out of convenience, since it's already prepared to collide with targets. By incrementing the position of the ray and having a short limit for it, we have a `Ray` instance that takes little steps forward in the game world, checking for collisions in each update.

If a collision has occurred, the returned `CollisionResult` contains information about where the collision has occurred, with what, and whether it can be used to build further functionalities.

Creating an RTS camera AppState object

In this recipe, we'll try to mimic the camera and controls that are common in RTS games. The camera will mostly look down on the scene, and aside from basic movement and rotation of the camera, there will also be automatic scrolling when the mouse reaches the edges of the screen.

Getting ready

We're going to set up the camera and camera handling in this recipe. Loading a scene to make sure the camera works as expected would be helpful.

How to do it...

To create an RTS camera `AppState` object, perform the following steps:

1. We start by creating a class that implements the `AnalogListener` and `ActionListener` interfaces so that we can receive user input from the mouse and keyboard. We'll use these to control the camera as follows:

```
public class RTSCameraAppState extends AbstractAppState implements
AnalogListener, ActionListener{
```

2. Next, we'll define what controls we'll handle. Using an `enum` will keep things tidy, so type the following code snippet:

```
public enum InputMapping{
MoveLeft, MoveRight, MoveUp, MoveDown,
    RotateLeft, RotateRight;
}
```

The following screenshot shows you the difference between the camera's position above the ground (half circle) and the camera's focus point (at the center):

3. We then set up some things in the `initialize` method. Rather than having a completely top-down perspective, we give the camera a little tilt with `lookAtDirection` and a unit vector. Then, we move the camera further away from the ground with the `camDistance` variable. There is a reason we do this and don't simply set the camera's location. By doing it this way, we can more easily get the location the camera is looking at. This will come in handy if we want to add more advanced features:

```
private Vector3f camLocation = new Vector3f(0, 20, 0);
private Vector3f lookAtDirection = new Vector3f(0, -0.8f, -0.2f);

public void initialize(AppStateManager stateManager, Application
app) {
  this.cam = app.getCamera();
  cam.lookAtDirection(lookAtDirection, Vector3f.UNIT_Y);
  camLocation.set(cam.getDirection().mult(-camDistance));
  cam.setLocation(camLocation);
  this.inputManager = app.getInputManager();
  addInputMappings();
}
```

4. Lastly, add the keys that we'll listen to `inputManager`:

```
private void addInputMappings(){
   inputManager.addMapping(InputMapping.MoveLeft.name(), new
      KeyTrigger(KeyInput.KEY_A), new KeyTrigger(KeyInput.KEY_
      LEFT));
   inputManager.addMapping(InputMapping.MoveRight.name(), new
      KeyTrigger(KeyInput.KEY_D), new KeyTrigger(KeyInput.KEY_
      RIGHT));
   ...[repeat for all keys]... InputMapping.MoveDown.
   name(),InputMapping.RotateLeft.name(),InputMapping.RotateRight.
   name()});
}
```

5. Now to the `onAction` method, where any calls to these mappings will end up. Since we have an `enum`, we can use a switch to see what kind of input it is and set our Booleans accordingly:

```
public void onAction(String name, boolean isPressed, float tpf) {
   InputMapping input = InputMapping.valueOf(name);
   switch(input){
      case MoveUp:
         moveUp = isPressed;
         break;
         [repeat for all actions]      case RotateRight:
         rotateRight = isPressed;
         break;
   }
}
```

6. Let's have a look at the `update` method, where we will put these Booleans to use. An `update` method is called automatically every frame, and we also get to know how much time (in seconds) has passed since the last update, in `tpf`. We start by storing the camera's current location and initialize a `Vector3f` object, which we'll use for our movement delta as follows:

```
public void update(float tpf) {
   super.update(tpf);
   camLocation = cam.getLocation();
   Vector3f tempVector = new Vector3f();
```

7. Next, we look to see if any of our `movement` Booleans are `true` and apply this to `tempVector` as follows:

```
if(moveUp){
   tempVector.addLocal(0, 0, 1f);
} else if(moveDown){
   tempVector.addLocal(0, 0, -1f);
}
if(moveLeft){
```

```
    tempVector.addLocal(1f, 0, 0);
  } else if (moveRight){
    tempVector.addLocal(-1f, 0, 0);
  }
```

8. To keep the movement speed constant, regardless of the frame rate, we multiply `tempVector` by the `tpf`, and then we also multiply it by our `moveSpeed` variable. Then, we add it to `camLocation` as follows:

```
tempVector.multLocal(tpf).multLocal(moveSpeed);
camLocation.addLocal(tempVector);
```

9. At the end of the method, we set the camera's location to the modified stored location as follows:

```
cam.setLocation(camLocation);
```

10. If we try `AppState` now, we would be able to scroll across the scene with our keys. We still have mouse controls and rotation to take care of.

11. Let's begin with rotation. We will handle it through a method called `rotate`. The supplied value is our `rotateSpeed` variable, from which we'll extract a `Quaternion` rotated around the *y* axis. We then multiply the Quaternion with the camera's rotation as follows:

```
private void rotate(float value){
  Quaternion rotate = new Quaternion().fromAngleAxis(FastMath.PI *
    value, Vector3f.UNIT_Y);
  rotate.multLocal(cam.getRotation());
  cam.setRotation(rotate);
}
```

12. Furthermore, we need to make a few alterations to the `update` method. First, we look to see whether the user has pressed any of the rotation keys and call the `rotate` method:

```
if(rotateLeft){
  rotate(rotateSpeed);
} else if (rotateRight){
  rotate(-rotateSpeed);
}
```

13. The next piece is a bit trickier, and we perform it just above the line where we multiply `tempVector` by `moveSpeed` (highlighted). We multiply `tempVector` by the camera's rotation to make sure that we get the movement across the correct axes. Then, since the camera is slightly tilted, we negate any movement along the *y* axis. The best way to understand what would happen is to probably remove this line and try it out as follows:

```
cam.getRotation().multLocal(tempVector);
tempVector.multLocal(1, 0, 1).normalizeLocal();
tempVector.multLocal(tpf).multLocal(moveSpeed);
```

14. That's rotation taken care of! It's pretty common in RTS or top-down games to scroll by moving the mouse to the extremes of the screen. So, let's add functionalities for that. The following code snippet should be added in the `update` method above the rotation checks:

```
Vector2f mousePos2D = inputManager.getCursorPosition();
if(mousePos2D.x > 0 && mousePos2D.x < cam.getWidth() / 10f){
  tempVector.addLocal(1f, 0, 0);
} else if(mousePos2D.x < cam.getWidth() && mousePos2D.x > cam.
getWidth() - cam.getWidth() / 10f){
  tempVector.addLocal(-1f, 0, 0);
}
if(mousePos2D.y > 0 && mousePos2D.y < cam.getHeight() / 10f){
  tempVector.addLocal(0, 0, -1f);
} else if(mousePos2D.y < cam.getHeight() && mousePos2D.y > cam.
getHeight() - cam.getHeight() / 10f){
  tempVector.addLocal(0, 0, 1f);
}
```

How it works...

The `AppState` object listens for the input from the player via `InputManager` and applies it to the application's camera. In just one short class, we've produced an RTS-like camera behavior.

Lastly, in this recipe, we added functionalities to pan the camera if the mouse cursor was near the edges of the screen. We used `InputManager.getCursorPosition()`, which is a very convenient method that returns the position of the mouse in the screen space. The bottom-left part of the screen has an x,y coordinate of 0,0. The top-left part of the screen has an *x, y* coordinate that is the same as the height and width of the screen in pixels. The next `if` statements check whether the cursor is in the 10 percent of the outermost portion of the camera (which in this case is the same as the screen) and modify `tempVector` accordingly.

There's more...

That's nice and all, but if we have terrain in our scene, which is not flat, the camera might very well end up below the ground level. How can we remedy this? An easy way is to use ray casting to check for the height of the terrain where the camera is looking. This can be implemented as follows:

1. First, we need to make sure the terrain has `CollisionShape`:

   ```
   terrain.addControl(new RigidBodyControl(0));
   ```

2. By supplying `0` to `RigidBodyControl`, we say that it doesn't have any mass (and it won't be affected by gravity, if there were any). Since we're not supplying `CollisionShape`, `MeshCollisionShape` will be created. Since the terrain is of an irregular shape, a primitive (such as a box) isn't usable.

3. Next, we need to create a field for the terrain in `AppState` and a setter as well.

4. To actually find out the height of the terrain, we create a method called `checkHeight`, which returns the height as float.

5. Inside `checkHeight`, we shoot `Ray`, which originates from the camera's location in the direction the camera is facing. An alternative could be to shoot it down to get the height directly below the camera, as follows:

```
Ray ray = new Ray(cam.getLocation(), cam.getDirection());
CollisionResults results = new CollisionResults();terrain.
collideWith(ray, results);
```

6. If we get a result from our ray, we get the `y` value from the collision point and return it as follows:

```
height = results.getClosestCollision().getContactPoint().y;
```

7. Now, in the `update` method, just above the line where we set the location, we call the `checkHeight` method. Be sure to apply the `camDistance` variable in order to get the correct offset! This is implemented as follows:

```
camLocation.setY(checkHeight() + camDistance);
cam.setLocation(camLocation);
```

Selecting units in RTS

In this recipe, we'll show you how the selection of units in an RTS can work and also implement functionalities to show you when a unit has been selected. We'll use `AppState`, which handles mouse selection and we will also create a new `Control` class to be used by any `spatial` we want to be made selectable. In the recipe, Control will display a marker at the feet of the selected `spatial`, but it can easily be extended to do other things as well.

Getting ready

This recipe will work fine if you have already started creating a game where you would like to select things by clicking on them or if you've completed the previous recipe. The least you will need for this recipe is a scene with something to click on. In the text, we will refer to `TestScene`, which was created in *Chapter 1, SDK Game Development Hub*, and the Jaime model which is used in it. It is assumed that you have some experience in action handling. If not, it's recommended that you refer to the *Attaching an input AppState object* recipe of this chapter to get an introduction to it.

How to do it...

Perform the following steps to select units in RTS:

1. Let's start by creating the Control class and name it `SelectableControl`. It should extend `AbstractControl`.

2. The class only has two fields: selected, which keeps track of whether the `spatial` field is selected or not (duh), and marker, which is another `spatial` field to show when selected is true.

3. The only logic in the class is in the `setSelected` method; we let it handle attaching or detaching the marker:

```
public void setSelected(boolean selected) {
  this.selected = selected;
  if (marker != null) {
    if (this.selected) {
      ((Node) spatial).attachChild(marker);
    } else {
      ((Node) spatial).detachChild(marker);
    }
  }
}
```

 The method assumes that the `spatial` is actually a `Node`. If it is not a `Node`, the class can do other things, such as changing the color parameter of `Material` to indicate that it is selected.

4. We might want to display different markers for different types of selections, so let's make it flexible by adding a setter method for the marker.

5. Now, we create a new `AppState` class called `SelectAppState`. It should extend `AbstractAppState` and implement `ActionListener` to receive mouse click events.

6. We'll add two fields, one static string to represent the mouse click, and a `List<Spatial>` called `selectables` where it will store anything that is selectable, as follows:

```
private static String LEFT_CLICK = "Left Click";
private List<Spatial> selectables = new ArrayList<Spatial>();
```

7. The `initialize` method should look familiar if you've read any of the other game control recipes. We add a mapping for `LEFT_CLICK` and register it with the application's `InputManager` to ensure it listens for it.

8. The only thing the `onAction` method will currently do is to trigger the `onClick` method when the left mouse button is pressed.

9. Mouse selection (or picking) works by shooting `Ray` from the position of the mouse cursor into the screen. We begin by getting the position of the mouse cursor on the screen as follows:

```
private void onClick() {
    Vector2f mousePos2D = inputManager.getCursorPosition();
```

10. Then, we get the position this represents in the game world as follows:

```
Vector3f mousePos3D = app.getCamera().
getWorldCoordinates(mousePos2D, 0f);
```

11. Now, we can see what direction this would be by extending the position deeper into the camera's projection, as follows:

```
Vector3f clickDir = mousePos3D.add(app.getCamera().
getWorldCoordinates(mousePos2D, 1f)).normalizeLocal();
```

The following figure shows you how `BoundingVolume`, in the shape of a box, can enclose the character:

12. We define `Ray` using `mousePos3D` as the origin and `clickDir` as the direction and a `CollisionResults` instance to store any collisions that will occur.

13. Now, we can define a `for` loop that goes through our `selectables` list and checks whether `Ray` intersects with any of `BoundingVolumes`. The `CollisionResults` instance adds them to a list, and we can then retrieve the closest collision which, for most cases, is the most relevant one, as follows:

```
for (Spatial spatial : selectables) {
    spatial.collideWith(ray, results);
```

```
}

CollisionResult closest = results.getClosestCollision();
```

 It's a good idea to have a look at the `CollisionResults` class as well as `CollisionResult`, as these classes already keep track of many useful things that will save valuable coding time.

14. After this, we can parse through our `selectable` list to see whether the `spatial` that was clicked on has any of the items in the list. If it is, we call the following code:

    ```
    spatial.getControl(SelectableControl.class).setSelected(true);
    ```

15. Depending on the requirements, we might want to deselect all other spatials at this point. If we're using nodes, we might also need to see whether it is any of the spatial's children that were hit by the ray as well.

16. To test this, we can use the same class used in the previous recipe, with a few additional lines.

17. First of all, we need to create and attach `SelectAppState` as follows:

    ```
    SelectAppState selectAppState = new SelectAppState();
    stateManager.attach(selectAppState);
    ```

18. Create `SelectableControl` and something that can be used as a marker (in this case, it will be a simple Quad).

19. Lastly, we need to add `SelectableControl` to our Jaime model, and then add Jaime as a selectable to `AppState` as follows:

    ```
    jaime.addControl(selectableControl);
    selectAppState.addSelectable(jaime);
    ```

20. If we now run the example and click on Jaime, the Quad should be rendered near his feet.

How it works...

This example shows you one of the strengths of using `Control` and `AppState`, as it's easy to add functionalities to a `spatial` object as long as the logic is kept modular. Another (although possibly less effective) way of performing the selection would be to run a collision check against all `spatial` objects in a scene and use `Spatial.getControl (SelectableControl. class)` to see whether any of the spatials should be possible to select.

In this recipe, the items in the `selectables` list extend the `Spatial` class, but the only actual requirement is that the objects implement the `Collidable` interface.

When shooting the ray, we get the position of the mouse cursor from `InputManager`. It's a `Vector2f` object, where `0,0` is the bottom-left corner, and the top-right corner equals the height and width of the screen (in units). After this, we use `Camera.getWorldCoordinates` to give us a 3D position of the mouse click (or any position on the screen). To do this, we must supply a depth value. This is between 0, which is closest to the screen, and 1f, into infinity. The direction would then be the difference between the nearest and farthest value, and it would be normalized.

Making the camera follow units

This recipe will cover some principles on how to make the camera follow something in the game world. While it might seem like an easy task at first, there are some tricky bits too.

Getting ready

The recipe will build upon the *Creating an RTS camera AppState object* recipe of this chapter. All of the steps described in this recipe will be applied to `AppState`.

How to do it...

To make the camera follow units, perform the following steps:

1. We start by adding two new variables, which we'll use for the new functionality. A Vector3f variable, called `targetLocation`, will be used to track the target, and a Boolean variable called `follow`, will be used to declare whether the camera should track the target or not. These are set from external classes.

2. Out of convenience, we also define a final Vector3f variable, called `UNIT_XZ`, which we set to `(1f, 0, 1f)`. We'll use this to convert 3D positions to 2D.

3. Then, we need to add some functionality in the `update` method just before `cam.setLocation(camLocation);`.

4. First, we add a check to see whether the camera has been moved by the player. If so, we turn off the tracking as follows:

```
if(tempVector.length() > 0){
   follow = false;
}
```

5. Since the camera is up in the air and the target is (most likely) on the ground, we transform the camera's location to a position on the same horizontal plane as the target. The `targetLocation` vector is pretty simple to handle. We just flatten it by zeroing on the `Y` value as follows:

```
Vector3f targetLocation2D = targetLocation.mult(UNIT_XZ);
```

6. The camera is a bit trickier; since we're interested in the target's position in relation to the point the camera is looking at, we need to first find out where it is looking. First, we get the relative position of the point the camera is looking at by multiplying the height with the direction as follows:

```
Vector3f camDirOffset = cam.getDirection().mult(camDistance);
```

7. Then, we add it to the camera's location (you can say that we project it on the ground) to get its world position. Finally, we flatten this as well with UNIT_XZ as follows:

```
Vector3f camLocation2D = camLocation.add(camDirOffset).
  multLocal(UNIT_XZ);
```

8. We're using a linear interpolation that moves the camera's focus point 30 percent closer to the target location each cycle. Then, we reverse the addition we did earlier (or unproject) to get a new 3D position for the camera. The distance check is optional, but since we're going to use interpolation, we might save a few calculations by only interpolating if the distance is above a certain threshold as follows:

```
if(targetLocation2D.distance(camLocation2D) > 0.01f){
    camLocation2D.interpolate(targetLocation2D, 0.3f);
    camLocation.set(camLocation2D);
    camLocation.subtractLocal(camDirOffset);
```

9. To show that these changes work, we need to change a few things in our test application. We can grab Jaime from our scene and use his translation as the target location. We use worldTranslation and not localTranslation in this case:

```
appState.setTargetLocation(jaime.getWorldTranslation());
appState.setFollow(true);
```

10. Then, in the update method of the test case, we make him slowly move along the x axis as follows:

```
jaime.move(0.2f * tpf, 0, 0);
```

11. While running the application, we should see the camera follow Jaime until we move it manually.

How it works...

Another way of handling it would be not to move the camera during the input but the actual point it looks at, and have the camera troll along. No matter which way you choose to do it though, practicing and thus getting a better understanding of these trigonometric problems is always a good idea.

Since we're using linear interpolation here, `camLocation2D` will never actually reach `targetLocation`; it'll just get infinitely closer. This is why an `if` statement can be useful in these cases to see whether it's worth actually changing the distance or not. Finding the right threshold to break off is empiric and varies from case to case.

Following a character with ChaseCamera

In this recipe, we'll explore jMonkeyEngine's `ChaseCamera` class. This camera is a bit different from the previous cameras we've explored since we don't have direct control over its position. It is not like the camera-on-a-stick method we tried in the *Creating a reusable character control* recipe. While it still follows and looks at the character, it can float around the character more freely and also be controlled by the player.

The default control for the camera is to hold down the left mouse button and drag it to rotate the camera around the character. This is a very common control pattern in third-person games on consoles, where you rotate the camera with the left stick and control the character with the right.

We will implement a behavior where the character moves in the direction the camera is facing rather than the direction the character is facing when you press the forward key. This is common in console games.

Getting ready

Out of convenience, we'll extend, or modify, the `GameCharacterControl` class from earlier. This way, we'll get some of the basic functionality and save some time.

How to do it...

To start off, we can create a new `SimpleApplication` class in which we'll apply the following steps:

1. To initialize the camera, you supply the application's camera, `spatial`, to be followed, and the input manager, as follows:

    ```
    ChaseCamera chaseCam = new ChaseCamera(cam, playerNode,
    inputManager);
    ```

2. The `ChaseCamera` class has lots of settings to suit different kinds of games. To start off, we turn off the need to hold down the left mouse button to rotate the camera. It's not something we want for this recipe. This is implemented as follows:

    ```
    chaseCam.setDragToRotate(false);
    ```

3. We do, however, want smooth movement for the camera. For this, type the following line of code:

    ```
    chaseCam.setSmoothMotion(true);
    ```

4. By default, the camera will focus on the origin point of `spatial`, which in this case, would be Jaime's feet. We can easily make it look at a higher-up point, such as `waist.chaseCam.setLookAtOffset(new Vector3f(0, 1f, 0));`.

5. Next, we set some distance restrictions for the camera. There is no guarantee that it will stay within those boundaries though. It especially seems to violate `minDistance`:

    ```
    chaseCam.setDefaultDistance(7f);
    chaseCam.setMaxDistance(8f);
    chaseCam.setMinDistance(6f);
    ```

6. The `ChasingSensitivity` method defines how quickly the camera will follow `spatial`. If it's 1, it will follow slowly and if it's 5, it will follow quickly. We want the camera to be pretty responsive in this recipe:

    ```
    chaseCam.setChasingSensitivity(5);
    ```

7. The following `RotationSpeed` method defines how quickly the camera moves when moving it:

    ```
    chaseCam.setRotationSpeed(10);
    ```

8. Now, we have a basic setup for `ChaseCamera`. Let's see what we need to do to the `GameCharacterControl` class to suit this kind of game.

9. We can easily apply the behavior where forward is the direction of the camera by replacing the two lines, and setting `modelForwardDir` and `modelLeftDir` in the `update` method:

    ```
    Vector3f modelForwardDir = cam.getRotation().mult(Vector3f.
      UNIT_Z).multLocal(1, 0, 1);
    Vector3f modelLeftDir = cam.getRotation().mult(Vector3f.UNIT_X);
    ```

10. Since we don't directly control the characters' view direction anymore, we can set it to always be the last direction the character faced (when moving) as follows:

    ```
    viewDirection.set(walkDirection);
    ```

11. At the end of the method, we mustn't forget to apply it to `PhysicsCharacter` as follows:

    ```
    setViewDirection(viewDirection);
    ```

How it works...

The `ChaseCamera` class is a convenient class that offloads a lot of camera handling from the coder. It has a lot of settings that can be tweaked to get the desired behavior. Camera tweaking is a delicate and time-consuming matter, and if you're working in a team, this is something a designer might do if the properties would be exposed in a text file and loaded during startup.

There's more...

If you press forward and then rotate the camera, the character will move in that direction, instead. In many games of this type, however, the character would keep running in the direction it had before the player rotated the camera. We can apply this behavior to our character with a few tweaks.

To do this, we need to change `modelForwardDir` and `modelLeftDir` into private fields in the class. Then, we make sure we only update these when the character isn't receiving any input from the player. In this recipe, this would mean an `if` statement, as follows:

```
if(!forward && !backward && !leftStrafe && !rightStrafe){
  modelForwardDir = cam.getRotation().mult(Vector3f.UNIT_Z).
    multLocal(1, 0, 1);
  modelLeftDir = cam.getRotation().mult(Vector3f.UNIT_X);
}
```

Adding a game controller or joystick input

So far, we've used the mouse and keyboard for input. It's the most common way to handle controls on a PC, but let's explore the game controller and joystick support in jMonkeyEngine a bit. Writing code for a game controller is not very difficult. The tricky part is being agnostic enough to support the wide range of devices out there. Gone are the days when a joystick only had four directions and a fire button.

Getting ready

Like in many recipes in this chapter, we'll use `InputAppState` from the *Attaching an input AppState object* recipe. This recipe will be fine to apply to any input handling class. Naturally, some kind of input device is necessary as well.

How to do it...

To add a game controller or joystick input, perform the following steps:

1. First of all, any controllers that the system recognizes will be available through `inputManager.getJoysticks()`. We'll create a new method called `assignJoysticks()` where we apply this.

2. These controllers might turn up differently, in no particular order. It also seems as if they can sometimes show duplicate axes or some axes as separate controls. How can we handle this? The safest way might just be to have a `for` loop, parsing all controllers and trying to map them to the controls as follows:

```
Joystick[] joysticks = inputManager.getJoysticks();
  if (joysticks != null){
    for( Joystick j : joysticks ) {
      for(JoystickAxis axis : j.getAxes()){
```

3. A difference between keyboard and mouse mapping is that we don't actually need to add new mappings to `InputManager`. Instead, we tell the joystick what actions to emit. In this case, it's the *x* axis on the left stick that is assigned the strafing action as follows:

```
axis.assignAxis(InputMapping.StrafeRight.name(), InputMapping.
StrafeLeft.name());
```

 The *x* and *y* axes are often simple to map, usually on the left stick on the controller. The right one might not be as obvious. In this example, it's mapped to the rotation-X and rotation-Y axes, but might be mapped to the *z* axis, or rotation-Z as well.

4. In the same way, we can assign buttons to emit specific actions:

```
button.assignButton("Fire");
```

How it works...

A joystick is an input device, just like the mouse or keyboard. While there is a way to map the actions in the same way, with `InputManager.addMapping()`, the recommended way is to do the reverse and assign actions to the joystick instead. Remember that `InputManager` still needs to listen to the mappings.

Mapping buttons is even trickier than axes. First of all, there are two types of buttons, analog and digital. On a controller, usually the lower-right and left buttons controlled by the index fingers are analog, whereas all other buttons usually are digital. In jMonkeyEngine, everything analog is an axis. So, you will find that most likely, these will be reported as an axis.

 On my controller, a Razer Hydra, left and right triggers are reported as the *z* axis.

As if that's not enough, all you have to work with is a button index. Fortunately, with most game controllers emulating one of the big brands of console makers, some kind of standard can be expected. However, there are exceptions, and for any serious game, an interface where the user can remap their device is a must.

There's more...

There's a good, visual test example in the jMonkeyEngine project called `TestJoystick`, where you can instantly see the mapping of the attached controller and the corresponding action of each input.

The following figure shows you a view in the TestJoystick example:

Leaning around corners

If you're making a sneaker or tactical shooter game, a common feature is to be able to lean around corners. This is used to scout without being seen or shooting without exposing yourself too much. In this recipe, we'll develop a way to do this with our `GameCharacterControl` class. We will implement functionalities to both handle leaning with keys (such as the shoulder buttons on a gamepad) and freeform leaning with the mouse.

Getting ready

This recipe will expand on the `GameCharacterControl` and `InputAppState` classes from the beginning of the chapter, but it should be easy to adapt to your own project. It is mostly used in FPS games, and this is what we will build it for.

Leaning in this example will emulate the player character moving the upper body. To achieve this and to save us some calculations on how much the camera should be offset when leaning, we will use the built-in behavior of spatials and how translation and rotation is propagated through in a node.

How to do it...

1. First of all, we need a new `Node` instance called `centerPoint` in our `GameCharacterControl`. This will be the origin of our leaning, so to speak:

   ```
   private Node centerPoint = new Node("Center");
   ```

2. We set the translation to be pretty much in the center of the character's body (half the distance to the camera). We also attach the head node to `centerPoint`. In the `setSpatial` method, we add the following lines of code:

   ```
   if(spatial instanceof Node){
     ((Node)spatial).attachChild(centerPoint);
     centerPoint.setLocalTranslation(0, 0.9f, 0);
     centerPoint.attachChild(head);
   }
   ```

   The following figure shows you the relation between the `head` and `centerPoint` nodes:

3. We continue to follow the pattern we have used in `GameCharacterControl` and use Booleans to define whether an action should happen and then handle any changes in the `update` method. So, let's start by adding three new Booleans to handle leaning as follows:

    ```
    private boolean leanLeft, leanRight, leanFree;
    ```

4. Now, before we add the actual leaning functionality, we need to introduce two more fields. The `leanValue` field stores the current amount of leaning for the character. We use the `maxLean` field to have some kind of limit to how much the player can lean. This is in radians and is set to corresponding 22.5 degrees. Sounds too little? Feel free to experiment using the following lines of code:

    ```
    private float leanValue;
    private float maxLean = FastMath.QUARTER_PI * 0.5f;
    ```

5. In the `onAction` method, we make sure that we handle the corresponding input. Again, after setting the Booleans like this, make sure our actions stay on until the key is released:

    ```
    if (binding.equals("LeanLeft")){
       leanLeft = value;
    } else if (binding.equals("LeanRight")){
       leanRight = value;
    } else if (binding.equals("LeanFree")){
       leanFree = value;
    }
    ```

6. Applying the leaning value is pretty straightforward. We do this in a method called `lean`, which takes a float value as the input. First, we clamp `leanValue` to make sure we don't exceed our `maxLean` value. Then, we set the rotation along the z axis to the negative value as follows:

    ```
    private void lean(float value){
       FastMath.clamp(value, -maxLean, maxLean);
       centerPoint.setLocalRotation(new Quaternion().fromAngles(0, 0,
          -value));
    }
    ```

7. One bit left now, and that's where to call this method from. In the `update` method, we add two blocks of code. This reads as: if the button for leaning left is pressed and the leaning value is less than the maximum leaning value, lean more. Otherwise, if the button for free leaning is not pressed and the lean value is more than 0, lean less:

    ```
    if(leanLeft && leanValue < maxLean){
       lean(leanValue+= 0.5f * tpf);
    } else if(!leanFree && leanValue > 0f){
       lean(leanValue-= 0.5f * tpf);
    }
    ```

8. This code block then needs to be mirrored to lean in the other direction.

9. That's it for controlling leaning with buttons only. To add leaning using the mouse when `leanFree` is pressed, the `onAnalog` method needs a bit of work as well. We need to hijack the `RotateLeft` and `RotateRight` inputs when `leanFree` is set to `true`. The character shouldn't turn then, but it should lean instead. This is easily done with an `if` statement. We apply the lean value instantly in this case. The code we added previously in the `update` method will take care of returning the leaning to zero when the button is released:

```
if(leanFree){
  if (name.equals("RotateLeft")) {
    leanValue += value * tpf;
  } else if (name.equals("RotateRight")) {
    leanValue -= value * tpf;
  }
  lean(leanValue);
}
```

10. We already have `InputAppState`, which handles our input, so let's add a few more buttons to it. Three more values to our `InputMapping` enum are `LeanLeft`, `LeanRight`, and `LeanFree`.

11. Then, we assign those to *Q* and *E* keys to lean left and right, and V for free, or analog leaning.

How it works...

This is an easy way to handle leaning since we have very few calculations to do. The scene graph takes care of that for us. This works for the same reason; the turning of the `head` node in the *Creating a reusable character control* recipe could control the camera, which is normally not available in the scene graph. By attaching the `head` node to the center point (which, in turn, is attached to the main player node), any rotation or movement that the node does will be propagated to the `head` node, and thus, the camera.

Detecting cover automatically in a third-person game

Cover shooters is an ever-popular genre in today's console games. How does one code a system that recognizes and allows players to take cover? There are several ways to do this, but basically, there are two main branches, each with their benefits and drawbacks. The first branch is one where a level designer places logical cover items around the environments or where they are baked into models by an artist. This could be as simple as a bounding volume, or it could be complex with directional data as well. This has a benefit for the programmer in that it's easy to recognize when a player is inside them by comparing bounding volumes. Another benefit is that the designer has full control over where there is cover and where there isn't. A drawback is that it is labor-intensive for the designer or artist and might be inconsistent to the player.

The method we'll implement is one where there is no pregenerated cover, and it's checked in runtime. No additional work is required for a designer or artist, except that the models that are used need to be of a certain height to be recognized as cover (and work with animations).

Normally, there are two different kinds of cover: a low cover that characters can crouch behind and shoot over. The other one is full height cover, where characters stand next to the edge of it and shoot around the corner. In some games, it's only possible to use full height covers where it's also possible to shoot from them, such as corners.

Once the character is in cover, certain movement restrictions usually apply. In most games, the player can move sideways along the cover. In some games, moving backwards will release the character from the cover, while in others, you have to toggle the cover button. We'll implement the latter.

Getting ready

Let's define in more detail what we'll implement and how. We'll use `Rays` to detect whether the player is covered or not and `KeyTrigger` to toggle the entering or exiting cover. If you're not familiar with the concept of Rays, you can, for example, have a look at the *Firing in FPS* or *Selecting units in RTS* recipes in this chapter. Cover can be anything in the scene above a certain height. All of the action in this recipe will be handled by `GameCharacterControl` from the *Following a character with ChaseCamera* recipe. There are two separate areas we need to look at. One is the cover detection itself, and the other is related to how the character should behave when in cover.

How to do it...

To implement automatic cover detection, perform the following steps:

1. There are a few new fields we need to introduce to keep track of things. It's not enough to simply send one ray from the center to detect the cover, so we'll need to cast from the edges or near edges of the player model as well. We call this offset `playerWidth`. The `inCover` variable is used to keep track of whether the player is in cover mode or not (toggled). The `hasLowCover` and `hasHighCover` variables are set in the cover-detection method and are a way for us to know whether the player is currently within limits of a cover (but not necessarily in the cover mode). The `lowHeight` and `highHeight` variables are the heights where we'll cast `Ray` from in order to check for cover. The `structures` variable is everything we should check for cover against. Don't supply `rootNode` here or we'll end up colliding with ourselves:

    ```
    private float playerWidth = 0.1f;
    private boolean inCover, hasLowCover, hasHighCover;
    private float lowHeight = 0.5f, highHeight = 1.5f;
    private Node structures;
    ```

2. Now let's move to the fun part, which is detecting cover. A new method called `checkCover` needs to be created. It takes `Vector3f` as the input and is the position from where the rays originate need to be originated.

3. Next, we define a new `Ray` instance. We don't set the origin yet; we just set the direction to be the same as the character's `viewDirection` and a maximum length for it (and this may vary depending on the context and game) as follows:

```
Ray ray = new Ray();
ray.setDirection(viewDirection);
ray.setLimit(0.8f);
```

4. We define two integer fields called `lowCollisions` and `highCollisions` to keep a track of how many collisions we've had.

5. Next, we populate a new field called `leftDir`. This is the direction that is to the left of the character. We multiply this by `playerWidth` to get the left extreme to look for cover in, as follows:

```
Vector3f leftDir = spatial.getWorldRotation().
getRotationColumn(0).mult(playerWidth);
```

6. We'll start by checking for low covers and set y to `lowHeight` as follows:

```
leftDir.setY(lowHeight);
```

7. Then, we create a `for` loop that sends three Rays: one at the left extreme of the player, one in the center, and one to the right. This is done by multiplying `leftDir` with `i`. The loop must then be duplicated for the upper Rays as well:

```
for(int i = -1; i < 2; i++){
  leftDir.multLocal(i, 1, i);
  ray.setOrigin(position.add(leftDir));
  structures.collideWith(ray, collRes);
  if(collRes.size() > 0){
  lowCollisions++;
  }
  collRes.clear();
}
```

8. In order to be considered to be inside range of a cover, all three (left, middle, and right) Rays must hit something. A high cover always has a low cover as well, so we can check to see whether we've hit the low cover first. If we did, we do one more Ray check to find out the normal of the actual triangle hit. This will help us align the model with the cover:

```
if(lowCollisions == 3){
  ray.setOrigin(spatial.getWorldTranslation().add(0, 0.5f, 0));
  structures.collideWith(ray, collRes);

  Triangle t = new Triangle();
  collRes.getClosestCollision().getTriangle(t);
```

9. The opposite of the triangle's normal should be the character's new `viewDirection`:

```
viewDirection.set(t.getNormal().negate());
```

10. Finally, we check whether we also have high cover and set the `hasLowCover` and `hasHighCover` fields accordingly.

11. To restrict movement, the `onAction` method needs some modifications. The first criterion we check is whether the toggle cover button is pressed. If we're already in cover, we'll release the character from the cover. If we're not in cover, we check whether it's possible to go into cover:

```
if(binding.equals("ToggleCover") && value){
  if(inCover){
    inCover = false;
  } else {
    checkCover(spatial.getWorldTranslation());
    if(hasLowCover || hasHighCover){
      inCover = true;
    }
  }
}
```

12. In the following bracket, we limit movement to left and right if we're inside cover. If neither of the preceding statements applies, movement should be handled as usual. If we didn't want the player to be able to move inside cover, we'd be done by now.

13. Since we want to mimic popular cover-based games though, we have some more work ahead of us.

14. At the top of the update method, we have code to set the direction of the character based on the camera's rotation. We need to change this a bit, since once the character is inside cover, it should move based on the direction of the cover rather than the camera. To achieve this, we add a `!inCover` criterion to the original `if` statement, since outside cover, this should work like it worked previously.

15. Then, if we are in cover, we base `modelForwardDir` and `modelLeftDir` on the rotation of the spatial, as follows:

```
modelForwardDir = spatial.getWorldRotation().mult(Vector3f.
UNIT_Z);
modelLeftDir = spatial.getWorldRotation().mult(Vector3f.UNIT_X);
```

16. Once the movement has been applied to the `walkDirection` vector but before it is applied it to the character, we check whether the character will still be inside cover after moving:

```
if(walkDirection.length() > 0){
 if(inCover){
  checkCover(spatial.getWorldTranslation().add(walkDirection.
    multLocal(0.2f).mult(0.1f)));
    if(!hasLowCover && !hasHighCover){
```

```
        walkDirection.set(Vector3f.ZERO);
    }
}
```

17. We add the current `walkDirection` vector to the position of the player and check for cover at that position. If there is none, the movement is not allowed and we set `walkDirection` to 0.

18. Now all that's needed is a new mapping for `ToggleCover`, which is added to `InputAppState`:

```
inputManager.addMapping(InputMapping.ToggleCover.name(), new
    KeyTrigger(KeyInput.KEY_V));
```

How it works...

Each time the player presses the `ToggleCover` key or button, a check will be run to see whether there is cover within range. Three rays are cast forward from a low height, one at the left edge of the model, one from the center, and one from the right. Since `leftDir` is multiplied by -1, 0, and 1 on the *x* and *z* axes, we get the offset to the left- and right-hand side of the center position. To be considered inside cover, all three must have collided with something. This ensures that the player model is wholly covered.

The Ray won't stop just because it collides with something, and if the cover is thin, it might continue through the back side of it, generating additional collisions. We only want to count one collision per ray, though (the closest), which is why we only increase `lowCollisions` by one.

The high cover is checked after the low cover, because in general, there is never any cover that only covers the upper body.

Once it's decided that the character is inside cover and the player wants to move, we need to check whether the player will still be inside cover at the new position. This is so that the player doesn't accidentally exit cover and end up getting killed. To avoid unnecessary performance hits, we don't want to do this every frame. We do this only if there has actually been some movement happening.

See also

▶ To get the most out of this, we will need suitable animations. Refer to *Chapter 4, Mastering Character Animations*, to get a few ideas on how to do this.

3
World Building

In this chapter, we'll go through some of the fundamentals behind generating a code-based world and its lighting before we go beyond the basics and discuss more advanced techniques.

This chapter contains the following recipes:

- ▶ Using noise to generate a terrain
- ▶ Lighting your world and providing it with dynamic lights
- ▶ Deforming a terrain in real time
- ▶ Automating trees' distribution
- ▶ Endless worlds and infinite space
- ▶ Flowing water with cellular automata
- ▶ The essentials of a cube-based world

Introduction

In *Chapter 1, SDK Game Development Hub*, we used Terrain Editor to manually create a heightmap and Scene Composer to put things together into scenes. Those were the two ways of creating worlds in jMonkeyEngine. In this chapter, we'll look into creating worlds using code or procedural generation. This can often be very quickly set up, but getting it right (and performant) can be tricky. To achieve this, we will make use of techniques such as custom meshes and batching. Batching is a method of taking several geometries using the same `Material` instance and creating one mesh out of all their meshes. This can significantly improve the performance of the application.

Using noise to generate a terrain

While noise is unwanted in many occasions, it is a great tool for procedural generation and has many uses. In this recipe, we'll explore jMonkeyEngine's `FractalSum` class and generate an image based on the output. This can be used as a heightmap for a terrain, but we are not limited by that. With some tweaking, we could get a basis to cover a forest or city.

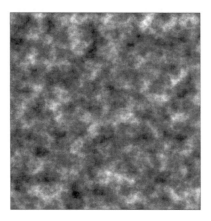

Getting ready

This recipe relies on a way to output an image. Either use your own method to do this or refer to the *The ImageGenerator class* section in *Appendix, Information Fragments*, which provides an example of how to do it.

How to do it...

To generate a heightmap, perform the following steps:

1. We will start by creating a class called `NoiseMapGenerator`.

2. In its constructor, define a new `FractalSum` instance and store it in a field called `fractalSum`.

3. Next, create a public method called `generateNoiseMap` that takes an integer parameter called `size`, a float parameter called `frequency`, and an integer parameter called `octaves` as inputs.

4. Inside the method, configure `fractalSum` with some of the values and set the amplitude to `0.5f` as follows:

    ```
    fractalSum.setFrequency(frequency);
    fractalSum.setAmplitude(0.5f);
    fractalSum.setOctaves(octaves);
    ```

5. Then, define a 2D float array called `terrain`. Its dimension should be [size] x [size].

6. Now, create a double `for` loop statement and parse through the size of both dimensions. Inside the loop, we get the value from `fractalSum`, which is based on your x and y coordinates; add `0.5f` to the value. Clamp it to get a value between `0f` and `1f` and set the value in the terrain array as follows:

```
for(int y = 0; y < size; y++){
   for(int x = 0; x < size; x++){
      float value = fractalSum.value(x, 0, y) + 0.5f;
      value = FastMath.clamp(value, 0f, 1f);
      terrain[x][y] = value;
   }
}
```

7. When you're done, call the `ImageGenerator` class to create the PNG image for us as follows:

```
ImageGenerator.generateImage(terrain);
```

How it works...

With this simple implementation, and by using the supplied `ImageGenerator` class, we have the basics for a heightmap. We can see the result in our `Projects` folder under `assets/Textures/heightmap.png`. It's an image that shifts smoothly between bright and dark areas; here, bright areas represent a high terrain and dark areas, a low terrain. Bright pixels have values that are close to 1, whereas dark pixels have values close to 0. Normally, noise outputs values between -1 and 1. This is why we change the amplitude to 0.5f so that it yields a range between -0.5 and 0.5, and then we add 0.5 to the result.

A noticeable problem is that no matter how much we change the speed and frequency of the noise, the same kind of rolling hills landscape will appear, only in different scales. By changing the octaves' value, we will generate noise in several iterations with decreasing amplitude. The value of each pixel for each iteration is multiplied with the previous one. The result is called fractal noise. Using octaves is a way of adding detail by iterating over the result with different frequencies. For each iteration, the frequency is doubled and the amplitude is halved.

Frequency can be thought of as a scale value where a higher frequency will generate more and smaller features. Having a higher frequency on its own will make peaks and valleys occur more frequently.

A normalization process is not strictly needed for a heightmap, unless we want to save it as an image. Also, if we were generating a large number of heightmaps (for example, during the runtime for a game), we would not want to normalize the terrain based on a particular heightmap's minimum and maximum values or we would end up with very similar and hilly landscapes.

There's more...

Now that we have generated a heightmap and exported it to an image, we can actually use it as a base in Terrain Editor. The process is similar to the one where we created a terrain for our scene in *Chapter 1, SDK Game Development Hub.*

After creating a new scene (by all means, we can use an existing scene as well) and opening it, we can right-click on the main node in the **SceneExplorer** window and select **Add Spatial..** and then select **Terrain...**.

It's important that we select the same total size as that of the pixels of our image. Then, in the **Heightmap** screen, we choose **Image Based** from the **HeightMap** drop-down menu and select our image.

The **Roughness** slider will define how much the heightmap will be smoothed out before it is added. A higher smoothness will remove finer details, and this is a must if we want to have characters that will run or drive on top of it.

The **Height Scale** option will define the maximum altitude that the heightmap can have and scale it accordingly.

Lighting your world and providing it with dynamic lights

This recipe will mostly be theories on different lighting types, but we'll also explore a way to easily control the movement of lights.

The four main types of lights that we can use to light up our world are as follows:

- **Ambient Light**: This lights up everything in the scene evenly. It's good for avoiding anything to be in a pitch-black state, but it doesn't create any shadows or nuances. Adding a too bright ambient light will give the world a bland look, while giving it a touch of color can set the mood.

- **Directional Light**: This shines from a particular direction with perfectly parallel rays and without any falloff. This is usually used to simulate a sun, a bright source of light located far away.

- **Point Light**: This shines equally in every direction but with a falloff, meaning this will eventually stop illuminating the surroundings. Usually, this forms most of the light sources in a game scene.

- **Spot Light**: This is exactly as it sounds. This produces a cone-shaped light in a specific direction from a specific location, and its light will eventually fall off. It has more settings than its sibling light types. Technically, it is more advanced than point lights and requires additional calculations in the shader to see what it illuminates.

A spotlight with the same `spotInnerAngle` and `spotOuterAngle` parameters will have a light cone that looks like this:

The `spotInnerAngle` and `spotOuterAngle` parameters define the size of the light cone that spotlight produces and both are set in radians. The `spotInnerAngle` parameter defines how far out the cone will shine at its maximum radiance. The `spotOuterAngle` parameter then defines how far the total extent of the radiance should be before it's been completely extinguished. Having a greater value for the `spotOuterAngle` parameter will produce a softer edge on the spotlight. A spotlight with a small `spotInnerAngle` parameter and a high `spotOuterAngle` parameter will have softer edges, as shown in the following image:

To ensure an object is affected by the lights in a scene, it must have a `Material` class that supports it. For most game objects, the default choice is the **Lighting** material. It supports a variety of lighting types from per pixel to lightmaps and vertex lighting. The latter two are optional but have their uses.

A lightmap is essentially an extra texture where lighting has been pre-rendered. Its resolution can rarely match real-time lighting, but from another perspective, it is very fast since lighting doesn't have to be calculated at runtime; also, it can be used for static scenes.

Normally, lighting is calculated on a per-pixel basis. This means that for each pixel visible on the screen, the processor has to calculate how it is affected by the available light sources. It is fairly expensive and even more so with many light sources, but it produces a more realistic result. Vertex lighting instead means that lighting is calculated for each vertex on a model. For low poly models, this is much faster although not as detailed. The quality will suffer noticeably when it is near the object, but it can give good enough results for objects some distance away.

How to do it...

Now that we have the basics covered, let's explore a pattern that allows us to move lights using objects in the scene graph:

1. First, create a new `PointLight` class called `pointLight` and set `radius` to `40`.

2. Then, call `rootNode.addLight(pointLight)` to add it to the scene graph.

3. Now, create a new `CameraNode` called `camNode` and then call `camNode.setControlDir(CameraControl.ControlDirection.CameraToSpatial);` before attaching it to the `rootNode`.

4. Next, create a new `LightControl` called `lightControl`, supplying `pointLight` to it to indicate that this is the light to control, as shown in the following code:

   ```
   LightControl lightControl = new LightControl(pointLight);
   ```

5. We set `controlDir` to be `LightControl.ControlDirection.SpatialToLight`. This means that the Spatial `camNode` will control the light's position:

   ```
   lightControl.setControlDir(LightControl.ControlDirection.
   SpatialToLight);
   ```

6. Finally, we add `lightControl` to `camNode`.

7. To test this out, we can load **Sponza** (Models/Sponza/Sponza.j3o) from the jMonkeyEngine's `test-data` library and apply the **Lighting** material to it.

How it works...

Lights are not `Spatials` in the scene graph, and it can be tricky to move them around. It can be added to nodes but then it will only illuminate the node (and its children) that it is added to. The `LightControl` class bridges the gap since it can be added as a control to `Spatial`, and it controls the position (and direction of a light). In this recipe, we used it so that the light will follow the camera around using a `CamNode`, but it works just as well for any other `spatial`.

There's more...

We touched on **Ambient Light** and **Directional Light** in the *Adding a sky box and lighting* recipe from *Chapter 1, SDK Game Development Hub*. In the *Creating a dynamic sky box with a moving sun* recipe from *Chapter 9, Taking Our Game to the Next Level*, we create **Directional Light** to simulate a day and night cycle.

Deforming a terrain in real time

A deformable terrain is something that can have a serious effect on the gameplay, or it can simply be a cosmetic bonus. It can be used for impact craters or games that require excavation.

We'll base the deformation around the `Control` class pattern as this allows us to offset the code in a manageable and reusable way. The recipe will trigger the deformation based on a mouse click, and it will use a ray to detect the collision point.

Getting ready

To get up and running quickly, unless there already is an application to apply this to, `TestTerrain.java` from the jMonkeyEngine's test cases will provide a good start for what we need. This example will expand on the code provided in that application, but it should work perfectly well with any terrain-based application.

How to do it...

With a base application already set up, we can get straight to the creation of the Control pattern:

1. Create a new class called `DeformableControl` that extends `AbstractControl`. It needs one private terrain field called `terrain`.

2. Override the `setSpatial` method and cast `Spatial` to fit your terrain field; use `terrain = (Terrain) spatial;` to do this.

3. Create a method called `deform` that takes the 2D location, the radius of the deformation, and the force as an input. Also, declare two lists that we'll use in the `heightPoints` and `heightValues` methods, as follows:

```
public void deform(Vector2f location, int radius, float force) {
    List<Vector2f> heightPoints = new ArrayList<Vector2f>();
    List<Float> heightValues = new ArrayList<Float>();
```

4. Now, we should create a nested `for` loop statement where we can iterate from `-radius` to `+radius` in both `x` and `y` (z to be correct). See how far from the center the point is and calculate the height to change at that location. The decrease of the force of the impact will be proportional to how far out it is from the center. Then, save the point in the `heightPoints` list and the new height in the `heightValues` list as follows:

```
for(int x = -radius; x < radius; x++){
  for(int y = -radius; y < radius; y++){
    Vector2f terrainPoint = new Vector2f(location.x + x,
    location.y + y);
    float distance = location.distance(terrainPoint);
    if(distance < radius){
      float impact = force * (1 - distance / radius) ;
      float height = terrain.getHeight(terrainPoint);
      heightPoints.add(terrainPoint);
      heightValues.add(Math.max(-impact, -height));
    }
  }
}
```

5. To wrap up the method, we need to apply the new heights. First, unlock the terrain and then lock it again as follows:

```
terrain.setLocked(false);
terrain.adjustHeight(heightPoints, heightValues);
terrain.setLocked(true);
```

6. Since we normally work with 3D vectors rather than 2D vectors, it can be a good idea to also create a convenience method called `deform`, which takes `Vector3f` as the input. It converts this input to `Vector2f` and in turn calls the other deform method as follows:

```
public void deform(Vector3f location, int radius, float force){
  Vector2f pos2D = new Vector2f((int)location.x, (int)location.z);
  deform(pos2D, radius, force);
}
```

7. Now, trigger the deformation from a method in our application. Firstly, it should create a new `ray` instance that originates from the camera, as shown in the following code:

```
Ray ray = new Ray(cam.getLocation(), cam.getDirection());
```

8. Next, create a new `CollisionsResults` object and check whether the ray intersects the terrain. If there is a collision, call `deform` on the terrain's `DeformableControl` object by supplying the `contactPoint` parameter of the collision as follows:

```
CollisionResultscr = new CollisionResults();
terrain.collideWith(ray, cr);
CollisionResult collision = cr.getClosestCollision();
```

```
if(collision != null){
  terrain.getControl(DeformableControl.class).deform(coll.
  getContactPoint(), 30, 30f);
}
```

How it works...

When deforming the terrain, we collect all the points we want to modify and the new heights in lists; then, we collectively update the terrain based on them. There is an `adjustHeight` method to update a single point as well, but it is assumed that it's faster using a list.

Locking the terrain means faster rendering. Whether to lock the terrain or not depends on the implementation. If it is a terrain that is changed with every frame, it probably doesn't need to be locked. On the other hand, if it changes only occasionally, it should probably be locked.

The formula that is used to calculate the change in height is *deltaHeight = force * (1 - distance / radius)*. This means that the change in height will be highest when it is closeest to the center; it will then fall off linearly as the distance increases and we get closer to the edge of the radius. A variation worth exploring is to use the root with *deltaHeight = force * FastMath.sqrt(1 - distance / radius)* instead. This will provide a rounder shape to the terrain.

Automating trees' distribution

Placing trees and bushes in an editor is fine for many types of games. There are many cases where you need objects to be in a very specific spot. When it comes to large-scale outdoor games, you might want to have a way of placing common objects in an automatic way, at least as a base. An artist or designer might then move items around to suit the needs of the game.

In this recipe, we'll create one such way that places trees using noise. Once the base is in, we'll take a look at how the pattern can be varied with different settings.

How to do it...

To produce automatic trees' distribution, perform the following steps:

1. We get right to the center of the things. Create a new class called `TreeControl` that extends `AbstractControl`.

2. Add a `TerrainQuad` field called `terrain`, a `FractalSum` field called `fractalSum`, a `Spatial` field called `treeModel`, and a `BatchNode` field called `treeNode`.

3. Override the `setSpatial` method. Here, we declare `treeNode`.

4. Then, assuming that the supplied `Spatial` is a `Node` class, parse its children looking for a `Spatial` that is an instance of `TerrainQuad`. Once found, set it to `terrain` as follows:

```
for(Spatial s: ((Node)spatial).getChildren()){
   if(s instanceof TerrainQuad){
     this.terrain = (TerrainQuad) s;
```

5. Using terrain's `terrainSize`, create a double `for` loop statement that parses from its negative height and width to its positive.

6. Inside this loop, grab a value from the `fractalSum` class based on the x and y coordinates. Then, look for the corresponding terrain height at that location as follows:

```
float value = fractalSum.value(x, 0, y);
float terrainHeight = terrain.getHeight(new Vector2f(x, y));
```

7. Now, we need to decide how many trees we want. The `FractalSum` class generates a value between -1 and 1. Start by saying that any value above 0.5 should generate a tree and create an `if` statement accordingly.

8. If this is fulfilled, start by cloning `treeModel`. Set its `localTranslation` to the x and y coordinates and the current `terrainHeight` field before attaching it to the `treeNode` field:

```
Spatial treeClone = treeModel.clone();
Vector3f location = new Vector3f((x), terrainHeight, (y));
treeClone.setLocalTranslation(location);
treeNode.attachChild(treeClone);
```

9. After parsing the whole terrain, tell the `treeNode` field to batch its contents to optimize the performance and then attach it to the supplied `Spatial`.

10. Now, create an application class to test this. It's recommended that you use a test case such as `TestTerrainAdvanced` to get a start.

11. Create a new `Node` class called `worldNode`, which we attach to `rootNode` and then attach the terrain to.

12. Then, create a new `TreeControl` class and load and set a suitable model that we can use as `treeModel`.

13. Finally, add the `TreeControl` class to `worldNode`.

After running the application, we will see trees spread out across the terrain—in valleys as well as on top of the mountains. Depending on the environment, trees might not grow on mountains. If we don't want this, we can add a simple check in the `TreeControl` class. By adding a field called `treeLimit`, we can clamp the growth of the tree above a certain height; also, make sure the `terrainHeight` field is lower than the value supplied from `fractalSum`.

How it works...

In this example, we let the noise do most of the work for us. All we did was parse through the terrain, and at regular intervals, check whether the noise value at that point indicated whether a tree should be placed.

The noise provides an almost endless amount of variation to our distribution of vegetation and an equally endless amount of tweaking possibilities.

The drawback of using these automatic generation techniques is that we don't have proper control over them, and changing a value ever so slightly might have a large impact on the terrain. Also, even if the generation process is cheap and can be repeated deterministically, we will have to start storing the data as soon as we want to modify it in any way.

There's more...

With the current settings, the example distributes trees across a landscape in a seemingly random pattern. At first glance, it might look natural but trees rarely are so evenly distributed as this. Outside of a forest, you will usually find trees clumped together. We can easily achieve this with noise by changing the frequency. The following examples show how changing the frequency can change the pattern:

- A frequency of 0.5 produces a very noisy and fairly uniform pattern, as shown in the following screenshot:

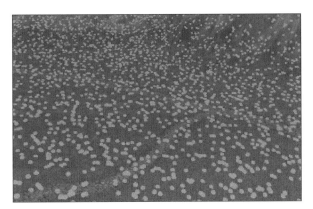

- ▶ With a frequency of 0.1, we can distinguish different patterns as follows:

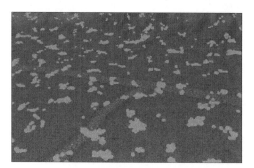

- ▶ A frequency of 0.02 yields even less but larger clumps of vegetation as follows:

Endless worlds and infinite space

There's really no such thing as endless or infinite in computer-generated worlds. Sooner or later, you're going to hit one limit or the other. However, there are some techniques that will get you further than others. The normal approach when creating a game is to move the player around the game world. Those who have tried to, for example, make a space exploration game in this way have noticed that pretty soon problems with regards to float numbers appear. This is because float values are not evenly spaced. As their values increase, their precision decreases. Using doubles rather than floats will only delay what's inevitable.

If you can't even have a solar system as a human-scaled game world, how can you then have a whole galaxy? As an old saying goes, "If Mohammed won't come to the mountain, the mountain must come to Mohammed." That is exactly the solution to our first problem! By making the game world move around the player, we ensure that the precision remains high. This is great for large-scale game worlds. The drawback is that it requires a different architecture. Switching how the game world is generated or loaded during the mid-development stage can be a huge task. It's better to decide this during the design phase.

Another problem is the sheer size of the worlds. You can't simply store all the terrain-based game world of a decent size in the memory at once. We can solve this problem by loading world data on demand and throwing it away when we don't need it any more. This recipe will use a simple method to generate the world on demand, but the principle can be applied to other methods, such as generating a heightmap or loading the world from a storage device.

How to do it...

Dynamic world loading can be created with the following steps:

1. Create a new class called `EndlessWorldControl`. It should extend `AbstractControl` and implement `ActionListener`.

2. We need to add a couple of fields to it as well. First of all, we need to keep track of the application's camera and store it in a parameter called `cam`. The class also requires a `Geometry` parameter called `currentTile` to represent the currently centered game area. A `Material` parameter called `material` will be used on the geometries and a `HashMap<Vector2f, Geometry>` parameter called `cachedTiled` will store the entire currently active game world.

3. The class implements `ActionListener` and will handle movements based on user input. To do this, add four Booleans as well: `moveForward`, `moveBackward`, `moveLeft`, and `moveRight`.

4. In the `onAction` method, add the following code to set the Booleans based on the input:

```
if (name.equals("Forward")) moveForward = isPressed;
else if (name.equals("Back")) moveBackward = isPressed;
else if (name.equals("Left")) moveLeft = isPressed;
else if (name.equals("Right")) moveRight = isPressed;
```

5. In the `controlUpdate` method, move the tiles based on the direction of the camera and the Booleans you just created. First, get the current forward direction of the camera and the direction which is to the left of it. Then, multiply it by `tpf` to get an even movement and an arbitrary value to increase the speed of the movement as follows:

```
Vector3f camDir = cam.getDirection().mult(tpf).multLocal(50);
        Vector3f camLeftDir = cam.getLeft().mult(tpf).
multLocal(50);
```

6. Using this, call a method called `moveTiles` if any movement should occur as follows:

```
if(moveForward) moveTiles(camDir.negate());
else if (moveBackward) moveTiles(camDir);
if(moveLeft) moveTiles(camLeftDir.negate());
else if (moveRight) moveTiles(camLeftDir);
```

7. Now, add the `moveTiles` method that takes a `Vector3f` object called `amount` as the input. First, parse through the values of the `cachedTiles` map and apply the `amount` value as follows:

```
for(Geometry g: cachedTiles.values()){
  g.move(amount);
}
```

8. Then, create an `Iterator` object and iterate through `cachedTiles` again; stop if any of the tiles contain `Vector3f.ZERO`, which is the location of the camera. This is our new `currentTile` object. This can be implemented as follows:

```
Vector2f newLocation = null;
Iterator<Vector2f> it = cachedTiles.keySet().iterator();
while(it.hasNext() && newLocation == null){
  Vector2f tileLocation = it.next();
  Geometry g = cachedTiles.get(tileLocation);
  if(currentTile != g && g.getWorldBound().contains(Vector3f.ZERO.
add(0, -15, 0))){
    currentTile = g;
    newLocation = tileLocation;
  }
}
```

9. The location of this tile will be used to decide which other tiles should be loaded. Pass this to two new methods: `updateTiles` and `deleteTiles`.

10. First, we take a look at the `updateTiles` method. It takes a `Vector2f` parameter called `newLocation` as the input. Create a nested `for` loop that goes from `x-1` and `y-1` to `x+1` and `y+1`.

11. Check whether `cachedTiles` already has the tile with `newLocation` and `x` and `y` combined. If it doesn't, we create a new tile and apply `BoundingBox` of the same size as the tile:

```
Vector2f wantedLocation = newLocation.add(new Vector2f(x,y));
if(!cachedTiles.containsKey(wantedLocation)){
  Geometry g = new Geometry(wantedLocation.x + ", " +
wantedLocation.y, new Box(tileSize * 0.5f, 1, tileSize * 0.5f));
```

12. We set location to be the delta distance from `newLocation`. If `currentTile` is not null, we add its `localTranslation` too:

```
Vector3f location = new Vector3f(x * tileSize, 0, y * tileSize);
if(currentTile != null){
  location.addLocal(currentTile.getLocalTranslation());
}
g.setLocalTranslation(location);
```

13. Finally, attach g to the control's spatial and put g in the `cachedTiles` map with `wantedLocation` as the key.

14. Now, for the `deleteTiles` method, it also takes a `Vector2f` parameter called `newLocation` as the input.

15. Like the `updateTiles` method, iterate through the `cachedTiles` map. Look for those tiles that are now more than two tiles away in either direction and add their location to a list called `tilesToDelete`:

```
Iterator<Vector2f> it = cachedTiles.keySet().iterator();
List<Vector2f> tilesToDelete = new ArrayList<Vector2f>();
while(it.hasNext()){
  Vector2f tileLocation = it.next();
  if(tileLocation.x>newLocation.x + 2 || tileLocation.
    x<newLocation.x - 2 || tileLocation.y>newLocation.y + 2 ||
    tileLocation.y<newLocation.y - 2){
    tilesToDelete.add(tileLocation);
  }
}
```

16. When you're done, simply parse through the `tilesToDelete` list, remove the tile from `cachedTiles`, and detach it from `Spatial`.

17. There is one more thing we need to do before leaving the class. In the `setSpatial` method, we should add a call to `updateTiles`, supplying `Vector2f.ZERO` to it to initialize the generation of the tile.

    For a larger implementation, we might want to introduce an `AppState` instance to handle this, but here we will manage it with a test application.

18. First of all, we need to disable `flyCam` with `flyCam.setEnabled(false)` and possibly move the camera to some distance from the ground.

19. Then, create a `Node` class called `worldNode` and an `EndlessWorldControl` instance called `worldControl`. Attach `worldNode` to `rootNode` and supply the `worldControl` object with a material before adding it to `worldNode` and setting the camera.

20. Finally, set up some keys to control the movement and add the `worldControl` object as a listener; refer to the following code on how to do this:

```
inputManager.addMapping("Forward", new KeyTrigger(KeyInput.KEY_
UP));
inputManager.addMapping("Back", new KeyTrigger(KeyInput.KEY_
DOWN));
inputManager.addMapping("Left", new KeyTrigger(KeyInput.KEY_
LEFT));
inputManager.addMapping("Right", new KeyTrigger(KeyInput.KEY_
RIGHT));
inputManager.addListener(worldControl, "Forward", "Back", "Left",
"Right");
```

How it works...

The process that we follow is that if a movement occurs, the `moveTiles` method will first move all the tiles to `cachedTiles`. It then checks to see whether there's a new tile that should be the center or whether it should be `currentTile`. If this happens, other tiles must be checked to see which ones should be kept and which ones need to be generated. This happens in the `updateTiles` method. Last in the chain is the `deleteTiles` method that checks which tiles should be removed because they are too far away.

If we print out the translation of the tiles, we can see that they are never very far from the center of their parent node. This happens because when we generate the tiles, we place them relative to `currentTile`. Since `currentTile` is also based on a relative position, things never move very far. It's almost like a conveyor belt.

Flowing water with cellular automata

Cellular automata is an n-dimensional set of cells that interact together with a given set of rules. Over time, these interactions have given way to patterns, and modifying the rules will modify the pattern. The most famous example is probably Conway's Game of Life where cells based on an extremely simple rule set create the most amazing, evolving patterns. In games, cellular automata is usually found simulating liquids in a tile- or block-based game worlds.

In this recipe, we'll explore such a liquid system based on a 2D grid. Since it's 2D, there can be no true waterfalls, but it can still be applied to a heightmap (which we'll show) to create natural-looking rivers.

Performance becomes an issue with large cellular automata, which will become evident as they're scaled up. To counter this, we'll also look at a couple of different techniques to keep the resource consumption down. The following image shows water running down the slope of a mountain:

Getting ready

This recipe requires height differences to make it interesting. A heightmap will work very well.

The model we'll develop will evolve around cells that are defined by two parameters: the height of the ground it resides on and the amount of water in it. If the height and amount of water combined are higher than a neighboring cell, water will pour out of it and into its neighbor. To make sure the cells are updated simultaneously, all of the water pouring into a cell will be stored in a separate field and applied at the end of the update cycle. This ensures that water can only move one tile through the field in one update. Otherwise, the same unit of water might travel across the whole grid in one update as we loop through the tiles.

The example mentions a `CellUtil` class. The code for this can be found in the *The CellUtil class* section in *Appendix*, Information Fragments.

How it works...

The following steps will produce flowing water:

1. First of all, let us create a class that contains the cell logic. We can call it `WaterCell`. It needs a float field called `amount`, another float field called `terrainHeight`, and one integer field for the current direction of the flow. It should also store any incoming water in a float field called `incomingAmount`.

2. In addition to the normal getter and setter for `amount`, add a method called `adjustAmount` that takes a float variable called `delta` as the input. The `delta` variable should be added to `amount`.

3. Create a method called `compareCells` that will move the water between cells. It takes another cell (where the water is coming from) as the input.

4. The first thing the method does is checks the difference in height between the two cells as follows:

   ```
   float difference = (otherCell.getTerrainHeight() + otherCell.
   getAmount()) - (terrainHeight + amount);
   ```

5. The method will only move the water in one way: from the supplied cell to this cell so it will only act if the difference is positive (and higher than an arbitrary small amount).

6. If so, it takes half of the difference since this would even out the amount between the two cells. Before applying it, make sure we don't move more water than there already is in the originating cell:

   ```
   amountToChange = difference * 0.5f;
   amountToChange = Math.min(amountToChange, otherCell.
     getAmount());
   ```

7. Add the calculated result to the `incomingAmount` field (we don't update the amount for this until everything has been calculated).

8. However, we must deduct the same amount from the originating cell or there would be a never-ending supply of water. It's done like this:

    ```
    otherCell.adjustAmount(-amountToChange);
    ```

9. Finally, return the deducted amount from this method.

10. We can leave this class for now and focus on creating a control that will use this class. Create a new class called `WaterFieldControl` that extends `AbstractControl`.

11. It needs two integer fields to control the width and height of the field as well as a 2D array of `WaterCell` called `waterField`. To display it, we'll add a `Node` class called `water` and a `Material` class called `material`.

12. The `setSpatial` method should be overridden and the `spatial` variable passed has to be an instance of `Node`. Look for a terrain among its children; once found, populate `waterField` with `WaterCells`, applying the height of the terrain for each tile as follows:

    ```
    for(int x = 0; x < width; x++){
      for(int y = 0; y < height; y++){
        WaterCell cell = new
        WaterCell();cell.setTerrainHeight(((Terrain)s).getHeight(new
        Vector2f(x, y)));
        waterField[x][y] = cell;
      }
    }
    ```

13. Now, create a new method called `updateCells`. For this example, define a source of water that will never run out right from the beginning by setting the amount of water in one of the middle tiles as 1.

14. Then, parse through each cell in the `waterField` array in a nested `for` loop.

15. If the cell has an amount that is larger than 0, we can go on and check where we should start moving the water. Start with the cell's direction, and if there is water left after checking one direction, continue to look through the other seven directions. This is what the implementation might look like:

    ```
    WaterCell cell = waterField[x][y];
      float cellAmount = cell.getAmount();
      if(cellAmount > 0){
        int direction = cell.getDirection();
        for(int i = 0; i < 8; i++){
          int[] dir = CellUtil.getDirection((direction + i) %
            8);
    ```

16. For each of these directions, we must first check that it is a valid location within the field. Then, retrieve the neighboring cell and call `compareCells` to try to dump water in it. If this try is successful, set the direction of the `neighborCell` object to the tested direction to represent the flow of water, as follows:

```
WaterCellneighborCell = waterField[x+dx][y+dy];
if(cell.getAmount() > 0.01){
    floatadjustAmount = neighborCell.compareCells(cell);
    if(adjustAmount > 0){
        neighborCell.setDirection(CellUtil.getDirection(dx,
            dy));
    }
}
```

17. Before you exit the method, parse through the `waterField` array once again. This time add `incomingWater` to the current amount of the cell and then set `incomingWater` to 0.

18. To handle the display of the result, create a new method called `createGeometry`.

19. The first thing we need to do is check whether the `Spatial` of the control has a child called **Water**. If it does, detach it.

20. Next, define a new `Node` class called `water`. Its name should be `Water` as this is an identifier in this example:

```
water = new Node("Water");
```

21. Again, parse the `waterField` array. If any cell's amount is more than 0, you should add a `Geometry` object that represents it.

22. We're going to add some logic to the `getGeometry` method to avoid recreating the `Geometry` field unnecessarily. First of all, set `geometry` to `null` if the `amount` value is 0.

23. Otherwise, if `geometry` is null, create a new `geometry` instance with a box-like shape as follows:

```
geometry = new Geometry("WaterCell", new Box(1f, 1f, 1f));
```

24. To adapt it to the amount of water we have, scale the resulting cube by typing the following code:

```
geometry.setLocalScale(1, 1f + amount, 1);
```

25. After this, return the `geometry` field, which might be null.

26. Coming back to the `WaterFieldControl` class, if the returned `geometry` variable is not null, set its location and attach it to the `water` node as follows:

```
g.setLocalTranslation(x, -1f + cell.getTerrainHeight() + cell.
getAmount() * 0.5f, y);
water.attachChild(g);
```

27. Apply the material to the `water` node and then batch it to increase the performance before attaching it to the control's `spatial`, as follows:

```
water = GeometryBatchFactory.optimize(water, false);
water.setMaterial(material);
((Node)spatial).attachChild(water);
```

28. To finish things off, update the `controlUpdate` method to call `updateCells` and `createGeometry`.

29. Now this can be used with a few lines in the application class. First of all, create a new `WaterFieldControl` class that we'll add to a `Node` class that contains a `Terrain` instance.

30. Next, we need to create the material for the water. This can be as simple as creating a `Material` instance with `Unshaded MaterialDefinition` and applying a blueish color to it or an advanced custom shader. It is then applied to the `WaterFieldControl` class via the `setMaterial` method.

How it works...

The beauty of cellular automata is the simplicity with which they work. Each cell has a very basic set of rules. In this example, each cell wants to even out the water level with a neighboring cell. As we go through iteration, the water moves downhill.

It's usually fairly easy to get the automation up and running, but it can take a while to get everything right. For example, even if each cell's amount is updated correctly, we will get weird oscillating water effects if the flow's direction doesn't work correctly. The reason is that there would be a preferred direction the water will take in a new cell. This direction might be the opposite of where it came from, making it want to move back to the cell it came from. Picking a random direction might work in that case, but it makes it more difficult to predict the behavior. This is why we use the direction of the water in the cell it came from. Naturally, the water will have some momentum and will continue to flow until it is stopped.

One thing that can be tricky to grasp at first is the reason why we don't update the water amount directly. The reason is that if water moves from cell x to cell x+1, that water would instantly become available for x+1 once the `update` method reaches there; also, it could be moved to x+2 and so on. We can't think of the water as real time, and that's why we first perform an outgoing operation on all the cells before we apply the incoming water. We also don't change the amount in the cell we're currently checking for the same reason. Instead, we move any water left in a cell to the `incomingWater` field.

The main challenge with the method is usually related to performance. Calculating can be expensive and rendering even more so. With a system like this, it's ever-changing and we might be forced to recreate the mesh in every frame. Rendering each cell on its own quickly becomes impossible, and we must use batching to create a single mesh. Even this is not enough, and in this example, we store the cell's `geometry` field so we don't have to recreate it unless the water level is 0 in a cell. We also scale the cell's `geometry` field if the water level changes as this is much quicker than creating a new `Mesh` class for it. The drawback is the additional memory that is used by storing it.

We also made it optional to update the water in every frame. By lowering it to a set amount of updates every second (in practice, its own frame rate), we could severely lessen the impact of the performance. This could also be taken further by only updating parts of the water field with every update, but efforts must be taken to conserve the amount of the water. We could also separate the field into smaller batches and check whether any of these need to be reconstructed.

There are ways to take this example further for those who wish. One could play around with the amount of water that each cell shares. This will make it more expensive to calculate but might give a smoother result. It's also possible to add pressure as a parameter, making it possible for water to move up the slopes. Evaporation might be a way to remove water from the system and clean up any puddles left by the main flow.

The essentials of a cube-based world

In this recipe, we'll build a small framework to generate optimized cube meshes, which can be used to create large-scale worlds. This framework will consist of an `AppState` object to handle user actions, a class called `CubeWorld` that will store the terrain data, and a class called `CubeCell` that will store the data for individual cells. In addition, there is a `CubeUtil` class that will help us to generate meshes.

Getting ready

This is an advanced recipe that requires an understanding the generation of a basic terrain, which can be found earlier in the chapter, and the building blocks of meshes and how to create custom meshes.

Before we begin, we will create a class called `CubeUtil` and populate it with some shaped data that we will need later. Since each of the cells is of a box shape, we can borrow some fields from the `Box` and `AbstractBox` classes and save some time in setting it up. Just copy the `GEOMETRY_INDICES_DATA`, `GEOMETRY_NORMALS_DATA`, and `GEOMETRY_TEXTURE_ DATA` fields to the `CubeUtil` class.

At the bottom of the class, there is a method called `doUpdateGeometryVertices` that contains a float array. Copy this float array too and call its vertices. This array contains data for the 24 vertices needed to create a cube with normal. It in turn relies on references to eight original vertex positions. We can get these from the `AbstractBox` class and the `computeVertices` method. The `Vector3f` center referenced here can be replaced with `Vector3f.ZERO`. The xExtent, yExtent , and zExtent parameters can be replaced with `0.5f` to get a square box with `1f` sides.

How to do it...

We start by creating the object that contains the cell data. This will have the following seven steps:

1. First, create a new class called `CubeCell`.

2. It contains a `Mesh` field call `mesh`, an array of six Booleans called `neighbors`, and another Boolean called `refresh`.

3. In addition, there is enum called `Type` where we can put names such as `Rock`, `Sand`, and `Grass`. Then, add a `Type` field called `type`.

4. Create a method called `hasNeighbor` that takes an integer parameter as an input and return the corresponding Boolean from the array.

5. Then, add a method called `setNeighbor` that takes both an integer parameter called `direction` and a Boolean parameter called `neighbor` as the input. If the current Boolean at the position of the direction is not the same as that of the neighbor, store the neighbor at that location and set `refresh` to `true`.

6. Add a method called `requestRefresh` that sets `refresh` to `true`.

7. For a mesh, add a `getMesh` method, and inside this, call a method called `CubeUtil.createMesh` if the mesh is null or refresh it if it is `true`. This will also set `refresh` to `false` as follows:

```
if(mesh == null || refresh){
  mesh = CubeUtil.createMesh(this);
  refresh = false;
}
return mesh;
```

Now, let's return to the `CubeUtil` class where we add some helper methods to generate the world. This section has the following steps:

1. First, add a `createMesh` method that takes a `CubeCell` parameter as the input. This method will create a mesh for the cell, and here you'll use the data we set up in the *Getting Ready* section of this recipe.

2. First of all, place the vertex data in the mesh with the following line of code:

```
m.setBuffer(VertexBuffer.Type.Position, 3, BufferUtils.
createFloatBuffer(vertices));
```

3. Add indices to the sides of the mesh that are exposed and check the neighbors to see which ones these are. Then, add six indices (for two triangles) for each mesh to a list using GEOMETRY_INDICES_DATA, as follows:

```
List<Integer> indices = new ArrayList<Integer>();
for(intdir = 0; dir < 6; dir++){
  if(!cube.hasNeighbor(dir)){
    for(int j = 0; j < 6; j++){
      indices.add(GEOMETRY_INDICES_DATA[dir * 6 + j]);
    }
  }
}
```

4. To add these to the mesh, first convert them into an array. Then, set the array as the index buffer, as follows:

```
m.setBuffer(VertexBuffer.Type.Index, 1, BufferUtils.
createIntBuffer(indexArray));
```

5. For texture coords and vertex normals, simply use the data we have already set up as follows:

```
m.setBuffer(VertexBuffer.Type.TexCoord, 2, BufferUtils.
createFloatBuffer(GEOMETRY_TEXTURE_DATA));
m.setBuffer(VertexBuffer.Type.Normal, 3, GEOMETRY_NORMALS_DATA);
```

6. Now, return the mesh to the calling method.

7. Add one more method called generateBlock to the CubeUtil class and create a 3D array of CubeCell and return it. The principle for it is the same as the heightmap we created in the *Using noise to generate a terrain* recipe, except here we use three dimensions instead of two. The following code with generate a CubeCell class in a 3D pattern:

```
CubeCell[][][] terrainBlock = new CubeCell[size][size][size];
for(int y = 0; y < size; y++){
  for(int z = 0; z < size; z++){
    for(int x = 0; x < size; x++){
      double value = fractalSum.value(x, y, z);
      if(value >= 0.0f){
        terrainBlock[x][y][z] = new CubeCell();
      }
    }
  }
}
```

We can now look at how to tie these two classes together and start generating some cubes. This will be performed in the following steps:

1. We turn our attention to the `CubeWorld` class that will hold the information about all our cubes. It has a `Node` field called `world`, an integer file called `batchSize`, and array of `Material` called `materials` and, for this example, a single `CubeCell[] [] []` array called `terrainBlock`.

2. After initializing the `worldNode` class in the constructor, create a public method called `generate`. Inside this, call `CubeUtil.generateBlock(4, batchSize)` and store it in `terrainBlock`.

3. Then, call and create another method called `generateGeometry` that will put all the `CubeCell` classes together into a `Node` class.

4. First, check whether the `worldNode` class already has a node with a given name. If it does, detach it. In either case, create a new `BatchNode` field with the same name we checked for.

5. Now, parse through the whole of the `terrainBlock` array and all the locations where there is a `CubeCell` class; we will check 6 directions (either side of it). For each side, check whether there is a neighbor there; there will be one if the position is not null. In that case, call `setNeighbor` on the cell you're checking for and supply the direction of the current as follows:

```
for(int y = 0; y < batchSize; y++){
   repeat for x and z
   if(terrainBlock[x][y][z] != null){
      for(inti = 0; i < 6; i++){
         Vector3f coords = CubeUtil.directionToCoords(i);
         if(coords.y + y > -1 && coords.y + y < batchSize){
            repeat for x and z
            if(terrainBlock[(int)coords.x + x][(int)coords.y
               y][(int)coords.z + z] != null){
               terrainBlock[x][y][z].setNeighbor(i, true);
            } else {
               terrainBlock[x][y][z].setNeighbor(i, false);
            }
         }
      }
   }
}
```

6. The next step is to create geometries for the `CubeCell` instances. Do this by again parsing through the `terrainBlock` field, and where the corresponding `CubeCell` is not null, create a new `Geometry` class by calling the `CubeCell'sgetMesh'` method. Then, move it to the right position using x, y, and z that we're iterating over, and apply a material and attach it to the batch node as follows:

```
Geometry g = new Geometry("Cube", terrainBlock[x][y][z].getMesh()
);
```

```
g.setLocalTranslation(x, y, z);
g.setMaterial(materials[0]);
node.attachChild(g);
```

7. Finally, in the `generateGeometry` method, call `node.updateModelBound()` and `node.batch()` to optimize it before attaching it to `worldNode`.

8. The basic of the generation process is now in place, and you can create a new class called `CubeWorldAppState` that extends `AbstractAppState`. In this case, add a `CubeWorld` field called `cubeWorld`.

9. Override the `initialize` method and declare a new `cubeWorld` instance.

10. Then, load a new material based on the **Lighting** material's definition and supply it to `cubeWorld`. After this, call `cubeWorld` and generate and attach `worldNode` through its getter method.

11. Also, add a light to see anything since we're using the **Lighting** material.

12. Now, create an application where we attach this `Appstate` instance and we should see our block of `CubeCell` in the world. It's static, however, and it's very common to want to change the world.

Let's see how we can add the functionality to pick up and place blocks. The following figure is of a resulting terrain block:

1. Begin in `CubeWorldAppState` by implementing `ActionListener` to handle user input. Add a `CubeCell` field called `takenCube` to store a `CubeCell` field that has been picked up.

2. Add mappings to `inputManager` to pick up and place a `CubeCell` field. Use the left and right mouse button as shown in the following lines of code:

```
inputManager.addMapping("take", new MouseButtonTrigger(MouseInput.
BUTTON_LEFT));
inputManager.addMapping("put", new MouseButtonTrigger(MouseInput.
BUTTON_RIGHT));
```

3. Then, create a method called `modifyTerrain` that takes a Boolean called `pickupCube` as the input.

4. To control what is picked up or aimed at, use a pattern that we have established in the *Firing in FPS* recipe of *Chapter 2, Cameras and Game Controls*. Use a ray that originates from the camera and moves toward the camera's direction.

5. Now, collide it with the `worldnode` class of `cubeWorld`. If it collides with something and the distance is lower than two (or some other arbitrary number) and `pickupCube` is true, we will pick up a cube. Get the `worldTranslation` vector of the geometry that the ray has collided with. Then, call a method called `changeTerrain` in `cubeWorld`. We'll create the method in a short while. Now, supply it with the coordinates of the geometry it collides with and the currently empty `takenCube` field as follows:

```
if(coll != null && coll.getDistance() < 2f && pickupCube){
  Vector3f geomCoords = coll.getGeometry().getWorldTranslation();
  takenCube = cubeWorld.changeTerrain(geomCoords, takenCube);
}
```

6. If instead, there is no collision or the collision is too far away, and at the same time `pickupCube` is `false` and `takenCube` is not null, try to place `takenCube` in the world. Since we don't have a collision point, move some way along the direction of the camera and round it off to the nearest integer. Then, call `cubeWorld.changeTerrain` again with the coordinates along with `takenCube`, as follows:

```
Vector3f geomCoords = cam.getLocation().add(cam.getDirection().
mult(2f));
geomCoords.set(Math.round(geomCoords.x), Math.round(geomCoords.y),
Math.round(geomCoords.z));
takenCube = cubeWorld.changeTerrain(geomCoords, takenCube);
```

7. In the `onAction` method, add the logic for the corresponding key press and call `modifyTerrain`, supplying either `true` if we're picking up or `false` if we're instead trying to place a `CubeCell` field.

8. In the `CubeWorld` class, create this `changeTerrain` method that takes a `Vector3f` parameter called `coords` and a `CubeCell` parameter called `blockToPlace` as the input. The `Coords` parameters represent the location of a `CubeCell` instance. The `changeTerrain` method returns a `CubeCell` instance.

9. The first thing we will do is define a `CubeCell` field called `changedBlock` where we store the incoming `blockToPlace`.

10. Then, do a check to make sure the supplied coordinate is within the bounds of the `terrainBlock` array and then check whether `changedBlock` is null. If it is, pick up the `CubeCell` instance from this location and populate `changedBlock` with the `CubeCell` instance. Then, set the location's `CubeCell` to null as follows:

```
if(changedBlock == null){
  changedBlock = terrainBlock[x][y][z];
  terrainBlock[x][y][z] = null;
}
```

11. If instead the `CubeCell` instance at this location is null (we already know that `changedBlock` is not null), set the `CubeCell` instance over here to `changedBlock` and `changedBlock` to null. Also, call `requestRefresh` on the `CubeCell` instance to force it to update the mesh, as follows:

```
else if(terrainBlock[x][y][z] == null){
  terrainBlock[x][y][z] = changedBlock;
  terrainBlock[x][y][z].requestRefresh();
  changedBlock = null;
}
```

12. Finally, if there has been a change made, call `generateGeometry` and return `changedBlock` to the calling method.

How it works...

This recipe is mostly about creating meshes that are as optimized as possible. Cubes are great building blocks, but each has 12 triangles, and rendering them all for hundreds or thousands will quickly slow down most systems. In the first part of the recipe, we implemented functionalities to create meshes that only had the exposed sides of the cube's generated triangles. We found this out by checking which of the positions next to the cube were occupied by other cubes.

Once all the cubes were generated, we added them to `BatchNode` and batched it to create one mesh for all the cubes. Even if the polygon count is the same, decreasing the number of objects greatly enhances the performance.

Having a single mesh means we can't change a single object in the mesh without regenerating the whole batch. If we plan to scale this up and generate a whole world, we need to keep the size of the batch to a size where we can regenerate it without creating slowdowns. Exploring a way to generate it on a separate thread might be a good next step.

4
Mastering Character Animations

In this chapter, we'll cover the following topics:

- ▸ Previewing animations in SDK
- ▸ Creating an animation manager control
- ▸ Extending the animation control
- ▸ Handling jump animations
- ▸ Creating a custom animation – leaning
- ▸ Creating a subanimation
- ▸ Lip syncing and facial expressions
- ▸ Eye movement
- ▸ Location-dependent animation – edge check
- ▸ Inverse kinematics – aligning feet with ground

Introduction

In this chapter, we'll take a closer look at skeleton-based animations. These are central features in many games, and having a good framework can save a lot of time (and money) in a project.

For those who are completely new to the subject of animations, it's recommended that you have a look at the jMonkeyEngine tutorials and Hello Animation in particular at `http://hub.jmonkeyengine.org/wiki/doku.php/jme3:beginner:hello_animation`.

Previewing animations in SDK

Before digging into the code, let's just briefly see how we can use SDK to see the animations that are supplied with a model.

How to do it...

Perform the following steps to see the animations that are supplied with the model:

1. Find the model in the **Projects** window. Right-click on it and select **Edit** in **SceneComposer** and you will get the following screenshot:

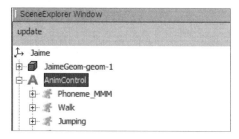

2. Find the **SceneExplorer** window and open the model's node. Look for **AnimControl** as seen in the preceding screenshot.

3. Open the **AnimControl** window and you will see the list of animations that are available. Then, navigate to the **Properties** window to select any of the animations and play them in the model, as shown in the following screenshot:

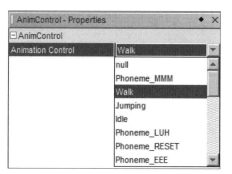

How it works...

The **SceneExplorer** window not only shows all the spatials that belong to a node, but also the controls that are attached to any spatial. Apart from adding new controls, it's also possible to change them. In the case of `AnimControl`, it's possible to set the current animation so it is played instantly. To stop playing it, we can select `null`.

Creating an animation manager control

We will create a control that will handle the animations of a character. It will follow jMonkeyEngine's control pattern and extend `AbstractControl`. We won't actually use most of the functions of `AbstractControl` right away, but it's a neat way to offset some of the code from a possible `Character` class. It will also be easy to add functionalities later on.

How to do it...

To create a control that will handle the animations of a character, perform the following steps:

1. Create a class called `CharacterAnimationManager` and have it extend `AbstractControl`. This class should also implement `AnimEventListener`, which `AnimControl` uses to tell our class when animations have finished playing.

2. We're going to map Jaime's animations into an enum. This is so we don't have to do a lot of string comparisons. While we're at it, we'll add some basic logic to the enum as well. The name of the animation, whether the animation should loop or not, and the time `AnimControl` should take to blend to a new animation using the following code:

```
public enum Animation{
    Idle(LoopMode.Loop, 0.2f),
    Walk(LoopMode.Loop, 0.2f),
    Run(LoopMode.Loop, 0.2f),
    ...
    SideKick(LoopMode.DontLoop, 0.1f);

    Animation(LoopMode loopMode, float blendTime){
        this.loopMode = loopMode;
        this.blendTime = blendTime;
    }
    LoopMode loopMode;
    float blendTime;
}
```

   We need two fields as well: an `AnimControl` field called `animControl` and an `AnimChannel` called `mainChannel`.

3. We set these in the `setSpatial` method, as shown in the following code. Don't forget to add the class to the `AnimControl` field as a listener, or we won't receive any calls when animations are finished:

```
public void setSpatial(Spatial spatial) {
    super.setSpatial(spatial);
    animControl = spatial.getControl(AnimControl.class);
```

```
    mainChannel = animControl.createChannel();
    animControl.addListener(this);
}
```

4. We define a new method called `setAnimation` in the following code. Inside this, we set the supplied animation to be `mainChannel` as the current one if it's not the same as the one playing now. We also set `loopMode` according to how it's defined in the enum:

```
public void setAnimation(Animation animation) {
    if(mainChannel.getAnimationName() == null || !mainChannel.
getAnimationName().equals(animation.name())){
        mainChannel.setAnim(animation.name(), animation.blendTime);
        mainChannel.setLoopMode(animation.loopMode);
    }
}
```

5. In the `onAnimCycleDone` method, we create a control so that all animations that don't loop return to the idle animation, with the exception of `JumpStart`, which should switch to `Jumping` (as in midair) as shown in the following code:

```
public void onAnimCycleDone(AnimControl control, AnimChannel
channel, String animName) {
    if(channel.getLoopMode() == LoopMode.DontLoop){
        Animation newAnim = Animation.Idle;
        Animation anim = Animation.valueOf(animName);
        switch(anim){
          case JumpStart:
            newAnim = Animation.Jumping;
            break;
        }
        setAnimation(newAnim);
    }
}
```

6. That's all that's needed to create a class that manages animations! To set this up from an application, we just need to load a model in the application and add the following line:

```
jaime.addControl(new AnimationManagerControl());
```

How it works...

The `AnimControl` class is responsible for playing and keeping track of the animations. `AnimChannel` has a list of `Bones` that the animation should affect.

Since we let the enum decide the animation parameters for us, we don't need much code in the `setAnimation` method. We do however need to make sure we don't set the same animation if it is already playing or it could get stuck, repeating the first frame in a loop.

The `onAnimCycleDone` method is called from `AnimControl` whenever an animation reaches the end. Here, we decide what will happen when this occurs. If the animation is not looping, we must tell it what to do next. Playing the idle animation is a good choice.

We also have one special case. If you look at the animation list, you will notice that Jaime's jump animation is split into three parts. This is to make it easier to handle jumps of different lengths or the falling animation.

We will tell `AnimControl` to change the animation to a jumping action once `JumpStart` is done. We never change to `JumpEnd` once the jumping action has taken place however. Instead, this should be called from elsewhere when Jaime hits the ground after he jumps. How this is measured is dependent on the game logic, but since we're using the `Control` pattern, we could use `controlUpdate` to check Jaime's whereabouts.

Extending the animation control

In the previous recipe, we built the basics for an animation by managing the `Control` class. This would be fine for many types of games, but for a game where a character is in focus, let's say an FPS, we would want a more detailed control. This is where the concept of `AnimChannel` comes in handy. `AnimChannel` is a way of dividing a skeleton into different groups of bones and applying an animation only to them. As we will find out in this recipe, this means we can have different animations playing on different parts of the body at the same time.

Applying animations only to certain channels can help reduce the workload tremendously for a character-focused game. Let's say we're making an FPS or RPG where the character can wield a number of different items and weapons, both one- and two-handed. Making full-body animations for all the combinations, including standing, walking, running, and more, is not feasible. If instead, you are able to apply the weapon animation only to the upper body and a walk animation to the lower body, you get a lot more freedom.

This recipe will also describe some other tricks that might help in developing the game.

How to do it...

We can have different animations playing on different parts of the body at the same time by performing the following steps:

1. First of all, we'll implement the `ActionListener` and `AnalogListener` interfaces in our animation's `manager` class. This will allow us to receive input directly from an input-handling class and decide which animations to play.

2. Next, we define two `AnimChannels`: one for the upper body called `upperChannel` and one for the lower called `lowerChannel`. We also create a `Channel` enum to easily choose whether to play an animation in a separate channel or the whole body, as shown in the following code:

```
public enum Channel{
    Upper, Lower, All,
}
```

❑ The SceneExplorer can be used to find suitable bones as shown in the following screenshot:

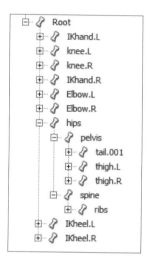

3. In the `setSpatial` method, we create the upper and lower channels in `AnimControl`. We let `AnimChannel` add all the bones recursively using the `addFromRootBone` method, as shown in the following code:

```
public void setSpatial(Spatial spatial) {
super.setSpatial(spatial);
    animControl = spatial.getControl(AnimControl.class);
    upperChannel = animControl.createChannel();
    lowerChannel = animControl.createChannel();
    upperChannel.addFromRootBone("spine");
    lowerChannel.addBone("Root");
    lowerChannel.addFromRootBone("pelvis");
```

4. In the same method, add this instance as `AnimEventListener` to `AnimControl` to receive events when animations change or cycle, as shown in the following code:

```
animControl.addListener(this);
```

5. To be able to set specific animations from other classes, we add a method called `setAnimation`, which takes an animation and `Channel` (enum) as the input, as shown in the following code:

```
public void setAnimation(Animation animation, Channel channel){
  switch(channel){
    case Upper:
      setAnimation(animation, upperChannel);
      break;
    ...
  }
}
```

6. In the `onAction` method, the control can receive input directly from `InputListener` and apply the logic on its own before setting the animation, as shown in the following code:

```
public void onAction(String name, boolean isPressed, float tpf) {
  if (name.equals("StrafeLeft")) {
    leftStrafe = isPressed;
  }
  ...
  } else if (name.equals("Jump") && isPressed) {
    jumpStarted = true;
    setAnimation(Animation.JumpStart);
  }
  if(jumpStarted || firing){
    // Do nothing
  } else if(forward || backward || rightStrafe || leftStrafe)  {
    setAnimation(Animation.Walk);
  } else {
    setAnimation(Animation.Idle);
  }
}
```

7. Finally, to test the concept of `AnimChannels`, we can implement `ActionListener` in our `SimpleApplication` instance and bind some keys to it, as shown in the following code:

```
public void onAction(String name, boolean isPressed, float tpf) {
  if (name.equals("Anim1") && isPressed) {
    jaime.getControl(AnimationChannelsControl.class)
.setAnimation(Animation.Walk, Channel.All);
  }
  ...
}
```

8. As an example of how the concept of `AnimChannels` can be used to create new animations out of combined ones, create a new application and set the walk animation on Jaime's `lowerChannel` while applying the jumping animation on `upperChannel`. Jaime will now commence a zombie walk impression.

How it works...

We can see that the `Animation` enum has had a field called `key` added. This is not necessary but is part of a way to not have to hard-code animation names.

By using the `addFromRootBone` method, the channel will automatically add all the bones recursively, starting with the bone that is supplied first. After adding spine to `upperChannel`, it will continue down the chain, adding shoulders, neck, arms, and hands, as shown in the following screenshot:

Different animations applied to the upper and lower parts of the body

Since we implemented `ActionListener`, there's also an `onAction` method in the class, which can receive an input from a number of external sources, such as `InputListener`. This also means it can apply logic by itself before deciding on what to play and not simply being an animation-playing control. We can recognize the pattern used here from the `GameCharacterControl` class from *Chapter 2, Cameras and Game Controls*.

By supplying a `Properties` file that maps the animation names, it's possible to use models with different naming conventions. It's also easier for a designer or artist to try out a number of different animations without consulting a programmer to make changes.

Handling jump animations

In this recipe, we'll show how the jumping animation can be handled in the animation manager control from previous recipes. Why does this require its own recipe? Animation-wise, jumping is usually a set of sequenced animations. If we look at Jaime, for example, there's `JumpStart`, `Jumping`, and `JumpEnd`. Normally, sequenced animations can be handled in the `onAnimCycleDone` method; when one animation ends, it can trigger the next. Jumping is different though since the middle jumping animation is indefinite and is on a loop. How long it plays depends on how long the character is in the air, which is driven by the gameplay or its physics.

How to do it...

You can handle jumping animations by performing the following steps:

1. For this, we'll need to add two more Booleans to our animation control: `jumpStarted` and `inAir`.

2. We trigger the first part of the animation in the `onAction` method, as shown in the following code. The `jumpStarted` Boolean is used to let the class know that other animations should not start while the character is the jumping state:

```
public void onAction(String binding, boolean value, float tpf) {
    if (binding.equals("Jump") && value) {
        jumpStarted = true;
        setAnimation(Animation.JumpStart);
    }
}
```

3. The `onAnimCycleDone` method should switch animations back to the jumping action once `JumpStart` has finished playing. We also set `inAir` to `true`, as shown in the following code:

```
public void onAnimCycleDone(AnimControl control, AnimChannel
channel, String animName) {
    if(channel.getLoopMode() == LoopMode.DontLoop){
        Animation newAnim = Animation.Idle;
        Animation anim = Animation.valueOf(animName);
        switch(anim){
            case JumpStart:
                newAnim = Animation.Jumping;
                inAir = true;
                break;
        }
        setAnimation(newAnim, channel);
    }
}
```

4. The `controlUpdate` method is suitable to check whether the character has landed after jumping (or falling). We check this directly in `BetterCharacterControl` and change the animation if it is back on the ground, as shown in the following code:

```
protected void controlUpdate(float tpf) {
  if(inAir){
    BetterCharacterControl charControl =spatial.getControl(BetterC
haracterControl.class);
    if(charControl != null && charControl.isOnGround()){
      setAnimation(Animation.Idle);
      jumpStarted = false;
      inAir = false;
    }
  }
}
```

How it works...

The implementation relies on the listener pattern where this control receives a notification of user actions from an external input class. In this project, we have a separate class that controls the character.

This `onAnimCycleDone` method is called by the `AnimControl` method when an animation has finished with one cycle (both looping and non-looping animations). Normally, when an animation ends, we'll want to switch to the idle animation to stop it from freezing. When `JumpStart` is finished, however, the character is most likely in midair and thus switches to a suitable looping animation. The `inAir` Boolean is used so the class knows it should start checking for when the character lands again.

Depending on the size of a project, the control class for the character and this animation-managing class might be merged into one. This should make some things easier, while the class itself might get bulky as more functions are implemented.

The `controlUpdate` class is called automatically with every tick, and here we can see whether the character is still airborne. In this implementation, `BetterCharacterControl` is used, and it has a method to see whether it is on ground. Jaime has a `JumpEnd` animation, but idle seems to work better with some blending.

Creating a custom animation - leaning

Custom animation is the concept of directly manipulating the bones of a character's skeleton to create animations. We will explore this by making a control that can be used together with *Chapter 2, Cameras and Game Controls*. Together with this recipe, leaning can be used on characters other than the player and in networked games.

Jaime leaning to the left

As in *Chapter 2, Cameras and Game Controls*, we have two ways to handle leaning: one is by using a key to lean toward the left and another to lean toward the right. The second one is to press a button and lean in any direction using the mouse, which is more common in computer games.

Getting ready

The control we are going to build will share some code with the recipe from *Chapter 2, Cameras and Game Controls*. The shared code will be explained there to save space, and it will most likely be used in tandem with thjs recipe, so being familiar with it is helpful.

How to do it...

1. We start by creating a new class that extends `AbstractControl` and implements `Action-` and `AnalogListener`.

2. Next, we define some values that will help us control the leaning. The `leanValue` is the current amount of leaning that is applied. There needs to be a limit on how much the character can lean, which is set in `maxLean`. For this example, it's 45 degrees in either direction. The two Booleans `leanLeft` and `leanRight` define whether we're currently leaning in either direction using keys, and `leanFree` defines whether the mouse is used. The `leaningBone` is the bone that we'll modify, and we'll also store the bone's original rotation in `boneRotation` and use it as a base when leaning.

3. When the control is added to a spatial, we need to look for a bone to apply the leaning to. We select spine as `leaningBone`, and clone its current rotation, as shown in the following code:

```
public void setSpatial(Spatial spatial) {
  super.setSpatial(spatial);
  Bone spine = spatial.getControl(SkeletonControl.class).
getSkeleton().getBone("spine");
  if(spine != null){
    leaningBone = spine;
    boneRotation = leaningBone.getLocalRotation().clone();
  }
}
```

4. The `onAction` method will receive the input and should set the controlling Booleans, namely, `leanLeft`, `leanRight`, and `leanFree`. The `onAnalog` option receives the mouse input when `leanFree` is active.

5. In the `controlUpdate` method, we check to see whether any leaning is to be applied, first to the left and then similarly to the right. If `leanValue` is near `0f`, we will round it off to `0`. If this happens, we give the control back to `AnimControl`, as shown in the following code:

```
protected void controlUpdate(float tpf) {
  if(leanLeft && leanValue < maxLean){
    leanValue += 0.5f * tpf;
  } else if(!leanFree && leanValue > 0f){
    leanValue -= 0.5f * tpf;
  }
  [mirror for right]
  if(leanValue < 0.005f && leanValue > -0.005f){
    leanValue = 0f;
  }
  if(leanValue != 0f){
    lean(leanValue);
  } else {
    leaningBone.setUserControl(false);
  }
}
```

6. In the `lean` method, which applies the leaning to the bone, the first thing we do is clamp the value to be inside the allowed threshold. Next, we call `setUserControl` on the bone to let it know that it shouldn't apply animations before creating a new `Quaternion` class based on the original rotation, as shown in the following code:

```
private void lean(float value){
  FastMath.clamp(value, -maxLean, maxLean);
```

```
    leaningBone.setUserControl(true);
    Quaternion newQuat = boneRotation.add(new    Quaternion().
fromAngles(-FastMath.QUARTER_PI * 0.35f, 0, -value));
    newQuat.normalizeLocal();
    leaningBone.setLocalRotation(newQuat);
}
```

How it works...

When selecting a bone to apply the leaning to, it should be close to the base of the upper body of the character. On Jaime, the spine is a suitable bone.

When `Bone.setUserControl(true)` is called, we tell the bone that no animations should be applied and that we will handle any rotation or translation manually. This has to be called before we set the rotation, or an exception will be thrown. Likewise, when we're done, we need to call `setUserControl(false)` to give the control back to the user (or no animation would be played).

Manually controlling bones is powerful and can be useful for many different applications, such as precision aiming and head tracking. Getting everything right can be tricky, however, and most likely it's not something that you will do frequently.

This class can be used separately from *Chapter 2, Cameras and Game Controls*, or they can be merged together. The benefit of having them separate is that we can also apply them separately. For example, the player's own character in a FPS won't need this control since you would never see it lean anyway. In this case, it's all about the camera. However, other players in the same (networked) FPS will need it, as would AI enemies who might use the same character control class.

To learn more about how `leanValue` is used and applied, have a look at the *Leaning around corners* recipe of *Chapter 2, Cameras and Game Controls*.

There's more...

If we're using an imported model and don't have access to a list of the bones, how do we know which bone to use? One simple way is to open the model in **Scene Explorer**. In **SkeletonControl**, we can see all the bones the character has but not their relative position on the model. By right-clicking and selecting **Get attachment node**, a new node will be created; also, by selecting it, we can see where it's located on the model. For more information on attachment nodes, have a look at the *Retrieving an attachment node* recipe of *Chapter 1, SDK Game Development Hub*.

Creating a subanimation

In this recipe, we're going to use SceneComposer to create subanimations. As the name implies, they're derived from an animation. Subanimations can be a good way to squeeze some extra out of stock models that don't have the exact animations you want, or if the modeler has gone home for the day. In this particular application, we'll prepare for the next recipe, which is about lip syncing. The **Extract sub animation** window in SDK looks, as shown in the following screenshot:

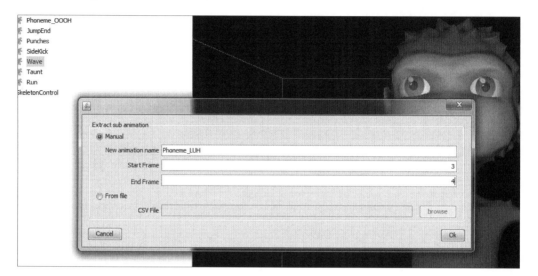

Getting ready

The biggest caveat when creating subanimations is that the jMonkeyEngine API uses relative time when interacting with models, while subanimations are created on a frame basis. So, the easiest way to find out which frames to extract is to open the model in an external editor and look at it in parallel.

How to do it...

Extracting a subanimation can be done by performing the following steps:

1. With the model opened in the Scene Composer, we expand **AnimControl**.

2. Now, we can see all the animations that are currently available. We right-click on an animation we would like to create a subanimation out of and choose the option, **Extract Sub-animation**.

3. Enter a start and end frame and it's done. The new animation is now available in the **AnimControl** option.

How it works...

An animation in jMonkeyEngine consists of a number of `BoneTracks`. Each of these has an array of floats with the times for the animations, an array of `Vector3f` with the positions of the bones, array of Quaternions with rotations, and another array of `Vector3f`'s with scales. Each instance of the arrays contains information about a frame.

A subanimation is a copy of an excerpt from all the `BoneTracks` in the parent animation.

Lip syncing and facial expressions

This recipe handles two important parts of making characters seem alive and sentient. Technically, they can be handled using `AnimChannel`, but they still deserve their own mention as they have some special requirements.

Lip syncing revolves around something called **Phoneme**, which is the distinct shape the mouth takes when making certain sounds. The number of phonemes a character has varies according to different needs, but there is a basic set that is used to create believable mouth movements.

Finally, we'll use jMonkeyEngine's **Cinematics** system to apply them in sequence and have the character speak (mime) a word. Cinematics is jMonkeyEngine's scripting system, and it can be used both to create in-game-scripted events and cutscenes. It is covered in more depth in *Chapter 9*, *Taking Our Game to the Next Level*.

We'll follow the control pattern in this recipe, and control can be merged into another animation controller or be kept alone.

Getting ready

Having a model with phoneme animations ready or creating them in an external modeling program is preferred. It's perfectly all right if the animations are one-frame static expressions.

If the previous options are not available, one method is to use the SDK's functionality to create subanimations. A version of Jaime with phoneme animations is supplied with the project for the sake of this recipe. For those interested in going through the process of creating subanimations themselves, there is a list of the ones used in the *Enabling nightly builds* section in *Appendix, Information Fragments*.

How to do it...

All the required functionalities can be implemented in a single class by performing the following steps:

1. To start off, we create a new class called `ExpressionsControl` that extends `AbstractControl`.

2. Inside this, we add `AnimControl` named `animControl`, one `AnimChannel` called `mouthChannel`, and another `AnimChannel` called `eyeBrowChannel`.

3. We define an enum to keep track of the phonemes that the controller supports. These are some of the most common ones, plus a `RESET` option for a neutral mouth expression, as shown in the following code:

```
public enum PhonemeMouth{
   AAAH, EEE, I, OH, OOOH, FUH, MMM, LUH, ESS, RESET;
};
```

4. We create another enum to set the expressions of the eyes, which is a simple way of adding emotions to what the character says, as shown in the following code:

```
public enum ExpressionEyes{
   NEUTRAL, HAPPY, ANGRY;
};
```

5. In the `setSpatial` method, we create `AnimChannel` for mouth animations and one for the eyes, then we add suitable bones to each of these, as shown in the following code. The list of bones available can be seen in `SkeletonControl` in `SceneComposer`.

```
mouthChannel = animControl.createChannel();
mouthChannel.addBone("LipSide.L");
. . .
```

6. Since the animations we'll use might just be one or a few frames each, we can set `LoopMode` to `Loop` or `Cycle`. The speed has to be higher than `0` or blending won't work. Set these for both `AnimChannels`.

7. Then, we have two setter methods to directly set an expression or phoneme in the control. The naming convention might differ depending on the assets, and it's good to have a small blending value:

```
public void setPhoneme(PhonemeMouth p){
   mouthChannel.setAnim("Phoneme_" + p.name(), 0.2f);
}
public void setExpression(ExpressionEyes e){
   eyeBrowChannel.setAnim("Expression_" + e.name(), 0.2f);
}
```

8. We can reuse any test class we might have from other recipes and just apply some new code to it as seen in the following code snippet. We set up a simple cinematic sequence that makes Jaime say (or mime) *Hello* and look happy.

 When this recipe was written, the following `AnimationEvent` constructor did not exist and `AnimChannels` were not applied properly. A patch has been submitted but may not have made it into a stable build. If required, the patch can be found in the *The AnimationEvent patch* section in *Appendix, Information Gathering*. It can also be acquired by turning on nightly builds in the SDK.

```
public void setupHelloCinematic() {
    cinematicHello = new Cinematic((Node)jaime, 1f);
    stateManager.attach(cinematicHello);
    cinematicHello.addCinematicEvent(0.0f, new AnimationEvent(jaime,
"Expression_HAPPY", LoopMode.Cycle, 2, 0.2f));
    cinematicHello.addCinematicEvent(0.1f, new AnimationEvent(jaime,
"Phoneme_EEE", LoopMode.Cycle, 1, 0.1f));
    cinematicHello.addCinematicEvent(0.2f, new AnimationEvent(jaime,
"Phoneme_LUH", LoopMode.Cycle, 1, 0.1f));
    cinematicHello.addCinematicEvent(0.3f, new AnimationEvent(jaime,
"Phoneme_OOOH", LoopMode.Cycle, 1, 0.1f));
    cinematicHello.addCinematicEvent(0.7f, new AnimationEvent(jaime,
"Phoneme_RESET", LoopMode.Cycle, 1, 0.2f));

    cinematicHello.setSpeed(1.0f);
    cinematicHello.setLoopMode(LoopMode.DontLoop);
    cinematicHello.play();
}
```

How it works...

The technical principles behind the phonemes are not that different from animating other parts of the character. We create `AnimChannels`, which handles different sets of bones. The first tricky bit is to organize the channels if you want to be able to control different parts of the body at the same time.

The pipeline for how to apply the phonemes can also be difficult. The first step will be to not set them directly in the code. It's not implausible that changing the expression of the character could be called directly from the code on certain events. Doing so for each phoneme in a sentence would be very cumbersome. Using the cinematics system is a good start as it would be relatively simple to write a piece of code that parses a text file and creates a cinematic sequence from it. Timing is really crucial, and it can take a lot of time to get the movements synced with sound. Doing it in a format that allows you to have a quick iteration is important.

Another more complex way would be to build up a database that maps words and phonemes and automatically applies them in a sequence.

The absolutely simplest approach is to not really care about lip syncing and just apply a moving mouth animation whenever the character speaks.

Eye movement

Eye contact is an important factor to make characters feel alive and aware of yours and other things' presence. In this chapter, we'll make a control that will follow a spatial with its eyes, as shown in the following screenshot:

How to do it...

Eye tracking can be implemented in a single control using the following steps:

1. We begin by creating a new class called `EyeTrackingControl` that extends `AbstractControl`.

2. It needs two `Bone` fields: one called `leftEye` and another called `rightEye`. Furthermore, we should add a spatial called `lookAtObject` and a related `Vector3f` called `focusPoint`.

3. In the `setSpatial` method, we find and store the bones for `leftEye` and `rightEye`.

4. We also need a method to set `lookAtObject`.

5. With this done, we add most of the other functionalities to the `controlUpdate` method. First of all, we need to take control of the bones or we won't be able to modify their rotation, as shown in the following code:

```
if(enabled && lookAtObject != null){
   leftEye.setUserControl(true);
   rightEye.setUserControl(true);
```

6. Next, we need to establish the `lookAtObject` position that is relative to the eyes. We do this by converting the position to model space and storing it in `focusPoint`, as shown in the following code:

```
focusPoint.set(lookAtObject.getWorldTranslation().
subtract(getSpatial().getWorldTranslation()));
```

7. Subtracting the eye position from `Vector3f` gives us the relative direction:

```
Vector3f eyePos = leftEye.getModelSpacePosition();
Vector3f direction = eyePos.subtract(focusPoint).negateLocal();
```

8. We create a new Quaternion and have it look in the direction of the `direction` vector. We can apply this on our eyes after modifying it a bit as its 0-rotation is up:

```
Quaternion q = new Quaternion();
q.lookAt(direction, Vector3f.UNIT_Y);
q.addLocal(offsetQuat);
q.normalizeLocal();
```

9. Then, we apply it by using `setUserTransformsWorld`. Finally, we give the control of the bones back to the system using the following code:

```
leftEye.setUserTransformsWorld(leftEye.getModelSpacePosition(),
q);
rightEye.setUserTransformsWorld(rightEye.getModelSpacePosition(),
q);
leftEye.setUserControl(false);
rightEye.setUserControl(false);
```

How it works...

The actual code is a fairly straightforward trigonometry, but knowing what values to use and the flow of doing it can be tricky.

Once the class receives an object to look at, it subtracts the model's `worldTranslation` from `lookAtObjects` so they end up in a coordinate system that is relative to the model's origo point also called **modelspace**.

Using `setUserTransformsWorld` also sets the position, but since we supply its current `modelSpacePosition`, no change will be applied.

Actually, the direction of each eye should be calculated separately for the result to be entirely correct.

There's more...

By now, the character has a very intent stare at the camera. This is an improvement, but it can be made more lifelike. Something that may not be so obvious is that we rarely look at the same point all the time even if we look at the same object. We can emulate this behavior by adding a random bit of flickering to the control:

```
private float flickerTime = 0f;
private float flickerAmount = 0.2f;
private Vector3f flickerDirection = new Vector3f();
```

By introducing these three fields, we have a base for what we want to do:

```
flickerTime += tpf * FastMath.nextRandomFloat();
if(flickerTime > 0.5f){
  flickerTime = 0;
  flickerDirection.set(FastMath.nextRandomFloat() * flickerAmount,
FastMath.nextRandomFloat() * flickerAmount, 0);
}
direction.addLocal(flickerDirection);
```

This piece of code goes in the middle of the `controlUpdate` method, right after calculating the direction. What we do is we increase `flickerTime` until it reaches 0.5f (note that this is not in seconds since we apply a random number). Once this happens, we randomize `flickerDirection` based on `flickerAmount` and reset `flickerTime`.

With each consecutive update, we will apply this to the calculated direction and slightly offset the focus point.

Location-dependent animation – edge check

In certain games, players traverse dangerous areas where a fall off from a ledge could lead to their deaths. Sometimes, in these games, the player is not meant to fall off and their movement is restricted when they are close, or the player gets an extra warning before they plummet.

The control we'll develop can be used for any of those things, but since this chapter is about animations, we'll use it to play a special animation when the player gets too close to the edge.

Getting ready

The recipe will use similar patterns that have been used before in this chapter and we'll also use the animation manager control from earlier in the chapter. Any animation control will be fine to use, but it should have separate channels for the upper and lower parts of the body.

How to do it...

We can implement almost everything we need in a single class as follows:

1. We begin by creating a class called `EdgeCheckControl`, which extends `AbstractControl` and contains the following fields, as shown in the following code:

```
private Ray[] rays = new Ray[9];
private float okDistance = 0.3f;
private Spatial world;
private boolean nearEdge;
```

2. We define the nine rays that will be used for collision detection. In the `setSpatial` method, we instantiate them and aim them downwards, as shown in the following code:

```
for(int i = 0; i < 9; i++){
  rays[i] = new Ray();
  rays[i].setDirection(Vector3f.UNIT_Y.negate());
}
```

3. In the `controlUpdate` method, we begin by placing one of the rays at the center of the character, as shown in the following code:

```
Vector3f origo = getSpatial().getWorldTranslation();
rays[0].setOrigin(origo);
```

4. We step around the character, placing the remaining rays in a circular shape. For each, we see whether it collides with something using the `checkCollision` method. If it doesn't, we don't need to check the rest and can exit the loop using the following code:

```
float angle;
for(int i = 1; i < 9; i++){
  float x = FastMath.cos(angle);
  float z = FastMath.sin(angle);
  rays[i].setOrigin(origo.add(x * 0.5f, 0, z * 0.5f));

  collision = checkCollision(rays[i]);
  if(!collision){
    break;
```

```
  }
  angle += FastMath.QUARTER_PI;
}
private boolean checkCollision(Ray r){
  CollisionResults collResuls = new CollisionResults();
  world.collideWith(r, collResuls);
  if(collResuls.size() > 0 && r.getOrigin().distance(collResuls.
getClosestCollision().getContactPoint()) > okDistance){
    return true;
  }
  return false;
}
```

5. In the last step in this method, we call the animation manager and tell it to play or stop playing the near-edge animation, as shown in the following code. We do this based on whether all the collisions have been detected or not, making sure we only send any change in state:

```
if(!collision && !nearEdge){
  nearEdge = true; spatial.getControl(AnimationManagerControl.
class).onAction("NearEdge", true, 0);
} else if(collision && nearEdge){
  nearEdge = false;  spatial.getControl(AnimationManagerControl.
class).onAction("NearEdge", false, 0);
}
```

6. Switching to our animation manager class, we modify it accordingly. The state is stored here so it can be used to see what other animations are allowed to be played, as follows:

```
if (binding.equals("NearEdge")) {
  nearEdge = value;
  if(nearEdge){
    setAnimation(Animation.Jumping, Channel.Upper);
  }
}
```

How it works...

With each update, the nine rays we create are placed in a circle around the character, with one in the center.

They will check for collisions with a surface below them. If any of them (this might be changed to two or three) does not hit something within okDistance, it will be reported as the character being close to a dangerous edge.

The `okDistance` has to be set to something suitable, higher than a step on a stair, probably at a height where the player could take damage.

When this happens, the animation manager will be called with the `NearEdge` action set to `true`. This will apply the jumping animation (wild flaying of the arms) to the upper body of the character while still allowing other animations to be played on the lower part.

The `NearEdge` Boolean is used to make sure that we only send the call to the animation manager once.

When doing collision checks, one should be careful about the amount and shape of the objects that are being collided. If the world is large or constructed from complex shapes (or even worse, if it has `MeshCollisionShape`), we should try to find optimized ways of applying the method. One way could be to separate the world into parts and have an auxiliary method to select which part to collide against. This method might use `contains` on `BoundingVolume` to see the part the player is located in.

Aligning feet with ground – inverse kinematics

Inverse kinematics is now a common part of animation systems in games and is a topic that might cover a chapter on its own. In this recipe, we'll look at placing a character's feet in accordance to the ground below. This is useful where an animation would otherwise place them in the air or on sloped ground.

Normally, animations work according to forward kinematics; that is, when a bone near the root of the skeleton rotates, it affects the bones further down the chain. As the name implies, Inverse Kinematics starts at the other end.

Here, we strive toward a desired position for the tip of a chain of bones, and bones further up the chain try to align themselves to suit this.

The most straightforward implementation of this rotates the bones by a small amount on all the axes. It then checks which of the rotations brings the tip closest to the desired position. This is repeated for all the bones in the chain and iterated until it has come close enough.

Getting ready

A model with `SkeletonControl` is needed for this recipe, and it's recommended that you be familiar with its setup. At the time of writing this recipe, the resident monkey, Jaime, is used.

This recipe uses an experimental feature that at the time of writing this is not part of a core build. To use it, you can build jMonkeyEngine yourself from the sources. You can also get it by enabling nightly builds. Refer to *Appendix, Information Fragments,* to find out how to change this setting.

How to do it...

Perform the following steps to get the basic IK functionality:

1. Let's begin by creating a new class that extends `AbstractControl`, and define a list that will contain the bones we want to use as tip bones.

2. In the `setSpatial` method, we add both the feet and toe bones to the list. We also supply some values that `KinematicRagdollControl` should work with when applying the IK and tell it which bones to work with, as shown in the following code:

```
setupJaime(spatial.getControl(KinematicRagdollControl.class));
   spatial.getControl(KinematicRagdollControl.class).
   setIKThreshold(0.01f); spatial.getControl(KinematicRagdollContr
ol.class).
   setLimbDampening(0.9f);
   spatial.getControl(KinematicRagdollControl.class)
   .setIkRotSpeed(18);
```

3. We create a method called `sampleTargetPositions` that goes through each of our targets and finds a position the control should try to reach, as shown in the following code:

```
public void sampleTargetPositions(){
   float offset = -1.9f;
   for(Bone bone: targets){
      Vector3f targetPosition = bone.getModelSpacePosition().
add(spatial.getWorldTranslation());
      CollisionResult closestResult = contactPointForBone(targetPosi
tion, offset);
      if(closestResult != null){
                  spatial.getControl(KinematicRagdollControl.class).
setIKTarget(bone, closestResult.getContactPoint().addLocal(0,
0.05f, 0), 2);
      }
   }
}
```

4. Finally, in the created method, we call `KinematicRagdollControl` and tell it to switch to the Inverse Kinematics mode:

```
spatial.getControl(KinematicRagdollControl.class).setIKMode();
```

5. To make it reusable, we use the `setEnabled` method to clear things up when the control is not in use; we make it apply IK when it's enabled again:

```
if(enabled){
   sampleTargetPositions();
} else {
```

```
                spatial.getControl(KinematicRagdollControl.class).
    removeAllIKTargets();
                spatial.getControl(KinematicRagdollControl.class).
    setKinematicMode();
    }
```

How it works...

The list we defined contains the bones that we want to have at the end of the chain. These are the bones that the control will try to get as close to the target position as possible. To get the feet at a suitable angle, we not only need the feet but also the toe bones. By trying to align both the feet and the toe bones, we get a better approximation of the ground below.

Unlike most of our controls, we don't actually do anything in the `controlUpdate` method. This is because the actual alignment is passed on to `KinematicRagdollControl`. Instead, we do a check each time the control is enabled and see what positions it should try to reach.

For each of the tip bones, we shoot a ray straight up, using an offset to start some way below the ground. The reason we don't just use the bones' position and check below it is because we can't be sure that the model is completely above the ground. Animations might very well push body parts inside the ground, and if we then shot a ray downwards, we wouldn't hit what we want.

Once a target position is found, we supply the bone to `KinematicRagdollControl`. Along with this is also an integer that defines how long the chain of bones should be that it can modify when trying to reach the target.

There are some more values we supply to `KinematicRagdollControl`. The `IKThreshold` value is the distance from the target point where it is okay for it to stop trying.

`LimbDampening` can be used to effect how much a bone should move in relation to others. Imagine we're stretching out for something on our desk. Our forearms are most likely to perform bigger movements (rotation-wise) than our upper arms. If `limbDampening` is lower than 1.0, the bones higher up in the chain (and likely bigger) will move less with each update than those closer to the tip bone.

`IKRotSpeed` defines the rotation steps the control should apply with each turn. A higher value means it'll get closer quicker, but it also means the margin of error becomes higher.

All these values require tweaking to get them right for the application. Implementation is just the first step. The `KinematicRagdollControl` method also needs some setting up, most importantly, it needs to know the bones it should be able to control.

There's more...

If we've implemented the recipe thus far, we can see that the result is not what we expected. On wobbly legs, resembling rubber or cooked spaghetti, our character slowly adjusts to the ground below it.

The most disturbing thing is probably that the legs seem to go in any direction. Fortunately, this can be remedied with some tweaking. The `KinematicRagdollControl` function has a method called `setJointLimit`, which does what it says. It can set the limits to how much rotation can be applied on each axis of a bone. Getting it right for all the bones will take some time though.

5
Artificial Intelligence

In this chapter, we'll cover the following recipes:

- ▸ Creating a reusable AI control class
- ▸ Sensing – vision
- ▸ Sensing – hearing
- ▸ Decision making – Finite State Machine
- ▸ Creating the AI using cover
- ▸ Generating NavMesh in SDK
- ▸ Pathfinding – using NavMesh
- ▸ Controlling groups of AI
- ▸ Pathfinding – our own A* pathfinder

Introduction

Artificial Intelligence (**AI**) is an extremely vast field. Even for games it can be very diverse, depending on the type of game and requirements.

Many developers enjoy working with AI. It gives you a sense of creating something alive, something intelligent, and rational. A good question to ask before designing AI for a game is what the expected behavior should be, from a player's perspective. In an FPS, it might be the case that the AI can separate the friend from the foe, find cover when attacked, flee when injured, and not get stuck on things as they move around. AI in an RTS might need to not only evaluate the current situation, but also plan ahead and divide resources between aggressive and defensive behavior. A group of soldiers and a tactical shooter might have advanced and dynamic group behavior. Another option is to have individual behaviors that still make them appear to work together, to the player.

The recipes in this chapter will, in most cases, work with isolated functionality, but revolve around a central AI control class. As such, the results might not always be impressive on their own, but at the same time, it should be quite easy to combine several of them into a more powerful AI.

Creating a reusable AI control class

In this recipe, we will create a control that is going to steer an AI character. Using `Control` to do this is beneficial since it can add the AI functionality and be used together with other `Controls` in the game. We can use `GameCharacterControl` from *Chapter 2, Cameras and Game Controls* for both the player and AI characters by adding `AIControl` to its spatial. To get a quick and visual result, we'll apply it to the bullet-based `BetterCharacterControl` class in this recipe.

How to do it...

We need to perform the following steps to get a basic, but functional attacking (or following) AI:

1. We begin by creating a new class called `AIControl`, extending `AbstractControl`. The core of the recipe will be based around an enum (enumeration) called `state`. For now it only needs two values: `Idle` and `Follow`.

2. Add fields for `BetterCharacterControl`, called `physicsCharacter`, Booleans `forward` and `backwards`, a `Vector3f` field for `walkDirection`, and another for `viewDirection`. If it's going to follow something, it also needs a `target` field, which can be `Spatial`.

3. The bulk of the logic is carried out in a `switch` statement in the `controlUpdate` method, as shown in the following code. The first case is `Idle`. In this case, the AI shouldn't do anything:

```
switch(state){
  case Idle:
    forward = false;
    backward = false;
  break;
```

4. In the `Follow` case, we should first check whether `target` is set. If there is a target, we find the direction to the target and make the AI face it by setting `viewDirection`, as shown in the following code:

```
case Follow:
  if(target != null){
    Vector3f dirToTarget = target.getWorldTranslation().
subtract(spatial.getWorldTranslation());
    dirToTarget.y = 0;
    dirToTarget.normalizeLocal();
    viewDirection.set(dirToTarget);
```

5. We check the distance to the target. If it's more than 5 the AI will try to get closer. If the distance instead is less than 3, it will try to back up a bit. The AI can also lose track of the target if it is more than 20 units away. In this case, it also changes state to `Idle`, as shown in the following code:

```
if (distance > 20f){
    state = State.Idle;
    target = null;
} else if(distance > 5f){
    forward = true;
    backward = false;
} else if (distance < 3f){
    forward = false;
    backward = true;
} else {
    forward = false;
    backward = false;
}
```

6. When it comes to movement, we can get the forward facing direction with the following line of code:

```
Vector3f modelForwardDir = spatial.getWorldRotation().
mult(Vector3f.UNIT_Z);
```

7. Depending on whether forward or backward is true, we can multiply this value with a suitable movement speed, and the call `setWalkDirection` on the `BetterCharacterControl` class with the result shown in the following code:

```
if (forward) {
    walkDirection.addLocal(modelForwardDir.mult(3));
} else if (backward) {
    walkDirection.addLocal(modelForwardDir.negate()
    .multLocal(3));
}
physicsCharacter.setWalkDirection(walkDirection);
```

8. Finally, we should also call `setViewDirection`, as shown in the following code:

```
physicsCharacter.setViewDirection(viewDirection);
```

How it works...

Using `BetterCharacterControl`, we get a lot of functionality for free. We only need a couple of Booleans to keep track of movement, and two `Vector3f` instances for directions. Target is what the AI will focus on (or follow, for now).

If we're familiar with `TestBetterCharacter` from jMonkeyEngine's test examples, we can recognize the movement handling from that class. For now, we only use the `forward/backward` functionality. It is a good idea to keep the rotation code as well, just in case we would like it to turn more smoothly in the future. The `walkDirection` vector is 0 by default. It can either be sent as it is sent to `physicsCharacter`, in which case the character will stop, or be modified to move in either direction. The `viewDirection` vector is simply set to look at the target for now, and passed on to `physicsCharacter`.

The logic in the `Follow` case mentioned previously is mostly there to have something to test with. Even so, it's AI behavior that seems to be sufficient for many MMOs. Once a target has been acquired, it will try to keep itself at a certain distance. It can also lose track of the target if it gets too far away. In this case, it falls back to the `Idle` state.

There's more...

By linking this recipe together with *Chapter 4, Mastering Character Animations*, we can easily make Jaime play some animations while he's moving.

Start by adding the `AnimationManagerControl` class to the AI character using the following code:

```
aiCharacter.addControl(new AnimationManagerControl());
```

We need to tell it to play animations. In `AIControl`, find the forward and backwards brackets inside the `controlUpdate` method and add the following lines:

```
if (forward) {
        ... spatial.getControl(AnimationManagerControl.class).setA
nimation(AnimationManagerControl.Animation.Walk);
   } else if (backward) {
        ... spatial.getControl(AnimationManagerControl.class).setA
nimation(AnimationManagerControl.Animation.Walk);
   } else {
spatial.getControl(AnimationManagerControl.class).setAnimation(Animati
onManagerControl.Animation.Idle);
}
```

There's more...

Let's create a test case world we can use for both this and many of the following recipes. First we need a world with physics:

```
BulletAppState bulletAppState = new BulletAppState();
stateManager.attach(bulletAppState);
```

We will need some kind of object to stand on. The `PhysicsTestHelper` class has a few example worlds we can use.

We load up good old Jaime. Again, we use the `BetterCharacterControl` class since it offloads a lot of code for us. Since the Bullet physics world is different from the ordinary scenegraph, Jaime is added to `physicsSpace` as well as to the `rootNode`, as shown in the following code:

```
bulletAppState.getPhysicsSpace().add(jaime);
rootNode.attachChild(jaime);
```

We also need to add our newly created AI control using the following code:

```
jaime.addControl(new AIControl());
```

There's one more thing we need to do for this to work. The AI needs to track something. The easiest way we can get a moving target is to add a `CameraNode` class and supply `cam` from the application, as shown in the following code:

```
CameraNode camNode = new CameraNode("CamNode", cam);
camNode.setControlDir(CameraControl.ControlDirection.CameraToSpatial);
rootNode.attachChild(camNode);
```

We set `camNode` to be the target, as shown in the following code:

```
jaime.getControl(AIControl.class).setState(AIControl.State.Follow);
jaime.getControl(AIControl.class).setTarget(camNode);
```

If we're familiar with cameras in OpenGL, we know they don't really have a physical existence. A `CameraNode` class in jMonkeyEngine gives us that. It tracks the camera's position and rotation, giving us something easy to measure. This will make it easier for us when we want the AI to follow it, since we can use the convenience of it being spatial.

For this reason, we can set `CameraNode` to be its target.

Sensing – vision

No matter how clever our AI is, it needs some senses to become aware of its surroundings. In this recipe, we'll accomplish an AI that can look in a configurable arc in front of it, as shown in the following screenshot. It will build upon the AI control from the previous recipe, but the implementation should work well for many other patterns as well. The following screenshot shows Jaime with a visible representation of his line of sight:

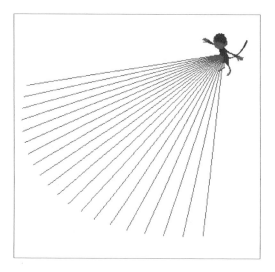

How to do it...

To get our AI to sense something, we need to modify the `AIControl` class from the previous recipe by performing the following steps:

1. We need to define some values, a float called `sightRange`, for how far the AI can see, and an angle representing the field of view (to one side) in radians.

2. With this done, we create a `sense()` method. Inside we define a Quaternion called `aimDirection` that will be the ray direction relative to the AI's `viewDirection` field.

3. We convert the angle to a Quaternion and multiply it with `viewDirection` to get the direction of the ray, as shown in the following code:

    ```
    rayDirection.set(viewDirection);
    aimDirection.fromAngleAxis(angleX, Vector3f.UNIT_Y);
    aimDirection.multLocal(rayDirection);
    ```

4. We check whether the ray collides with any of the objects in our `targetableObjects` list using the following code:

```
CollisionResults col = new CollisionResults();
for(Spatial s: targetableObjects){
  s.collideWith(ray, col);
}
```

5. If this happens, we set the target to be this object and exit the sensing loop, as shown in the following code. Otherwise, it should continue searching for it:

```
if(col.size() > 0){
  target = col.getClosestCollision().getGeometry();
  foundTarget = true;
  break;
}
```

6. If the sense method returns true, the AI now has a target, and should switch to the `Follow` state. We add a check for this in the `controlUpdate` method and the `Idle` case, as shown in the following code:

```
case Idle:
  if(!targetableObjects.isEmpty() && sense()){
    state = State.Follow;
  }
break;
```

How it works...

The AI begins in an idle state. As long as it has some items in the `targetableObjects` list, it will run the `sense` method on each update. If it sees anything, it will switch to the `Follow` state and stay there until it loses track of the target.

The `sense` method consists of a `for` loop that sends rays in an arc representing a field of view. Each ray is limited by `sightRange` and the loop will exit if a ray has collided with anything from the `targetableObjects` list.

There's more...

Currently, it's very difficult to visualize the results. Exactly what does the AI see? One way of finding out is to create `Lines` for each ray we cast. These should be removed before each new cast. By following this example, we will be able to see the extent of the vision. The following steps will give us a way of seeing the extent of an AI's vision:

1. First of all, we need to define an array for the lines; it should have the same capacity as the number of rays we're going to cast. Inside the `for` loop, add the following code at the start and end:

```
for(float x = -angle; x < angle; x+= FastMath.QUARTER_PI * 0.1f){
if(debug && sightLines[i] != null){
```

```
                    ((Node)getSpatial().getParent()).
detachChild(sightLines[i]);
}
...Our sight code here...
if(debug){
  Geometry line = makeDebugLine(ray);
  sightLines[i++] = line;      ((Node)getSpatial().getParent()).
attachChild(line);
}
```

2. The `makeDebugLine` method that we mentioned previously will look like the following code:

```
private Geometry makeDebugLine(Ray r){
  Line l = new Line(r.getOrigin(),
  r.getOrigin().add(r.getDirection().mult(sightRange)));
  Geometry line = new Geometry("", l);
  line.setMaterial(TestAiControl.lineMat);
  return line;
}
```

This simply takes each ray and makes something that can be seen by human eyes.

Sensing – hearing

The hearing we'll implement is one of the more basic models you can have. It's not as direct as vision, and requires a different approach. We'll assume that hearing is defined by `hearingRange`, and that the hearing ability has a linear fall off to that radius. We'll also assume that the sound emits something (in this case, footsteps), the volume of which is relative to the object's velocity. This would make sense in a stealth game, where sneaking should emit less sound than running. Sound is not blocked by obstacles or modified in any other way, apart from the distance between the target and the listener.

How to do it...

We will start by defining a class that all objects emitting sounds will use. This will require the following steps to be performed:

1. We create a class called `SoundEmitterControl`, extending `AbstractControl`.

2. It needs three fields, a `Vector3f` called `lastPosition`, a float for `noiseEmitted`, and another float called `maxSpeed`.

3. In the `controlUpdate` method, we sample the velocity the spatial has. This is the distance between the current `worldTranslation` and `lastPosition`. Divided by tpf (time-per-frame) we get the distance per second, as shown in the following code:

```
float movementSpeed = lastPosition.distance(spatial.
getWorldTranslation()) / tpf;
```

4. If it's actually moving, we see how much it moves compared to `maxSpeed`. Normalized between 0 and 1, this value becomes `noiseEmitted`, as shown in the following code:

```
movementSpeed = Math.min(movementSpeed, maxSpeed);
noiseEmitted = movementSpeed / maxSpeed;
```

5. Finally, we set `lastPosition` to current `worldTranslation`. Now we will implement the changes to detect sound in `AIControl`. This will have five steps. We start by defining a float called `hearingRange`. In the `sense()` method, we parse the list of `targetableObjects` and see if they have `SoundEmitterControl`. If any does, we check the distance between it and the AI using the following code:

```
float distance = s.getWorldTranslation().distance(spatial.
getWorldTranslation());
```

6. We get the `noiseEmitted` value from `SoundEmitterControl` and see how much is picked up by the AI, as shown in the following code:

```
float distanceFactor = 1f - Math.min(distance, hearingRange) /
hearingRange;
float soundHeard = distanceFactor * noiseEmitted;
```

7. If the threshold of 0.25f is exceeded, the AI has heard the sound and will react.

How it works...

The `SoundEmitterControl` class is meant to define how much sound a moving character makes. It does this by measuring the distance traveled each frame, and translates it to speed per second by dividing by the time-per-frame. It's been adapted slightly to work for the free-flying camera used in the test case. That's why `maxSpeed` is set to `25`. It uses `maxSpeed` to define how much noise the spatial is causing, on a scale of 0 to 1.

In the AI control class, we use the `sense()` method to test whether the AI has heard anything. It has a `hearingRange` field, with the range falling in a linear fashion from the location of the AI. Outside this range, no sound would be detected by the AI.

The method measures the distance from the sound emitting spatial, and factors this with the noise value it emits. For this example, a threshold of 0.25 is used to define whether the sound is loud enough for the AI to react.

Decision making – Finite State Machine

Decision making for AI can be handled in many different ways, and one common way is to use a **Finite State Machine** (**FSM**). An FSM contains a number of predefined states. Each state has a set of functionality and behavior tied to it. Each state also has a number of conditions for when it can change to another state.

In this recipe, we'll define a state machine that will emulate a common AI behavior in games. In fact, it will be more advanced than many games, which usually have AI that can only either move around on a path, or attack. Our AI will have three states, **Patrol**, **Attack**, and **Retreat**, as shown in the following diagram:.

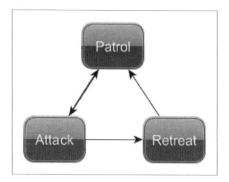

State diagram

The `PatrolState` will be the default and fallback state. It will perform random movement and will switch to `AttackState` if it spots an enemy.

The `AttackState` will handle firing and ammunition and will attack a target as long as it's visible and it has ammunition left. Then it will either return to `PatrolState` or flee using `RetreatState`.

The `RetreatState` will try to get away from a target for a set amount of time. After this, it will return to `PatrolState`, forgetting any fears it might previously have had.

All of our states will extend an abstract class called `AIState`, which we will also create in this recipe. This class in turn extends `AbstractControl`.

Worth noting is that all AI decision making and actions are handled from within the states. The states only relies on the AI control class to supply it with sensing updates (although this could also be handled by the states themselves).

How to do it...

We will start by creating the `AIState` class. This will have two steps, as follows:

1. We add a field to store `AIControl` and give it two abstract methods called `stateEnter` and `stateExit`.

2. These should be triggered when enabling and disabling the class, respectively. We override `setEnabled` to achieve this, as shown in the following code:

```
public void setEnabled(boolean enabled) {
  if(enabled && !this.enabled){
    stateEnter();
```

```
    }else if(!enabled && this.enabled){
      stateExit();
    }
    this.enabled = enabled;
}
```

With `AIState` done, we can look at the first behavior, `PatrolState`. We can implement this by performing the following steps:

1. First of all we add a `Vector3f` field called `moveTarget`. This is the position it will try to reach, relative to the current position.

2. We add an `if` statement with three outcomes in the `controlUpdate` method, which is the main bulk of the logic in the class. The first clause should disable it and enable the `AttackState` if `AIControl` has found a suitable target using the following code:

    ```
    if(aiControl.getTarget() != null){
      this.setEnabled(false);
      Vector3f direction = aiControl.getTarget().
    getWorldTranslation().subtract(spatial.getWorldTranslation());
      this.spatial.getControl(BetterCharacterControl.class).
    setViewDirection(direction);
      this.spatial.getControl(AttackState.class).setEnabled(true);
    }
    ```

3. If its location is close enough to the `moveTarget` vector, it should pick a new one nearby, as shown in the following code:

    ```
    else if(moveTarget == null || this.spatial.getWorldTranslation().
    distance(moveTarget) < 1f){
      float x = (FastMath.nextRandomFloat() - 0.5f) * 2f;
      moveTarget = new Vector3f(x, 0, (1f - FastMath.abs(x)) - 0.5f).
    multLocal(5f);
      moveTarget.addLocal(this.spatial.getWorldTranslation());
    }
    ```

4. Otherwise, it should keep moving towards the target, as shown in the following code:

    ```
    else {
      Vector3f direction = moveTarget.subtract(this.spatial.
    getWorldTranslation()).normalizeLocal();
      aiControl.move(direction, true);
    }
    ```

5. Finally, in the `stateExit` method, we should make it stop moving using the following code:

    ```
    aiControl.move(Vector3f.ZERO, false);
    ```

That's one state out of three; let's look at the `AttackState`. We can implement this by performing the following steps:

1. The `AttackState` keeps track of values related to firing. It needs to have a float for `fireDistance`, which is how far the AI can fire; an integer called `clip`, which is how many rounds it has in the current clip; another integer called `ammo`, which defines how many rounds it has in total; and finally, a float called `fireCooldown`, which defines the time between each shot the AI fires.

2. In the `stateEnter` method, we give the AI some ammunition. This is mostly for testing purposes, as shown in the following code:

    ```
    clip = 5;
    ammo = 10;
    ```

3. In the state's `controlUpdate` method, we do a number of checks. First we check whether `clip` is 0. If this is true, we check whether `ammo` is also 0. If this is also true, the AI must flee! We disable this state and enable `RetreatState` instead using the following code:

    ```
    if(clip == 0){
        if(ammo == 0){
            this.setEnabled(false);
            this.spatial.getControl(RetreatState.class).setEnabled(true);
        }
    ```

4. If the state still has ammo, it should refill the clip. We also set a longer time until it can fire again, as shown in the following code:

    ```
    else {
        clip += 5;
        ammo -= 5;
        fireCooldown = 5f;
    }
    ```

5. In the main `if` statement, if the state has lost the target, it should disable the state and switch to `PatrolState`, as shown in the following code:

    ```
    else if(aiControl.getTarget() == null){
        this.setEnabled(false);
        this.spatial.getControl(PatrolState.class).
        setEnabled(true);
    }
    ```

6. If it still has a target and is in a position to fire, it should fire, as shown in the following code:

    ```
    else if(fireCooldown <= 0f && aiControl.getSpatial().
    getWorldTranslation().distance(aiControl.getTarget().
    getWorldTranslation()) < fireDistance){
    ```

```
    clip--;
    fireCooldown = 2f;
}
```

7. Finally, if it is still waiting for the weapon to cool down since the last shot, it should keep waiting, as shown in the following code:

```
else if(fireCooldown > 0f){
    fireCooldown -= tpf;
}
```

The third and final state for our AI is `RetreatState`. We can implement this by performing the following steps:

1. Like the `PatrolState`, it should have a `moveTarget` field that it tries to reach.

2. We also add a float called `fleeTimer` that defines for how long it will try to get away.

3. In its `controlUpdate` method, if `fleeTimer` has not reached 0 yet, and it still feels a threat, it will pick a location opposite from the target and move towards it, as shown in the following code:

```
Vector3f worldTranslation = this.spatial.getWorldTranslation();
if (fleeTimer > 0f && aiControl.getTarget() != null) {
  if (moveTarget == null || worldTranslation.distance(moveTarget)
< 1f) {
    moveTarget = worldTranslation.subtract(aiControl.getTarget().
getWorldTranslation());
    moveTarget.addLocal(worldTranslation);
  }
  fleeTimer -= tpf;
  Vector3f direction = moveTarget.subtract(worldTranslation).
normalizeLocal();
  aiControl.move(direction, true);
}
```

4. Otherwise, it's all clear, and it will switch to `PatrolState`.

How it works...

The first thing we did was define an abstract class called `AIState`. It's convenient to use the control pattern since it means we have access to the spatial and familiar ways to attach/detach states and turn them on and off.

The `stateEnter` and `stateExit` methods are called when the state is enabled and disabled, and happens on transition from and to other states. The class also expects there to be some kind of AI control class.

The first state extending `AIState` was the `PatrolState`. Its update method has three outcomes. If the AI has spotted something it can attack, it will change to the `AttackState`. Otherwise, if it's close to the place it has selected to move to, it will select a new target. Or, if it still has some way to go, it will just continue moving towards it.

The `AttackState` has a bit more functionality, as it also handles firing and ammunition management. Remember, if it has come here, the AI has already decided it should attack something. Hence, if it has no ammunition, it will switch to the `RetreatState` (although we generously give it some ammo every time it enters the state). Otherwise, it will attack or try attacking.

The `RetreatState` only has one goal: to try to get as far away from the threat as possible. Once it has lost sight of the target, or has fled for the specified amount of time, it will switch to `PatrolState`.

As we can see, the logic is all contained within the associated state, which can be very convenient. The flow of the states will also always make sure the AI ends up in the `PatrolState` in the end.

Creating the AI using cover

Having AI using cover is a huge step towards making characters seem more believable and it usually makes them more challenging as they don't die as quickly.

There are many ways to implement this functionality. In the simplest form, the AI is not aware of any cover. It's simply scripted (by a designer) to move to a predefined favorable position when they spot an enemy. A player playing the sequence for the first time can't possibly notice the difference between an AI taking the decision by itself. Hence, the task of creating a believable AI (for that situation) is accomplished.

A much more advanced way would be to use the same principles for cover, which was established in *Chapter 2, Cameras and Game Controls*. However, evaluating options also becomes far more complex and unpredictable. Unpredictable AI might be good from the player's perspective, but it's a nightmare from a designer's perspective.

In this recipe, we'll go for a middle ground. First of all, we will base the AI on the FSM created in the previous recipe, and add a new state that handles finding cover. We will then add cover points to a scene, from which the AI can pick a suitable one and move there before attacking.

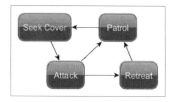

State diagram

How to do it...

Let's begin by defining a class called `CoverPoint`, extending `AbstractControl` by performing the following steps:

1. For now we can add a `Vector3f` called `coverDirection`. With getters and setters, that's all that's needed.

2. We create a class called `SeekCoverState`, extending our `AIState` class from the previous recipe.

3. It needs a list of `CoverPoints` called `availableCovers`, and a `CoverPoint` called `targetCover`.

4. In the `stateEnter` method, it should look for a suitable cover point. We can do this with the following piece of code. It parses the list and takes the first `CoverPoint` where the dot product of the direction and `coverDirection` is positive:

```
for(CoverPoint cover: availableCovers){
   if(aiControl.getTarget() != null){
      Vector3f directionToTarget = cover.getSpatial().
getWorldTranslation().add(aiControl.getTarget().
getWorldTranslation()).normalizeLocal();

      if(cover.getCoverDirection().dot(directionToTarget) > 0){
         targetCover = cover;
         break;
      }
   }
}
```

5. In the `controlUpdate` method, the AI should move towards `targetCover` if it has one.

6. Once it gets close enough, `targetCover` should be set to null, indicating it should switch to `AttackState`.

7. When this happens, `stateExit` should tell the AI to stop moving.

8. After adding the new state to the AI control class, to let it know it has the ability to seek cover, we also need to modify other states to enable it.

9. Most suitable is `PatrolState`, where it can switch to `SeekCoverState` instead of `AttackState` when it spots a target.

10. If we have a test case for the Finite State Machine, all we would now need to do is to add some `CoverPoints` to a scene and see what happens.

How it works...

The `CoverPoint` class we created adds the behavior to any `Spatial` instances to act as a cover. In a game, you would most likely not see the `CoverPoint` spatial, but it's good for debug and editing purposes. The concept can be expanded to cover other types of interest points for AI, as well as modified to handle volumes, rather than points using the spatial's geometry.

Once the `SeekCoverState` is enabled, it will try to find a suitable cover point that's relative to the target's position (at that time). It does this using the dot product between `coverDirection` and the direction to the target. If this is positive, it means the target is in front of the cover, and it picks this as `targetCover`.

When the AI reaches this, it sets `targetCover` to `null`. This means that when `controlUpdate` is called the next time, it will exit the state and enable `AttackState` instead. In a real game, the AI would most likely use some kind of navigation or pathfinding to get there. You can get an introduction to navigation in the next recipe. There is also the *Pathfinding: Our own A* pathfinder* recipe that covers implementing pathfinding later in the chapter.

With the current implementation of the AI, the result might be a bit erratic, since it doesn't remember the target's position. It might very well be that it doesn't see the target once it reaches the cover and instantly switches to `PatrolState`.

Generating NavMesh in SDK

Automatic NavMesh generation is a feature of the SDK available in the SceneExplorer. The NavMesh, as its name implies, is a mesh in which pathfinding can be applied to have AIs navigate through the game world. The generator takes a set of input values and, based on these, will create a mesh that stretches around obstacles. It can be seen as painted lines that the AI can use to know where it's safe to walk.

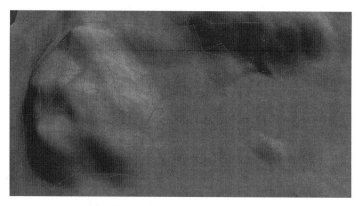

NavMesh on top of the terrain

Getting ready

The feature is available through a plugin, which we have to download first. Refer to the *Downloading the plugins* section in *Appendix, Information Fragments*.

How to do it...

1. Once the plugin has been downloaded, we can open any scene in the **SceneComposer** window, as shown in the following screenshot:

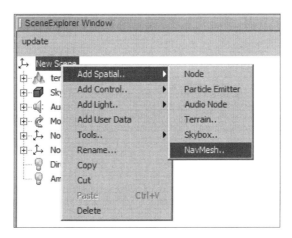

2. In the **SceneExplorer** window, right-click on the top node, and navigate to **Add Spatial.. | NavMesh..** to bring up the **options** window.

3. The simplest procedure from here is to click on **Finish** and see what happens.

4. A geometry called NavMesh will shortly appear in the list, and selecting it will display its reach. Blue lines indicate navigable paths.

5. If we're happy with it (which might be difficult to say if it's the first time we see one), we save the scene.

How it works...

The method by which the generator works is controllable by the large number of settings available. It can be difficult to know how they all affect the result, and what kind of result we're after, anyway. The best way is simply to test different parameters until a desired result is achieved. Each line is a path the pathfinder can follow, and there should be no isolated islands. The less lines there are in the mesh, the more restricted the AI will be. Remember, that different settings are optimal for different scenes.

Pathfinding – using NavMesh

Pathfinding can be done in many different ways, and in this recipe we'll look at how to use the NavMesh generated in the previous recipe for pathfinding. We'll use jMonkeyEngine's AI plugin, which has a pathfinder designed to navigate NavMeshes.

We achieve this using the Control pattern, and will also implement a way to generate paths in a thread-safe way separate from the main update thread, to not impact the performance of the application.

Getting ready

We'll need a scene with a NavMesh geometry in it. We also need to download the AI library plugin. Instructions on how to download a plugin in the SDK can be found in the *Downloading the plugins* section in *Appendix, Information Fragments*. The plugin is called `jME3 AI Library`. Once we have downloaded the plugin, we need to add it to the project. Right-click on the project and select **Properties**, then select **Libraries**, and then select **Add Library...**. Select **jME3 AI Library** and click on **Add Library**.

How to do it...

We start by defining the class that will generate the paths for us. This part will be implemented by performing the following steps:

1. We create a new class called `PathfinderThread`, which extends the `Thread` class.

2. It needs a couple of fields, a `Vector3f` called `target`, a `NavMeshPathfinder` called `pathfinder`, and two Booleans, `pathfinding` and `running`, where `running` should be set to `true` by default.

3. The constructor should take a `NavMesh` object as input, and we instantiate the `pathfinder` with the same, as shown in the following code:

```
public PathfinderThread(NavMesh navMesh) {
    pathfinder = new NavMeshPathfinder(navMesh);
    this.setDaemon(true);
}
```

4. We override the `run` method to handle `pathfinding`. While running is `true`, the following logic should apply:

```
if (target != null) {
    pathfinding = true;
    pathfinder.setPosition(getSpatial().
    getWorldTranslation());
    boolean success = pathfinder.computePath(target);
```

```
    if (success) {
      target = null;
    }
    pathfinding = false;
  }
```

5. If `target` is not `null`, we set `pathfinding` to `true`.

6. Then we set the start position of the pathfinder to the AI's current position, as shown in the following code:

```
pathfinder.setPosition(getSpatial().getWorldTranslation());
```

7. If the pathfinder can find a path, we set `target` to `null`.

8. In either case, pathfinding is done, and `pathfinding` is set to `false`.

9. Finally, we tell the thread to sleep for one second until trying again, as shown in the following code:

```
Thread.sleep(1000);
```

That's the first step of the pathfinding handling. Next, we'll define a class that will use this. This will be implemented by performing the following steps:

1. We create a new class that extends `AbstractControl` called `NavMeshNavigationControl`.

2. It needs two fields, a `PathfinderThread` called `pathfinderThread` and a `Vector3f` called `waypointPosition`.

3. Its constructor should take a node as input, and we use this to extract a `NavMesh` from, and pass it on to `pathfinderThread`, which is instantiated in the constructor as follows:

```
public NavMeshNavigationControl(Node world) {
  Mesh mesh = ((Geometry) world.getChild("NavMesh")).getMesh();
  NavMesh navMesh = new NavMesh(mesh);
  pathfinderThread = new PathfinderThread(navMesh);
  pathfinderThread.start();
}
```

4. Now, we create a method to pass a position it should pathfind to using the following code:

```
public void moveTo(Vector3f target) {
  pathfinderThread.setTarget(target);
}
```

5. The `controlUpdate` method is what does the bulk of the work.

6. We start by checking whether `waypointPosition` is `null`.

7. If it is not null, we project `waypointPosition` and the spatials `worldTranslation` onto a 2D plane (by removing the `y` value), to see how far apart they are as follows:

```
Vector2f aiPosition = new Vector2f(spatialPosition.x,
spatialPosition.z);
Vector2f waypoint2D = new Vector2f(waypointPosition.x,
waypointPosition.z);
float distance = aiPosition.distance(waypoint2D);
```

8. If the distance is more than `1f`, we tell the spatial to move in the direction of the waypoint. This recipe uses the `GameCharacterControl` class from *Chapter 2, Cameras and Game Controls*:

```
if(distance > 1f){
  Vector2f direction = waypoint2D.subtract(aiPosition);
  direction.mult(tpf);
  spatial.getControl(GameCharacterControl.class).
setViewDirection(new Vector3f(direction.x, 0, direction.y).
normalize());
  spatial.getControl(GameCharacterControl.class).
  onAction("MoveForward", true, 1);
}
```

9. If the distance is less than `1f`, we set `waypointPosition` to null.

10. If `waypointPosition` is null, and there is another waypoint to get from the pathfinder, we tell the pathfinder to step to the next waypoint and apply its value to our `waypointPosition` field as shown in the following code snippet:

```
else if (!pathfinderThread.isPathfinding() && pathfinderThread.
pathfinder.getNextWaypoint() != null && !pathfinderThread.
pathfinder.isAtGoalWaypoint() ){
  pathfinderThread.pathfinder.goToNextWaypoint();
  waypointPosition = new Vector3f(pathfinderThread.pathfinder.
getWaypointPosition());
}
```

How it works...

The `PathfinderThread` handles pathfinding. To do this in a thread-safe way, we use the pathfinding Boolean to let other threads know it's currently busy, so that they don't try to read from the pathfinder.

Target is the position the pathfinder should try to reach. This is set externally and will be used to indicate whether the thread should attempt to pathfind or not. This is why we set it to null once pathfinding is successful.

We keep the thread running all the time, to avoid having to initialize it every time. The thread will wake up once a second to see whether there is any pathfinding to perform. If the delay was not there, it would use up resources, unnecessarily.

This class uses the `waypointPosition` field to store the current waypoint we're trying to reach. This is so that we don't need to look it up in the pathfinder every time, and thus risk interrupting an ongoing pathfinding. It also allows the AI to keep moving even if it's currently contemplating a new path.

The `controlUpdate` method first checks whether the `waypointPosition` is `null`. Null indicates it has no current goal, and should go to the pathfinder to see whether there is a new waypoint for it.

It can only get a new waypoint if `pathfinderThread` currently is not actively `pathfinding` and if there is a next waypoint to get.

If it already has a `waypointPosition` field, it will convert both the spatials position and the `waypointPosition` to 2D and see how far apart they are. This is necessary as we can't guarantee that `NavMesh` is exactly on the same plane as the spatial.

If it finds out that the distance is further than `1f`, it will find out the direction to the `waypointPosition` field and tell the spatial to move in that direction. Otherwise (if it's close enough), it will set the `waypointPosition` field to `null`.

Once it has reached the final waypoint, it will tell the spatial to stop.

Controlling groups of AI

In this recipe, we'll kill two birds with one stone and implement both an interface for group AI management and look at weighted decision making.

In many ways, the architecture will be similar to the *Decision making – Finite State Machine* recipe. It's recommended to have a look at it before making this recipe. The big difference from the normal state machine is that instead of the states having definite outcomes, an AI Manager will look at the current needs, and assign units to different tasks.

This recipe will also make use of an `AIControl` class. This is also an extension of the `AIControl` that can be found in the *Creating a reusable AI control class* recipe.

As an example, we'll use resource gathering units in an RTS. In this simplified game, there are two resources, wood and food. Food is consumed continuously by the workers and is the driving force behind the decision. The AI Manager will try to keep the levels of the food storage at a set minimum level, taking into account the current consumption rate. The scarcer the food becomes, the more units will be assigned to gather it. Any unit not occupied by food gathering will be assigned to wood gathering instead.

How to do it...

We'll start by defining a `GatherResourceState` class. It extends the same `AIState` we defined in the *Decision making – Finite State Machine* recipe. This will be implemented by performing the following steps:

1. First of all it needs access to the AIControl called `aiControl`.

2. It needs two additional fields, a `Spatial` defining something to pick up called `resource`, and an integer called `amountCarried`.

3. In `controlUpdate` method, we define two branches. The first is for if the unit isn't carrying anything, `amountCarried == 0`. In this case, the unit should move towards `resource`. Once it gets close enough, it should pick up some, and `amountCarried` should be increased, as shown in the following code:

   ```
   Vector3f direction = resource.getWorldTranslation().subtract(this.
   spatial.getWorldTranslation());
   if(direction.length() > 1f){
     direction.normalizeLocal();
     aiControl.move(direction, true);
   } else {
     amountCarried = 10;
   }
   ```

4. In the other case, `amountCarried` is more than `0`. Now, the unit should move towards the HQ instead. Once it's close enough, `finishTask()` is called.

5. The `finishTask` method calls the AI Manager via `aiControl` to increase the resource amount that the state handles with the supplied amount as follows:

   ```
   aiControl.getAiManager().onFinishTask(this.getClass(),
   amountCarried);
   amountCarried = 0;
   ```

6. Finally, we create two new classes that extend this class, namely `GatherFoodState` and `GatherWoodState`.

With the new state handled, we can focus on the `AIControl` class. It will follow the pattern established elsewhere in the chapter, but it needs some new functionality. This will be implemented by performing the following three steps:

1. It needs two new fields. The first is an `AIAppState` called `aiManager`. It also needs to keep track of its state in an `AIAppState` called `currentState`.

2. In the `setSpatial` method, we add the two gathering states to our control, and make sure they're disabled, as shown in the following code:

   ```
   this.spatial.addControl(new GatherFoodState());
   this.spatial.addControl(new GatherWoodState());
   ```

```
this.spatial.getControl(GatherFoodState.class).setEnabled(false);
this.spatial.getControl(GatherWoodState.class).setEnabled(false);
```

3. We also add a method to set the state, `setCurrentState`. Sidestepping conventions, it should not set an instance of a state, but enable an existing state the AI control class has, while disabling the previous state (if any), as shown in the following code:

```
public void setCurrentState(Class<? extends AIStateRTS> newState)
{
    if(this.currentState != null && this.currentState.getClass() !=
newState){
        this.currentState.setEnabled(false);
    }
    this.currentState = state;
    this.currentState.setEnabled(true);
}
```

Now we have to write a class that manages the units. It will be based on the `AppState` pattern, and consists of the following steps:

1. We begin by creating a new class called `AIAppState` that extends `AbstractAppState`.

2. It needs a `List<AIControl>` of the units it controls, called `aiList`. We also add `Map<Class<? extends AIStateRTS>, Spatial>` called `resources` that contains the resources in the world that can be gathered.

3. It then needs to keep track of its stock of `wood` and `food`. There are also fields for the current `foodConsumption` value per second, `minimumFoodStorage` it would like to keep, and a `timer` for how long before it wants to reevaluate its decisions.

4. The `update` method is pretty simple. It starts by subtracting `foodConsumption` from the storage. Then, if `timer` has reached `0`, it will call the `evaluate` method, as shown in the following code:

```
food -= foodConsumption * tpf;
food = Math.max(0, food);
timer-= tpf;
if(timer <= 0f){
    evaluate();
    timer = 5f;
}
```

5. In the `evaluate` method, we begin by establishing the food requirement, as shown in the following code:

```
float foodRequirement = foodConsumption * 20f +
minimumFoodStorage;
```

6. Then we decide how urgent food gathering is, on a factor of 0.0 - 1.0, as shown in the following code:

```
float factorFood = 1f - (Math.min(food, foodRequirement)) /
foodRequirement;
```

7. Now we decide how many workers should be assigned to food gathering by taking that factor and multiplying it by the total amount of workers, as shown in the following code:

```
int numWorkers = aiList.size();
int requiredFoodGatherers = (int) Math.round(numWorkers *
factorFood);
int foodGatherers = workersByState(GatherFoodState.class);
```

8. We create a helper method, called `workersByState`, that returns the number of workers assigned to a given state, as shown in the following code:

```
private int workersByState(Class<? extends AIStateRTS> state){
   int amount = 0;
   for(AIControl_RTS ai: aiList){
      if(ai.getCurrentState() != null && ai.getCurrentState().
getClass() == state){
         amount++;
      }
   }
   return amount;
}
```

9. Comparing the current gathers with the required amount, we know whether to increase or decrease the number of food gatherers. We then set the state to change according to whether more or less food gatherers are required, as shown in the following code:

```
int foodGatherers = workersByState(GatherFoodState.class);
int toSet = requiredFoodGatherers - foodGatherers;
Class<? extends AIStateRTS> state = null;
if(toSet > 0){
   state = GatherFoodState.class;
} else if (toSet < 0){
   state = GatherWoodState.class;
   toSet = -toSet;
}
```

10. We can create another method, called `setWorkerState`, that loops through `aiList` and calls `setCurrentState` of the first available worker. It reruns `true` if it has successfully set the state of a unit, as shown in the following code:

```
private boolean setWorkerState(Class<? extends AIStateRTS> state){
  for(AIControl_RTS ai: aiList){
    if(ai.getCurrentState() == null || ai.getCurrentState().
getClass() != state){
      ai.setCurrentState(state);
      ((GatherResourceState)ai.getCurrentState()).
        setResource(resources.get(state));
      return true;
    }
  }
  return false;
}
```

11. The example implementation also requires that we set the resource for that state in the form of a spatial. This is so that the units know where they can pick up some of the resource. It can be set somewhere in the application, as shown in the following code:

```
aiAppState.setResource(GatherFoodState.class, foodSpatial);
aiAppState.setResource(GatherWoodState.class, woodSpatial);
```

How it works...

At the beginning of the game, we add one green food resource, and one brown wood resource, some distance away from the HQ (at 0,0,0). The `AIAppState` starts by looking at the current food storage, seeing it's low, it will assign an AI to go to the food resource and bring back food.

The `AIAppState` evaluate method starts by establishing the need for food gathering. It does this by dividing the food stores by the current requirement. By setting the food in the algorithm to not be able to exceed the requirement, we make sure we get a figure between 0.0 and 1.0.

It then takes the amount of units available, and decides how many of those should be gathering food, based on the `factorFood` figure, rounding it off to the nearest integer.

The result is compared to how many are currently on a food gathering mission, and adjusts the number to suit the current need, assigning them to either food or wood gathering.

The worker AI is completely controlled by the state they're set to by the manager, and in this recipe, all they can do is move to one resource or the other. They have no idle state, and are expected to always have some task.

The two states we use in the recipe are actually the same class. Both resources are gathered in the same way, and `GatherFoodState` and `GatherWoodState` are only used as identifiers. In a real game, they might well behave differently from each other. If not, it might be a good idea to use a parameterized version of `GatherResourceState` instead.

There's more

This recipe only has two different states, where one is the deciding one. What do we do if we have, let's say five equally important resources or tasks to consider? The principles are very much the same:

- Begin by normalizing the need for each task between 0.0 and 1.0. This makes it easier to balance things.

- Next, add all the values together, and divide each value by the sum. Now, each value is balanced with each other, and the total of all values is 1.0.

In this recipe, the evaluation is done continuously, but it might just as well be applied when an AI has finished a task, to see what it should do next. In that case, the task could be picked at random among the distributed values to make it more dynamic.

Pathfinding – our own A* pathfinder

Using the built-in functions of the `NavMesh` package might be enough for some, but in many cases we need customized pathfinding for our projects. Knowing how to implement, or even better, understanding A* (a-star) pathfinding, can take us a long way in our AI endeavors. It's easy to implement and very versatile. Correctly set up, it will always find the shortest path (and pretty fast too!). One of the drawbacks is that it can be memory-intensive in large areas if not kept in check.

A* is an algorithm that finds the shortest path in a graph. It's good at finding this quickly using **heuristics**, or an estimation of the cost to get from a position in the graph to the goal position.

Finding a good value for the heuristic (H) is very important in order to make it effective. In technical terms, H needs to be **admissible**. This means that the estimated cost should never exceed the actual cost.

Each position, called a node, will keep track of how the cost from the starting node to itself, using the current path. It will then choose the next node to go to base on this, cost plus the cost to the next node plus the estimated cost to the goal node.

A* could be said to work something like this; imagine that we're trying to find our way to a castle, through a maze. We're at an intersection, and can choose either the left path or the right path. We can see the castle in the distance to our left. We don't know anything about either path beyond the point where we're standing, but at least, taking the left path brings us closer to the castle, so it's natural to test that path.

Now, it could very well be that the left path is wrong, and much longer. That's the reason it also keeps track of how far it's travelled along the path. This is called G. The longer it travels along a path, the higher G will become. If the path also starts to deviate from the way to the castle, H will rise again. At some point G plus H might be higher than it would be at the entrance to the right path at the intersection. Then it will hop back to that point and see where the other path leads, until the point where G plus H along that path is higher.

This way, the AI using A* knows it's always traveled the shortest path once it exits the maze.

In this recipe, we'll use an estimated cost to the goal, H, that is the distance as-the-bird-flies between two nodes. This will guarantee that H is admissible and always equal to or less than the actual distance to travel.

We'll use the distance between nodes to calculate the cost to travel between them. This will be a lot to take in, but once done, we have a pathfinder we can use for many different applications.

How to do it...

We'll start by defining the node object, in a bean pattern. This will be implemented by performing the following steps:

1. We create a new class called `WaypointNode` that extends `AbstractControl`.

2. It needs three integers, `f`, `h`, and `g`.

3. We also have to add two Booleans, `open` and `closed`, to aid the pathfinder, a list of other nodes, called `connections`, it's current position stored in `Vector3f` and another node as `parent`.

Now we can create the pathfinder itself. This will be implemented by performing the following steps. We create a new class called AStarPathfinder.

1. The pathfinder class needs a list of nodes, called `openList`, which are the nodes currently considered.

2. It has to know of the `startNode` and `goalNode`.

3. The `pathfind` method is the heart of the class. We can take a look at it in full, before explaining it, as shown in the following code:

```
private void pathfind() {
  openList.add(startNode);
  WaypointNode current;
  while(!openList.isEmpty()) {
    current = openList.get(0);
    for (WaypointNode neighbor : current.getConnections()) {
      if (!neighbor.isClosed()) {
        if (!neighbor.isOpen()) {
          openList.add(neighbor);
```

```
                    neighbor.setOpen(true);
                    setParent(current, neighbor);
                  } else if (current.getG() + neighbor.getPosition().
           distance(goalNode.getPosition()) < neighbor.getG()) { // new path
           is shorter
                    setParent(current, neighbor);
                  }
                }
              }
              openList.remove(current);
            current.setClosed(true);
            if (goalNode.isClosed()) {
              break;
            }
            // sort list
            Collections.sort(openList, waypointComparator);
          }
        backtrack();
      }
```

4. It should begin by adding the `startNode` to `openList`.

5. Next, we define a while loop that always picks the first node in `openList`.

6. Inside this loop, we create another `for` loop that iterates through all the currently selected connected nodes, called neighbors.

7. If the neighboring node is not in `openList`, it should be added there. It should also set the current node to `parentNode` of the `neighbor` node, as shown in the following code:

```
openList.add(neighbor);
neighbor.setOpen(true);
neighbor.setParent(current);
```

8. While doing this, `g` of the neighbor should be set to current node's G plus the distance between the two nodes, as shown in the following code:

```
neighbor.setG(current.getG() + (int) (current.getPosition().
distance(neighbor.getPosition()) * multiple));
```

9. Also, if H has not already been calculated for `neighbor`, it should, by measuring the distance between `neighbor` and `goalNode`. F should be updated by adding G and H together, as shown in the following code:

```
if(neighbor.getH() == 0){
  neighbor.setH((int) (neighbor.getPosition().distance(goalNode.
getPosition()) * multiple));
}
neighbor.updateF();
```

10. It might also be that a shorter path has been discovered since `neighbor` was calculated. In this case, the neighbor should be updated again with the `current` node as `parent`. Do that and repeat the previous two steps.

11. If `neighbor` is closed, it shouldn't do anything with it.

12. Once the neighbors have been parsed, the current node should be removed from `openList`. `openList` should then be reordered according to the total cost, `F`, of the nodes.

13. The looping of `openList` should exit, either when it's empty, or when the `goalNode` has been reached, which is indicated by when it's closed.

14. When the pathfinding is done, the shortest path can be extracted by going through the parent nodes starting with the `goalNode`, as shown in the following code. Reversing the resulting list will yield the best path, from `startNode` to `goalNode`. This can be implemented as follows:

```
private void backtrack() {
    List<WaypointNode> path = new ArrayList<WaypointNode>();
    path.add(goalNode);
    WaypointNode parent = goalNode;
    while (parent != null) {
        parent = parent.getParent();
        path.add(parent);
    }
}
```

How it works...

The node bean that we created stores information about the state of the node, which is set by the pathfinder as it passes, or considers passing a node. The `g` value is the total cost to this node, along the current path, from the starting node. `h` is the estimated value left to the `goalNode`. In this recipe, it's the shortest distance possible. To be the most effective, it should be as close to the actual distance as possible, without exceeding it. This is to guarantee that it finds the shortest path. `F` is simply `g` and `h` added together, becoming the total estimated cost of the path using this node, and is the value used by the algorithm to consider.

These values are stored as integers, rather than floats. This is better both for memory and processing purposes. We get around lower-than-one distances by multiplying them with 100.

It also keeps track of whether it's currently open or closed. It's quicker to query the node itself, than seeing if the list contains it. The node actually has three states, either open, closed, or the standard, neither which is when it has not yet been considered for the path. The parent of a node defines from which other node the path came to this node.

openList contains all the nodes the pathfinder is currently considering. It starts with only the startNode, adding all its neighbors, since none are either open or closed at this stage. It also sets the parent of the node, calculates the cost to get to this node, and estimates the cost left to the goal (if it has not been calculated before). It only needs to do this once per node, as long as the goal is not moving.

Now, openList has a few new nodes to work with, and the current node is removed from the list. At the end of the while loop, we sort openList according to f-cost of the nodes, so that it always starts looking at the node with the lowest total cost. This is to make sure it doesn't spend any unnecessary time looking at paths which are not optimal.

The algorithm can be considered to be successful once the goalNode has been put in openList and is set to closed. We can't end searching just because the goalNode enters openList. Since we also reconsider nodes if we find a shorter path to the node, we want to check all the goalNodes neighbors as well before ending the search.

If there is no path available to the goalNode, openList will become empty before the goalNode is closed, and the search will fail.

6
GUI with Nifty GUI

First of all, what is **Nifty GUI**? It's not the only GUI available in jMonkeyEngine, but it is the one that is officially supported. It is not developed by the jMonkeyEngine team but is an independent open source effort that has implementations in other engines as well.

In this chapter, we'll cover the following topics:

- Initializing Nifty and managing an options menu
- Loading the screen
- Creating an RPG dialog screen
- Implementing a game console
- Handling a game message queue
- Creating an inventory screen
- Customizing the input and settings page
- Using offscreen rendering for a minimap

Introduction

Nifty GUI is operated using screens. A screen could be, for example, an in-game (**HUD) heads-up display** or the same game's main menu. Screens are built using XML and Nifty's own set of tags. On each screen, there can be layers that are drawn on top of each other according to their order.

On a screen, objects cascade similarly as on a web page, that is, from top to bottom or left to right, depending on the settings. The following code is an example of what a simple screen might look like:

```
<nifty xmlns="http://nifty-gui.sourceforge.net/nifty-1.3.xsd"
        xmlns:xsi="http://www.w3.org/2001/XMLSchema-instance"
```

```
        xsi:schemaLocation="http://nifty-gui.sourceforge.net/nifty-
    1.3.xsd http://nifty-gui.sourceforge.net/nifty-1.3.xsd">
        <useStyles filename="nifty-default-styles.xml" />
        <useControls filename="nifty-default-controls.xml" />

        <registerSound id="showWindow" filename="Sound/Effects/Beep.ogg" />

        <screen id="main" controller="gui.controller.MainScreenController">
            <layer id="layer0" childLayout="absolute" backgroundColor="#000f">
                <!-- add more content -->
            </layer>
        </screen>
    </nifty>
```

Each screen has a `Controller` class tied to it. This is the link between the XML and Java that allows Nifty to control functions in the code and the other way around.

Another important concept is `Controls` (not to be confused with `Controller` classes or jMonkeyEngine's Control interface). Using `Controls` is a very convenient way to make screen files smaller and create reusable components. Anyone familiar with, for example, components in JSF will see the similarities. It's highly recommended that you become accustomed to using these early on, or screen files will quickly become unmanageable.

A UI's implementation is often very specific to the game in question. This chapter will try to show and explain the different functions and effects available in Nifty GUI. Even if the title of a recipe does not appeal to you, it could still be worth to glance through the content to see whether it covers some features that could be suitable for your project.

Initializing Nifty and managing an options menu

To start things off, let's begin with a simple recipe that will provide us with the basics of setting up the application to use Nifty GUI and tell us how to manage the options menu. An options menu is usually found in games; it acts as a link between different screens. For this reason, it's suitable to create it using the control pattern so it can be easily handled across screens.

We'll initialize Nifty GUI inside `AppState` to offset it from the main application code and then access the application from Nifty and control Nifty through code.

Getting ready

Let's look at how to initialize Nifty in an application. We start off by defining a new `AppState` to handle our Nifty functions. We can call it `NiftyAppState` and have it extend `AbstractAppState`.

In the `initialize` method, we need to create the Nifty display with the following line of code, giving Nifty access to various functionalities within the application and telling it to render o in the GUI view:

```
NiftyJmeDisplay niftyDisplay = new NiftyJmeDisplay(app.
getAssetManager(),
                app.getInputManager(),
                app.getAudioRenderer(),
                app.getRenderManager().getPostView("Gui Default"));
```

We should also store the Nifty instance in the class for use later, using `niftyDisplay. getNifty()`. With this done, we need to add `niftyDisplay` as a processor to the same view we just specified, using the following code:

```
app.getRenderManager().getPostView("Gui Default").
addProcessor(niftyDisplay);
```

The last thing that needs to be done before Nifty could show anything is to tell it what to draw. We do this with `nifty.fromXml` and pass the XML file to be used as well as the name of the screen (if several screens are stored in the same XML).

How to do it...

We start by defining the XML files for our options menu and the screen that will contain it. Perform the following steps to do this:

1. First of all, we should create a new file called `optionsMenu.xml`. It should reside in the `Interface/Controls` folder.

2. The first tag we need to have is a `<nifty-controls>` tag to let Nifty know that the elements inside should be parsed as controls.

3. Then, we add `<controlDefinition name="options">`, which is the actual options menu instance.

4. This is where the actual layout starts, and it does so with a `<panel>` element, as shown in the following code:

```
<panel id="optionsPanel" childLayout="vertical"
width="40%" height="60%" align="center" valign="center"
backgroundColor="#333f">
```

5. At the top, we'll have `<panel>` that will include `<control name="label">` element with text="Options".

6. To the right of this panel, there should be a small button with the familiar **x** to close the menu and an interact element to call a method in the `Controller` class, as shown in the following code:

```
<control name="button" id="closeButton" align="right" label="x"
height="30px" width="30px" >
  <interact onClick="toggleOptionsMenu()"/>
</control>
```

7. After this, we can have as many `<control name="button">` elements we want for our options menu to work. There should at least be one that calls `quit()` in the `Controller` class to stop the application.

8. Now, we can define a screen to contain our options menu. If we right-click on the **Projects** window and select **New/Empty Nifty GUI file**, we will get a basic setup for a screen.

9. Clean out everything between the `<layer>` tags, and change the controller of the `<screen>` element to `gui.controls.NiftyController`.

10. Next, we need to define what styles to include using the `<useStyles>` tag, which should appear before the `<screen>` element.

11. We add `<useControls filename="nifty-default-controls.xml" />` to include access to basic nifty controls such as buttons, and we should add another `<useControls>` tag for our options menu. These should also be added before the `<screen>` element.

Now, we can start looking at the `Controller` code for this. Perform the following five steps to do this:

1. We should define a class that implements the `ScreenController` interface, which will become the link between the GUI and the code. We can make it abstract and call it `NiftyController`.

2. It should have two protected fields, namely, `Nifty nifty` and `Screen screen`, which will be set from the values provided in the `bind` method.

3. We also need a Boolean field called `optionsMenuVisible`.

4. We need to add methods for each of the methods specified in the `optionsMenu.xml` file, and `toggleOptionsMenu()` should either show or hide the menu depending on whether `optionsMenuVisible` is true or not. A handy way to get hold of an element is by using the following code:

```
nifty.getCurrentScreen().findElementByName("options");
```

5. Then, we can call either `hide()` or `show()` on the element to control visibility.

Normally, the application is shut down when *Esc* is pressed. Let's make the options menu handle this instead; this consists of the following four steps:

1. Start by deleting the related mapping by adding the following line to the `NiftyAppState` initialization method:

   ```
   app.getInputManager().deleteMapping(SimpleApplication.INPUT_
   MAPPING_EXIT);
   ```

2. Now, we need to add our own mapping for the Esc key, as shown in the following code:

   ```
   app.getInputManager().addMapping("TOGGLE_OPTIONS", new
   KeyTrigger(KeyInput.KEY_ESCAPE));
   app.getInputManager().addListener(this, "TOGGLE_OPTIONS");
   ```

3. The `NiftyAppState` method also needs to implement `ActionListener` and handle the key press:

   ```
   public void onAction(String name, boolean isPressed, float tpf) {
      if(name.equals(TOGGLE_OPTIONS) && isPressed){
     ((NiftyController)nifty.getCurrentScreen().
   getScreenController()).toggleOptionsMenu();
      }
   }
   ```

4. With the normal shut down routine removed, we need to add functionality inside `NiftyController` to handle this instead. Since this class will be shared by the screens, we provide the application with static access and a setter method. The `quit` method just has to call `app.stop()` to shut it down.

How it works...

Nifty was initialized inside `AppState` to offset the code from the main application and make it more modular. This also made it easier to add some more general functionalities related to controlling the GUI.

Every nifty `Controller` class must implement the `ScreenController` interface for Nifty to be able to find it. Since some functions will be shared across the screens, we created an abstract class called `NiftyController` to avoid duplicating the code. Apart from handling the generic Options menu, it was also given access to the application itself.

The link between the XML file and the `Controller` class doesn't need to be specified beyond providing the qualified name of the controller in the screen. Likewise, Nifty will find methods automatically using the name provided in the `interact` tag of `ButtonControl`.

The `<panel>` elements are versatile objects that can be used for many parts of the layout and can contain most other types of layout items.

It's OK to contain several `<controlDefinition>` elements within a `<nifty-controls>` tag.

There's more...

It's very easy to use a `properties` file to back a Nifty file for localization purposes, as given in the following points:

- First of all, the following tag needs to be present to link the properties file:
  ```
  <resourceBundle id="localization" filename="packagename.filename"
  />
  ```
- It can be called, for example, from a `label` control:
  ```
  <control name="label" text="${localization.STR_HELLO_WORLD}"/>
  ```

Loading the screen

In this recipe, we'll develop a loading screen along with a controller for the game. It'll cover the most important aspects of the loading screen, such as showing a text and image for what it's loading and an indicator that shows the system is working.

Before starting this, it's recommended that you have a basic understanding of how to set up Nifty in an application and how to create screens and controllers. Have a look at the previous recipe, *Initializing Nifty managing an options menu*, if you are unsure about this.

How to do it...

We begin by creating the XML for the loading screen. Perform the following nine steps to do this:

1. Create a new file called `loadingScreen.xml` and load `Nifty-default-styles` and `Nifty-default-controls`. Optionally, we can also include `optionsMenu` from the previous recipe.

2. The first element we need is a `<screen>` element:
   ```
   <screen id="loadingScreen" controller="gui.controller.
   LoadingScreenController">
   ```

3. Inside this, we define a `<layer>` element:
   ```
   <layer id="layer0" childLayout="center" backgroundColor="#000f">
   ```

4. Inside this `<layer>` element, we define `<panel>` that will contain our layout. Note that we set `visible` to `false`:

```
<panel id="loadingPanel" childLayout="vertical" visible="false">
```

5. Since we want a smooth transition to the screen, we'll add a fade effect to this panel:

```
<effect>
  <onShow name="fade" start="#00" end="#ff" length="500"
inherit="true"/>
  <onEndScreen name="fade" start="#ff" end="#00" length="200"
inherit="true"/>
</effect>
```

6. To add a movie-style and non-interactive feel to it, we will have three `<panel>` elements inside this file. At the top and bottom, there will be two black bars captioning the loading image, which will appear in the central panel.

7. Inside the `topPanel` element, we define `<control name="label">` that will contain the name of the scene that is being loaded.

8. The `bottomPanel` element will have an animated indicator that will show the system hasn't frozen. We will define another panel inside this, aligned to the right of the screen. We will use an `imageSizePulsate` effect to animate this and have it fade in as well, as shown in the following code:

```
<effect>
  <onShow name="fade" start="#00" end="#ff" length="1000"/>
  <onShow name="imageSizePulsate" startSize="100%" endSize="50%"
pulsator="SinusPulsator" activated="true" timeType="infinite"/>
</effect>
```

9. Optionally, we can also add another `<layer>` tag beside the previous one that will contain the `options` control from the previous recipe.

Now, we have a complete XML. Let's have a look at the controller for this. We will create it by performing the following seven steps:

1. We begin by creating a new class called `LoadingScreenController` that extends the `NiftyController` class we created in the previous recipe.

2. We define two strings, `loadingText` and `loadingScreen`, and setters for these as well.

3. Next, we override the `onStartScreen()` method and add the following three lines to it:

```
screen.findNiftyControl("caption", Label.class).
setText(loadingText); screen.findElementByName("central
Panel").getRenderer(ImageRenderer.class).setImage(nifty.
createImage(loadingScreen, true));
screen.findElementByName("loadingPanel").setVisible(true);
```

4. The controller is now done. However, there are some more things we need to do before we can look at it.

5. First, we need to add the screen to Nifty. If we have the `NiftyAppState` method from the previous recipe, we should add the following line just after the `nifty.fromXml` call:

```
nifty.addXml("Interface/Screens/loadingScreen.xml");
```

6. We can also add a `convenience` class to access `nifty.gotoScreen()`.

7. Now, before calling `gotoScreen("loadingScreen")` from our main class, we can add the following lines to set `lodingText` and `loadingImage`:

```
((LoadingScreenController)niftyState.getNifty().
getScreen("loadingScreen").getScreenController()).
setLoadingText("Loading Test Scene"); ((LoadingScreenController)
niftyState.getNifty().getScreen("loadingScreen").
getScreenController()).setLoadingImage("Interface/Image/
loadingScreen.png");
```

How it works...

Most of the work in this recipe consists of getting the XML layout right. It's a good idea to sketch it on paper first and visualize the flow of the elements.

The reason the fade effect is shorter is because by the time it fades out, the game is ready to be played and the player doesn't need to wait longer than necessary. When the loading screen is first shown, the player has to wait for the game to load.

There is a reason why we set `loadingPanel` to `visible="false"` at the beginning and used `onShow` rather than `onScreenStart` effects. The `onStartScreen` method in the controller is called after the screen has been started and `onScreenStart` effects have been fired (and completed). This means that any fading will occur before we set the images, and they would pop into existence after some time has passed. Since the `onShow` effects are called once the element becomes visible, we get around that problem this way.

Another possible gotcha here, especially if we use a test case to show the screen, is that we can't call `nifty.gotoScreen` just after initializing `NiftyAppState`. Since the `AppState` initialization method is called in a thread-safe way, it doesn't run until the next update cycle. This means that if we try to change the screens on the next line, we will get `NullPointerException`.

Creating an RPG dialog screen

As the title implies, we'll explore a method to create a dialog screen, similar to those found in many RPGs. It'll display an image of the character being talked to, but this could be replaced by using some clever camera work to zoom in on a character instead.

It will use a Nifty `ListBox` to display the player's available dialog options and a listener to find out the result of the player's choice.

There most likely has to be some dialog tree system that backs the implementation. For this example, we'll use a template class called `DialogNode`. This will have information about a character's name, image, and what it says. It also contains the player's options as a string array, as shown in the following screenshot. What's missing from it is the callbacks for each option. It will, however, be possible to call it from the controller's listener method.

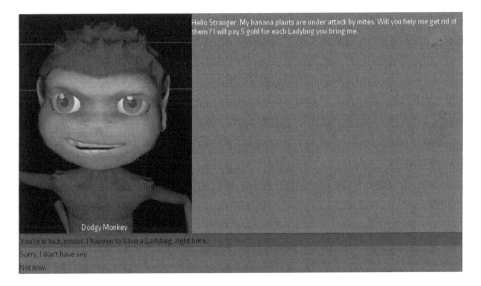

How to do it...

Before we work on the screen, we should define a new reusable Nifty control to contain the character information of the character the player is talking to; perform the following steps to do this:

1. Create a new file called `characterDialogControls.xml` with the `<nifty-controls>` tag, and inside it, create a new `<controlDefinition name="characterControl">` class.

2. The layout for this is fairly simple; it needs one `<panel>` element that contains another `<panel>` for the character image and a `<control name="label">` element for the name.

Now, let's build the dialog screen. We do this by performing the following nine steps:

1. Create a new file called `dialogScreen.xml` and load `nifty-default-styles` and `nifty-default-controls`. It should also load the `characterDialogControls.xml` file. We can also include `optionsMenu` from the previous recipe.

2. The first element we need is a `<screen>` element:

   ```
   <screen id="dialogScreen" controller="gui.controller.
   DialogScreenController">
   ```

3. Inside this, we define a `<layer>` element:

   ```
   <layer id="layer0" childLayout="center" backgroundColor="#0000">
   ```

4. Inside the `<layer>` element, we define `<panel>`, which will contain the rest of our layout:

   ```
   <panel id="dialogPanel" childLayout="vertical" visible="false">
   ```

5. We'll add a short fade effect to this panel as well:

   ```
   <effect>
     <onShow name="fade" start="#00" end="#ff" length="200"
   inherit="true"/>
     <onEndScreen name="fade" start="#ff" end="#00" length="200"
   inherit="true"/>
   </effect>
   ```

6. The dialog panel will have four `<panel>` elements inside it. At the top and bottom, we should add two thin panels with black background to give it a cinematic feel.

7. The upper part of the two central panels will contain the `characterControl` we just created:

   ```
   <control name="characterControl" id="character"/>
   ```

8. The lower one will have a listbox that contains the player's dialog options:

   ```
   <control id="dialogOptions" name="listBox" vertical="off"
   horizontal="off" displayItems="3" selection="Single"/>
   ```

9. If we also want support for the options menu, it should go in a separate layer to make it show on top of the rest of the GUI.

The controller code for it can be created by performing the following 12 steps:

1. Begin by defining a new class called `DialogScreenController` that extends `NiftyController` or implements `ScreenController` if an abstract `Controller` class is not available.

2. Next, we add two fields: one for the current `DialogNode`, `dialogNode`, and a reference to `ListBox` in the XML called `dialogOptions`.

3. The `onStartScreen()` method should be overridden; here, it should set `dialogOptions` by calling `screen.findNiftyControl`:

   ```
   dialogOptions = screen.findNiftyControl("dialogOptions", ListBox.class);
   ```

4. Finally, `onStartScreen` should also call `onDialogNodeChanged()` if `dialogNode` is set.

5. Now, we need to define the method called `onDialogNodeChanged` that will apply the dialog information to the layout.

6. We should begin this by setting the name of the character; again, we will use `screen.findNiftyControl` to do this:

   ```
   screen.findNiftyControl("characterName", Label.class).setText(dialogNode.getCharacterName());
   ```

   Likewise, the dialog text is set in the same manner.

7. To set the image, we need to create `NiftyImage` and pass it on to `ImageRenderer` of an element using the following code:

   ```
   screen.findElementByName("characterImage").getRenderer(ImageRenderer.class).setImage(nifty.createImage(dialogNode.getCharacterImage(), true));
   ```

8. Next, we clear `dialogOptions` and use `dialogOptions.addItem` to apply the values available in `DialogNode`.

9. Finally, we call `dialogOptions.refresh()` and `screen.layoutLayers()` and set the `dialogPanel` element to be visible.

10. To find out which item is pressed in `dialogOptions`, we add a listener method to the class:

    ```
    public void onDialogOptionSelected(final String id, final ListBoxSelectionChangedEvent event)
    ```

11. Then, we add an annotation to let it know which element to listen to:

    ```
    @NiftyEventSubscriber(id="dialogOptions")
    ```

12. Using `event.getSelectionIndices()`, we can find out which item the player has pressed.

How it works...

Getting the layout exactly as we want can be tricky sometimes, but in general, it's important to know that Nifty really likes the width and height to be defined.

Using the ListBox here gives us a lot for free since it handles a dynamic number of options, and callbacks to the code are easily handled with the `listener` method. By default, it has scrollbars and handles multiple selection, which is why we explicitly defined it to be `selection="Single"` and used `vertical="off"` and `horizontal="off"` to turn off the scrollbars. It also supports item selection by using the up, down, and *Enter* keys.

The listener method in the controller can be referred to as anything; what Nifty looks for is the annotation and the method's parameters. From here, we can call the next `DialogNode` or other code based on the player's choices.

Implementing a game console

A console can be a very powerful tool that allows a player to have control over game functions that might either not have a functional UI yet, or where setting up a UI is simply not be feasible due to its complexity.

This recipe will implement a console in the main screen from the first recipe in this chapter and also use the `Move` effect to slide it in and out of view. Moreover, it will describe how to use console commands to let the player control the game functions.

How to do it...

Just as before, we begin by defining a control that will host the console. It can be done by performing the following four steps:

1. Inside the `<nifty-controls>` tags, we add a new `<controlDefinition name="consoleControl">` class.

2. Then, we add a small console, aligning it with the bottom of the screen:

   ```
   <control id="console" name="nifty-console" lines="10" width="100%"
   valign="bottom" backgroundColor="#6874" visible="true">
   ```

3. To spice up the simple console, we give it a `Move` effect when it's being shown or hidden:

   ```
   <effect>
     <onShow name="move" mode="fromOffset" offsetY="100" length="300"
   inherit="true"/>
     <onHide name="move" mode="toOffset" offsetY="100" length="200"
   inherit="true"/>
   </effect>
   ```

4. In `mainScreen.xml`, we add `controlDefinition` inside a new layer:

   ```
   <layer id="consoleLayer" childLayout="center"
   backgroundColor="#0000">
     <control name="consoleControl"/>
   </layer>
   ```

That's it for XML hacking. Now, we can turn our attention to the `NiftyController` class from the *Initializing Nifty and managing an options menu* recipe and add a console to handle to it. This can be done by performing the following 10 steps:

1. We need to add a new field, `Console console`, and bind it using the following code:

   ```
   nifty.getScreen("main").findNiftyControl("console", Console.
   class);
   ```

2. Next, we add a method about the output text to the console from external sources. We call it `outputToConsole`, and it takes a string as an input. It then calls `console.output` to display the message.

3. Another new method is `toggleConsole()`. It should check whether `console.getElement()` is visible or not and then hide or show it accordingly.

4. Then, we add a `subscriber` method that will receive anything entered in the console. It needs the `@NiftyEventSubscriber` annotation with the console as its ID. It also needs a method declaration that looks like the following code:

   ```
   public void onConsoleCommand(final String id, final
   ConsoleExecuteCommandEvent command)
   ```

5. Define a new class called `HideCommand` that implements `ConsoleCommand`.

6. Add a field `NiftyController controller` together with a setter method to the `HideCommand` class.

7. In the implemented `execute` method, we call `controller.toggleConsole()`.

8. Going back to `NiftyController`, we instantiate a new `HideCommand` method and set the controller.

9. We then create a new `ConsoleCommands` instance and call `registerCommand`; thereafter, we supply/hide the instance and call `commandText`, and `HideCommand` as `ConsoleCommand`.

10. Finally, we call `enableCommandCompletion(true)` in the `ConsoleCommands` instance.

How it works...

In this recipe, we implemented two ways of handling the input in the console. The most straightforward way is the `onConsoleCommand` method where we get the raw input and can do whatever we want with it.

The more intricate way of doing this is using `ConsoleCommands`. With this, we get a nice layered pattern to handle the input. Once the console is shown or hidden, it will quickly slide in or out of the screen with the move effect. It will move the `offsetY` distance, and based on the mode, it will either move to that offset or from it. The `inherit="true"` value ensures that child elements move together with the component in question.

Handling a game message queue

It is possible to relay most game-related information to the player using a console. However, it's a very basic form of communication. Modern players often expect more graphical ways of receiving information. In this recipe, we'll explore one way of doing this using Nifty. We'll create a dynamic message queue with messages moving in from the right of the screen and fading out once clicked.

It actually doesn't require that many lines of code.

How to do it...

The XML for this recipe can be completed by performing the following five steps:

1. We start by defining a new `<controlDefinition name="gameMessage">`.

2. Inside this, we should add a `panel` element, and inside this `panel` element, add two `<control name="label">` elements with the ID `#title` and other contents.

3. The panel should also have two effects, one `onShow` trigger and one `onHide` trigger with move and fade effects respectively, as shown in the following code:

   ```
   <onShow name="move" mode="fromOffset" offsetX="1500" length="100"
   inherit="true"/>
   <onHide name="fade" start="#ff" end="#00" length="100"
   inherit="true"/>
   ```

4. In addition to the `gameMessage` control, we can define another control to be our `messageQueue` element. It just needs a horizontally aligned panel, spanning the whole screen.

5. To make them align with each other, the `messageQueue` control is added to the `mainScreen.xml` file inside the same layer as the console.

   Inside `MainScreenController`, we need to do the following changes:

6. First, add a new `int` field called `messageIndex`.

7. Then, we need two methods. One of these is called `addMessage` that should take a string as an input.

8. Inside the `addMessage` method, we define a `ControlBuilder` method called `messageBuilder`. This will create `gameMessage` controls:

   ```
   messageBuilder = new ControlBuilder("gameMessage") {{
       id("message"+messageIndex);
       interactOnClick("removeMessage("+messageIndex+")");
   }};
   ```

9. After calling the `build` method on this and supplying the `messageQueue` element as the parent, we can call `element.findNiftyControl` to set the title and the text on the labels inside the `gameMessage` control.

10. Then, we call `element.show()` and increase `messageIndex` for the next message.

11. The second method we create is `removeMessage`. It takes a string called `id` as the input.

12. Inside this, we use `screen.findElementByName` to find the message, and call `hide`.

13. While doing this, we supply a new `EndNotify` object, which in its `perform` message should call `markForRemoval()` on the message and also `layoutElements()` on the parent `messageQueue` control.

How it works...

Once the `addMessage` method is called in the `Controller` class, `ControlBuilder` creates a new `gameMessage` instance. The `interactOnClick` element tells `gameMessage` to call `removeMessage` when clicked, supplying its index as `id`.

After its built and added to `messageQueue`, we populate the title and content elements of the message. Using # in the ID of these elements is preferred by Nifty for non-unique IDs.

The `gameMessage` instance is not visible upon creation, and we call `show()` to make it play the `onShow` effect we defined.

The `Move` effect is set up to have `offsetX`, which is outside of the screen. If it's too low, there will be a pop effect as it comes into existence. It's set to reach the target position in 100 ms. Messages will stack up nicely without any additional work when they are added.

The messages are set to disappear when clicked, as defined in the builder, through the `interactOnClick` method. Instead of just removing them, we want to play a short fade effect to make the transition smoother. Simply hiding them won't be enough in this case either. Since they still occupy a position in the `messageQueue` panel, the remaining messages won't align properly.

Hence, we want to call `markForRemoval` on the `gameMessage` element. Doing this instantly, however, would remove it before our hide effect is played. This why we supply an `EndNotify` object that is handled once the hide effect is done with playing; then, we add the `markForRemoval` call in here instead.

Let's say we would like to be able to show messages in a window, either when clicking the message in the queue, or any time. In that case, we can use Nifty's window control.

We can define a new `controlDefinition` in our `gameMessageControls.xml` file and call it `messageWindow`. Inside this, we'll add `<control name="window">`, inside which we can add any content we'd like. For now, we can settle with `<control name="label">` for text content and a short fade effect when showing or hiding the window.

Then, we can copy the `addMessage` method to `MainScreenController`, and instead of having `ControlBuilder` make `gameMessage`, we can tell it to build a `messageWindow` window instead.

We don't need an `interactOnClick` element, as the window can be closed by default. Instead, we can use it to set the title of the window:

```
set("title", "Window"+windowIndex);
```

Windows are also draggable by default, but the parent element must have `childLayout="absolute"` for it to work, as it lets the element decide its position itself.

Creating an inventory screen

In this recipe, we'll create an inventory screen, which is very common, mostly in RPGs. To do this, we'll use the `Droppable` and `Draggable` components in Nifty and create an `InventoryItem` class to help us differentiate different the types of items (and hence, where they can be attached). This time, we'll use both XML to create the static components and the Java Builder interface to build the inventory (or backpack) slots. The reason is that in many games, the amount of inventory a character has varies.

How to do it...

We begin by creating the controls, which are the key components of this method. This can be done by performing the following four steps:

1. First, we create a new controls file, `inventoryControls.xml`, with the `<nifty-controls>` tag.

2. Inside this, we first define `<controlDefinition name="itemSlot">` with the following content:

   ```
   <control name="droppable" backgroundColor="#fff5" width="64px"
   height="64px" margin="1px" childLayout="center"/>
   ```

3. Then similarly, we create a draggable control to be the item, and name it `<controlDefinition name="item" >`.

4. This item contains both the draggable component and a label with the item's name:

```
<control name="draggable" backgroundColor="#aaaf" width="64px"
height="64px" childLayout="center" valign="top">
  <text id="#itemLabel" text="" color="#000f" valign="center"
width="100%" style="nifty-label"/>
</control>
```

Next, we can turn our attention to the screen itself. It can be created by performing the following five steps:

1. First, we make sure that the styles we want to use are loaded, and add our `inventoryControls.xml` file is loaded with `<useControls>`.

2. Then, we add a `<screen>` element with a link to our controller file:

```
<screen id="inventoryScreen" controller="gui.controller.
InventoryScreenController">
```

3. Inside this, we need a `<layer>` element:

```
<layer id="layer0" childLayout="center" backgroundColor="#0000">
```

4. Inside the `<layer>` element, we need a `<panel>` element that will contain the rest of our layout:

```
<panel id="inventoryPanel" childLayout="horizontal">
```

5. The next element is a panel that will keep our dynamically created `itemSlots`:

```
<panel id="inventorySlots" childLayout="horizontal"/>
```

The following screenshot shows us the dynamically created item slots:

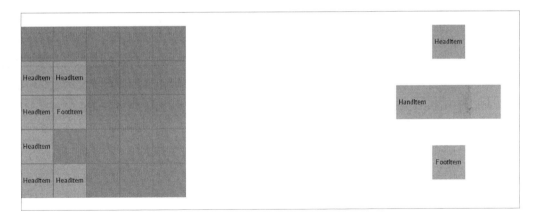

After this, we create a simple representation of a humanoid with two hands and feet, using the `itemSlot` control. We use `align` and `childLayout` to make the components appear where we want them to.

6. First, add a panel to contain the components:

```
<panel id="characterPanel" childLayout="vertical">
```

7. Then, add the head using the following command:

```
<panel id="character" backgroundColor="#000f" childLayout="center"
align="center" valign="top">
  <control name="itemSlot" id="Head"/>
</panel>
```

8. Add one left and right hand using the following command:

```
<panel id="hands" backgroundColor="#000f" childLayout="horizontal"
width="25%" align="center" valign="bottom">
  <control name="itemSlot" id="HandLeft" align="left" />
  <panel width="*" height="1px"/>
  <control name="itemSlot" id="HandRight" align="right" />
</panel>
```

9. Finally, we have one `itemSlot` for the legs/feet:

```
<panel id="legs" backgroundColor="#000f" childLayout="horizontal"
align="center" valign="bottom">
  <control name="itemSlot" id="Foot"/>
</panel>
```

With the XML elements done, we can turn to the Java code. The following nine steps are necessary:

1. We create a class called `InventoryItem`. This has an enum (enumeration) for different body parts: head, hand, foot, and a name.

2. Next, we'll create the `Controller` class, `InventoryScreenController`, and have it extend `NiftyController`; also, implement `DroppableDropFilter`.

3. We need to add a map to contain our `InventoryItems`, with the name as the key. It can be called `itemMap`.

4. The `bind` method should be overridden, and in here, we should find different `DropControls` in the `InventoryScreen` and add this class as a filter using the following code:

```
screen.findNiftyControl("HandLeft", Droppable.class).
addFilter(this);
```

Now, we can generate the item slots in the inventory in a 5 x 5 grid.

5. We define two builders: `ControlBuilder` for the itemSlot controls and `PanelBuilder` to make columns that will contain five itemSlots each.

6. We can use a `for` loop to iterate five times over the following block:

```
panelBuilder = new PanelBuilder("") {{
   id("inventoryColumn"+posX);
   childLayoutVertical();
}};
panelBuilder.build(nifty, screen, screen.findElementByName("invent
orySlots"));
```

7. While still inside this `for` loop, we run another `for` loop, generating the five item slots for that column:

```
slotBuilder = new ControlBuilder("itemSlot") {{
   id("itemSlot"+index);
}};
Element e = slotBuilder.build(nifty, screen, screen.findElementByN
ame("inventoryColumn"+posY));
```

8. For each of the item slots, we also need to add the following class as a DropFilter:

```
e.findNiftyControl("itemSlot"+index, Droppable.class).
addFilter(this);
```

9. The implemented method that is accepted needs some logic. Once an item has been dropped on an `itemSlot`, we should check whether it's allowed, and we can do it with the following lines of code:

```
InventoryItem item = itemMap.get(drgbl.getId());
if(drpbll.getId().startsWith(item.getType().name()) || drpbll.
getId().startsWith("itemSlot")){
   return true;
```

With the item slots done, we can generate some items for testing.

10. First we use a `for` loop to create 10 `InventoryItems` with different types and names.

11. For each of these, we create a Nifty control using `ControlBuilder` and the item control we defined earlier, as shown in the following code:

```
itemBuilder = new ControlBuilder("item") {{
   id("item"+index);
   visibleToMouse(true);
}};
Element e = itemBuilder.build(nifty, screen, screen.findElemen
tByName("itemSlot"+index)); e.findElementByName("#itemLabel").
getRenderer(TextRenderer.class).setText(item.getName());
```

12. Then, we put each of the inventory items in the itemMap with the ID of the control as the key. This ensures we can easily find out the link to the inventory item where a nifty item has been dragged or dropped.

How it works...

The Java Builder interface we use to create item slots takes a while to get used to, but it's a really powerful tool when we have the need to create nifty elements dynamically. In this case, we still use a predefined control. This saves us a couple of lines of code and allows someone else than a coder to edit the layout and style of the component since it's exposed in the XML file.

By default, a `Droppable` control will always accept the `Draggable` control that is being dropped. The `accept` method in `DroppableDropFilter` enables us to define what should be accepted or not. It's illustrated in this recipe by only accepting `InventoryItems` of a certain type. The method parameters for the accept method can be described, as the first `Droppable` is the control that the `draggable` control is being picked up from. The `Draggable` control is the item that is being moved. The second `Droppable` control is the target where `Draggable` has been dropped.

 At the time of writing this, the first `Droppable` control tends to be null the first time a `Draggable` control is being moved.

Customizing the input and settings page

Just about every modern game lets the player customize the input according to their own preferences. This recipe will rely on jMonkeyEngine to do the work for us, and we will use Nifty GUI as a visual aid. We'll use `RawInputListener` to work out which keys have been pressed and divide them between key codes and characters using the `Keyboard` class.

Getting ready

The recipe will depend on there being some bindings in `InputManager`. If you already have a game, this would not be a problem. If not, it will describe how to add a couple of bindings for the example to work.

How to do it...

Following the pattern from previous recipes, we'll start defining the controls, then move on to the screen, and finally work on the controller. Adding the controls and screen will consist of the following eight steps:

1. Inside a `<nifty-control>` tag, we define a new `<controlDefinition name="keyBindingControl">`.

2. Here, we'll add a horizontal spanning panel with some margin to the edges of its container and enough height to contain text:

```
<panel childLayout="horizontal" width="80%" height="25px"
backgroundColor="#666f" marginLeft="10px" marginRight="10px"
marginTop="4px" align="center" >
```

3. This panel will have three elements. The first is a label control that contains the text for the key binding, as shown in the following code:

```
<control name="label" id="#command" width="150px" text=""/>
```

4. Then, it will have a button to change the binding, displaying the current key:

```
<control name="button" id="#key" width="100px" valign="center"/>
```

5. In between them, it will have a simple panel with `width="*"`.

6. Now, we can define another `<controlDefinition name="settingsControl">` that will contain a number of our `keyBindingControls`.

7. This will contain a panel, and inside this, four `keyBindingControls` for each moving direction. The IDs of these controls should be representative of the direction and end with a key as follows:

```
<control name="keyBindingControl" id="forwardKey"/>
```

8. The following points are needed for the screen:

   ❏ The ID should be settings, and controller should be `gui.controller.SettingsController`

   ❏ The `settingsControl` class we just created should be added inside a layer element

That's all with regards to XML. To create the `Controller` class, perform the following steps:

1. As usual, we create a new class that extends `NiftyController`. We call it `SettingsController`.

2. We'll have `Element` fields for each of the key bindings we would like to track and one `Element` field for the current `selectedElement`.

3. In addition, we should add `Map<Integer, String>` called `mappings` where we can keep the relations between key inputs and input bindings.

4. From here, we should call a `bindElements` method, which we'll define as well.

5. Inside this, we'll add the current key bindings to the `mappings` map using the key code as key and the actual binding as the value. This can usually be found in the class that handles the input.

6. Next, for each of the keys we would like to handle, we find the reference in the settings screen and populate their values accordingly. For example, for the forward key use the following code:

```
forwardMapping = screen.findElementByName("forwardKey");
forwardMapping.findNiftyControl("#command", Label.class).
setText("MoveForward");
forwardMapping.findNiftyControl("#key", Button.class).
setText(Keyboard.getKeyName(KeyInput.KEY_W));
```

7. Next, we define a new inner class called `KeyEventListener` that implements `RawInputListener`.

8. In `onKeyEvent`, add an `if` statement for if the incoming `KeyInputEvent` is pressed and `selectedElement` is not null.

9. Here, we add a reference to the yet-to-be-created `changeMapping` method and add the following line:

```
selectedElement.findNiftyControl("#key", Button.class).
setText(Keyboard.getKeyName(evt.getKeyCode()));
```

10. Finally, we should set `selectedElement` to `null`.

Now, we can turn our attention to the `changeMapping` method.

11. This method has the pressed key code as an input parameter, and we use this to see whether we already have a binding in our `mappings` map. If `inputManager` of the application also has this, we should delete the old binding.

12. Next, we need to iterate through all the values in our `mappings` map and check whether any of the bindings match the one that the selected element is handling. If you find a match, it should be deleted.

13. Finally, we create a new `KeyTrigger` class using `keyCode` and add it to `inputManager` using `addMapping`.

The last thing we need to do in this class is add an event subscriber to the buttons in `keyBindingControls`.

14. We define a new method, `keyClicked(String id, ButtonClickedEvent event)`, and give it the following annotation:

```
@NiftyEventSubscriber(pattern=".*Key#key")
```

15. When the button is clicked, the corresponding element should be selected, so we use `event.getButton().getElement().getParent()` to find out which one that is.

How it works...

This recipe explains that when a button that represents a key binding is clicked, the corresponding element is selected. By using a pattern in the annotation for the `keyClicked` method, rather than an ID, we can capture all the keys using the wildcard `.*`. This is also why the naming of the elements is important.

Once an element is selected, `KeyEventListener` will start to listen for a key to be pressed on the keyboard. We set the text of the button to be the text representation of the key. In many cases, we can use the `getKeyChar` method of `KeyInputEvent` for this; however, not all the methods have a character like representation, hence the use of the `Keyboard` class and `getKeyName` method instead. This method tends to output a string representation instead.

The `changeMapping` method first sees whether there is a current binding for the key pressed and deletes it if that is the case. This is not enough, however, since we also need to delete any previous bindings for that input. This is why we also iterate over the current mappings to see whether any of them match the binding that this key press was for; if yes, it deletes them too.

There's more...

This recipe uses a static representation of the different input bindings. This would most likely be fine for many games, but modern first person shooters for example, can have 20 and more key bindings; adding all of these manually to the XML can be cumbersome and not good from a maintenance perspective. In this case, it might be better to use the Java Builder interface described in the *Creating an inventory screen* recipe to let Java do the repetitious work.

Using offscreen rendering for a minimap

There are generally two ways of creating minimaps. One way is to let an artist draw a representation of the map, as shown in the following screenshot. This usually ends up beautifully as it gives considerable freedom to the artist when it comes to style. The method is not that viable during development when scenes might be changing a lot, or for games with procedural content where the end result is not known beforehand.

Minimap with unit marker

In those cases, taking a snapshot of the actual scene can be very helpful. The resulting image can then be run through various filters (or shaders during rendering) to get a less raw look.

In this recipe, we'll achieve this by creating a new `ViewPort` port, and `FrameBuffer` to store a snapshot of a camera. Finally, we'll create `NiftyImage` out of it and display it as a GUI element.

How to do it...

We're going to start by creating a `Util` class to handle the rendering of our minimap. This will consist of the following 15 steps:

1. Define a new class called `MinimapUtil`.

2. It will only have one static method, `createMiniMap`, with the following declaration:

   ```
   public static void createMiniMap(final SimpleApplication app,
   final Spatial scene, int width, int height)
   ```

3. The first thing we do is create a new camera called `offScreenCamera` with the same width and height that were supplied to the method.

4. The camera should have the parallel projection set to true, and a frustrum that spans between 1 and 1000 in depth, `-width` to `width`, and `-height` to `height`, as shown in the following code:

   ```
   offScreenCamera.setParallelProjection(true);
   offScreenCamera.setFrustum(1, 1000, -width, width, height,
   -height);
   ```

5. It should be located at some distance above the scene and rotated downwards, as shown in the following code:

   ```
   offScreenCamera.setLocation(new Vector3f(0, 100f, 0));
   offScreenCamera.setRotation(new Quaternion().fromAngles(new
   float[]{FastMath.HALF_PI,FastMath.PI,0}));
   ```

6. Next, we create a new `ViewPort` by calling the application's `RenderManager` and its `createPreView` method using `offScreenCamera`:

   ```
   final ViewPort offScreenView = app.getRenderManager().
   createPreView(scene.getName() + "_View", offScreenCamera);
   offScreenView.setClearFlags(true, true, true);
   offScreenView.setBackgroundColor(ColorRGBA.DarkGray.
   mult(ColorRGBA.Blue).mult(0.3f));
   ```

7. Now, we need a `Texture2D` class to store the data in, so we create a class called `offScreenTexture` with the same width and height as before and set `MinFilter` to `Trilinear`:

   ```
   final Texture2D offScreenTexture = new Texture2D(width, height,
   Image.Format.RGB8);
   offScreenTexture.setMinFilter(Texture.MinFilter.Trilinear);
   ```

8. A `FrameBuffer` class is needed as a medium for the data, so we create one with the same width and height, and `1` sample, as shown in the following code:

   ```
   FrameBuffer offScreenBuffer = new FrameBuffer(width, height, 1);
   ```

9. We set `DepthBuffer` to be `Image.Format.Depth` and `offScreenTexture` to be `ColorTexture`:

   ```
   offScreenBuffer.setDepthBuffer(Image.Format.Depth);
   offScreenBuffer.setColorTexture(offScreenTexture);
   ```

10. Then, we set `outPutFrameBuffer` of `offScreenView` to be `offScreenBuffer`:

    ```
    offScreenView.setOutputFrameBuffer(offScreenBuffer);
    ```

11. Unless the scene we supplied already has some lights, we should add at least one `Light` class to it.

12. Then, we attach the scene to `offScreenView`:

    ```
    offScreenView.attachScene(scene);
    ```

13. To store the texture, we can add it to `AssetManager` with the following line:

    ```
    ((DesktopAssetManager)app.getAssetManager()).addToCache( new
    TextureKey(scene.getName()+"_mini.png", true), offScreenTexture);
    ```

14. Now, we can do the actual rendering by calling the application's `renderManager` and `renderViewPort` methods:

    ```
    app.getRenderManager().renderViewPort(offScreenView, 0);
    ```

15. After this, we're done and can call `removePreview` to discard `offScreeenView`:

    ```
    app.getRenderManager().removePreView(offScreenView);
    ```

With the `Util` class done, we can create a screen `Controller` class. Perform the following additional six steps to do this:

1. Create a new class called `GameScreenController` that extends `NiftyController`.

2. For now, it only needs one public method called `createMinimap` that takes a scene as the input.

3. The first thing the `createMinimap` method should do is call `MiniMapUtil.createMinimap`.

4. With the scene rendered, we can create `NiftyImage` with the `nifty.createImage` method.

5. Then, we can apply the image to our minimap element in the Nifty screen with the following line:

```
screen.findElementByName("minimap").getRenderer(ImageRenderer.
class).setImage(image);
```

6. Now, all we need to do is add a panel element called `minimap` to a screen that uses `GameScreenController` as the controller.

How it works...

Offscreen rendering is just what it sounds like. We render something in a view that is not related to the main view that the player sees. To do this, we set up a new viewport and camera. It's not possible to render something directly to a texture, which is why `FrameBuffer` is used as the medium.

Once the texture object is created and added to the asset manager, it's possible to keep changing it if we would like to at a later stage. It's even possible to have a live view of the scene in the minimap, although this would probably cost unnecessary resources. In this case, we remove the view as soon as we've rendered it once.

The example is limited in some sense, like it expects that there is a correlation between the size of the scene and the size of the minimap.

Nifty uses its own image format, `NiftyImage`, so we need to convert the image we saved; however, Nifty's `createImage` will automatically find the texture in the asset manager based on the name (key).

There's more...

Usually, on a minimap, players will want some kind of indication about their (and others) whereabouts. Let's implement that in the minimap we just created:

1. First of all, we need to change the `minimap` element in our screen a bit. We set `childLayout` to `absolute` and add another panel inside it called `playerIcon` with a small width and height.

2. Next, we add a new `Element` field called `playerIcon` to the `GameScreenController` and use `findElementByName` in the `bind` method to set it.

3. Then, we add another method called `updatePlayerPosition` with two integers, `x` and `y`, as the input.

4. This method should use `setConstraintX` and `setConstraintY` on the `playerIcon` element to set the position. Those methods take `SizeValue` as the input, and we supply the x and y values with the `"px"` definition.

5. Finally, in the same method, we need to call `layoutElements()` on the `minimap` element to make it update its child elements.

For other things, such as visible enemies, we can use the builder interface to create them as and when we need them and then use `markForRemoval` to remove them when they're not needed anymore. An example of this process can be seen in the *Handling a game message queue* recipe.

7
Networking with SpiderMonkey

This chapter will be all about using the networking engine of jMonkeyEngine, SpiderMonkey, to take our games beyond the isolation of our own computers to the Internet. Don't worry if you're not well versed in networking, we'll take it from the very beginning.

This chapter contains the following recipes:

- ▶ Setting up a server and client
- ▶ Handling basic messaging
- ▶ Making a networked game – Battleships
- ▶ Implementing a network code for FPS
- ▶ Loading a level
- ▶ Interpolating between player positions
- ▶ Firing over a network
- ▶ Optimizing the bandwidth and avoiding cheating

Introduction

Data sent over the network is organized in packets, and protocols handle them differently. Packets can look different depending on protocols, but they contain the data itself along with control information, such as addresses and formatting information.

SpiderMonkey supports both TCP and UDP. In SpiderMonkey, TCP is referred to as reliable. TCP is reliable because it verifies each network packet sent, minimizing problems due to packet loss and other errors. TCP guarantees that everything arrives safely (if at all possible). Why ever use anything else then? For speed. Reliability means that TCP can be slow. In some cases, we're not dependent on every packet reaching the destination. UDP is more suitable for streaming and low-latency applications, but the application will have to be prepared to compensate for the unreliability. This means that when a packet is lost in FPS, the game needs to know what to do. Will it just stop in its tracks, or stutter along? If a character is moving and the game can predict the movement between the messages that arrive, it will create a smoother experience.

Learning how to use the API is fairly easy, but we will also see that networking is not something you add to a game; the game needs to be adapted for it from the planning stage.

Setting up a server and client

In this recipe, we'll look at the absolute minimum in order to get a server and client up and running and be able to talk to each other.

This is accomplished in just a few lines of code.

The server and client will share some common data that we'll store inside a `properties` file for easy access and external modification. First and foremost, the client must know the address of the server, and both server and client need to know which port to listen on and connect to. These would most likely be editable from within a game.

How to do it...

Perform the following steps to set up a server and client:

1. In the constructor of the server class, we start by loading the properties file. Once done, we can initialize the server with the following lines of code:

    ```
    server = Network.createServer(Integer.parseInt(prop.
    getProperty("server.port")));
    server.start();
    ```

    In the static block, we must also make sure that the server doesn't shut down immediately.

2. The client is set up in a similar way, shown as follows:

    ```
    client = Network.connectToServer(prop.getProperty("server.
    address"), Integer.parseInt(prop.getProperty("server.port")));
    client.start();
    ```

3. To verify that a connection has taken place, we can add `ConnectionListener` to the server, as follows:

```
public void connectionAdded(Server server, HostedConnection conn)
{
    System.out.println("Player connected: " + conn.getAddress());
}
```

4. If we connect to the server again, we should see the message printed in the server's output window.

How it works...

The `Network` class is the main class used when setting up and connecting our components. This particular method is the simplest way to create a server, simply stating a port to listen to. Let's set different ports for TCP and UDP and supply the name and version of the server.

The `connectToServer` method creates a client and connects it to the specified address and port. Like in the server case, there are other convenient methods in `Network` that let us specify more parameters if we want.

That's actually all that's needed. When running the two programs in parallel, we should see the client connected to the server. There is no verification, however, that anything has happened. That's why we added `ConnectionListener` at the end. It's an interface with two methods: `connectionAdded` and `connectionRemoved`. These methods will be called whenever a client connects or disconnects. These methods gave the server a way to communicate to us that a connection has happened. These methods will be sources for a chain of events in more advanced recipes.

Once the server is started, it begins to listen for incoming connections on the specified port. If the network address is considered the street name, the port will be the door that will be opened and made passable. So far, a mere handshake between the server and client has been made at the doorstep.

Handling basic messaging

So far, we've learned the basics to set up a server and connecting a client. However, they don't do much, so let's look into what it takes to get them to communicate with each other.

Getting ready

In SpiderMonkey, communication is handled via messaging and the message interface. When a server sends a message, it uses the `broadcast()` method, while a client uses `send()`. The side that is supposed to receive the message has to have a suitable `MessageListener` class. To try all these things out, let's have our server greet the connecting player by sending them a message, which will be displayed once received.

How to do it...

Perform the following steps to connect and handle basic messaging:

1. We begin by defining our message. It's a simple serializable bean with just one field, as shown in the following code snippet:

```
@Serializable()
public class ServerMessage extends AbstractMessage{
    private String message;

    public String getMessage() {
        return message;
    }

    public void setMessage(String message) {
        this.message = message;
    }
}
```

2. Next, we create a class that implements `MessageListener`. It's a very simple class that will print the message to the console when received, as follows:

```
public class ServerMessageHandler implements
MessageListener<Client>{

    public void messageReceived(Client source, Message m) {
        ServerMessage message = (ServerMessage) m;
        System.out.println("Server message: " + message.
getMessage());
    }
}
```

3. We instantiate `ServerMessageHandler` and add it to the client, telling it to only listen for `ServerMessages`, as follows:

```
ServerMessageHandler serverMessageHandler = new
ServerMessageHandler();
client.addMessageListener(serverMessageHandler, ServerMessage.
class);
```

It is also possible to let `ServerMessageHandler` handle all incoming messages by using the following line of code:

```
client.addMessageListener(serverMessageHandler);
```

4. We now tell the server to create a message and send it to all the players when someone connects:

```
ServerMessage connMessage = new ServerMessage();
String message = "Player connected from: " + conn.getAddress();
connMessage.setMessage(message);
server.broadcast(connMessage);
```

5. There is one more thing we need to do. All the message classes used need to be registered before being used. We do this before the application starts, as follows:

```
public static void main(String[] args ) throws Exception {
    Serializer.registerClass(ServerMessage.class);
```

How it works...

Spending time and defining what messages should contain is a good way to get a grip of the project as a lot of the architecture will revolve around them. The message we created in this recipe is called `ServerMessage`, because it is used to send a lot of information from the server to the client.

The next class we created was `MessageListener`. The only thing it does upon receiving the message is print it to the console. We added it to the client, and also stated that it should specifically listen for `ServerMessages`.

By default, calling `broadcast` will send the message to all the connected clients. In this case, we just want to send a message to a specific client or a group of clients (like a team). Broadcast can also be called with `Filter`. It can also send messages to a specific channel, to which a team or group of players might be assigned.

Making a networked game – Battleships

In the previous recipes, we looked at how to set up a server, and connect and handle basic messaging. In this recipe, we'll reinforce this knowledge and expand it by adding server verification and applying it to a real game.

A turn-based board game is perhaps not what you would normally develop using a 3D game SDK, but it's a very good game to learn networking. The Battleships game is a good example not only because the rules are simple and known to many but also because it has a hidden element, which will help us understand the concept of server verification.

 If you're unfamiliar with the Battleships game, visit `http://www.wikipedia.org/wiki/Battleship_(game)`.

Since we're mainly interested in the networking aspects of the game, we'll skip some of the verification normally needed such as looking for overlapping ships. We also won't write any graphical interface and use the command prompt to obtain input. Again, to focus on the networking API, some of the plain Java logic for game rules won't be explained.

The game will have a client and server class. Each class will have a `MessageListener` implementation and share messages and game objects.

Getting ready

It is highly recommended to familiarize yourself with the content of the previous recipes in the chapter, if you haven't already.

The amount of messages will increase greatly compared to the previous recipes. Since both the server and client need to keep a track of the same messages and they need to be registered in the same order, we can create a `GameUtil` class. It has a static method called `initialize()`. For every new message type we create, we add a line like this:

```
Serializer.registerClass(WelcomeMessage.class);
```

The game revolves around a couple of objects that we'll define before getting into the networking aspect.

We need a `Ship` class. For this implementation, it only needs the `name` and `segments` fields. We add methods so that once a tile containing `Ship` is hit, we can decrease the segments. When segments reach zero, it's sunk. Likewise, `Player` can be a simple class, with only an ID necessary for identification with the server, and the number of ships still alive. If the number of ships reaches zero, the player loses.

Many of the message types extend a class called `GameMessage`. This class in turn extends `AbstractMessage` and needs to contain the ID of the game, and state that the message should be reliable, thus using the TCP protocol.

How to do it...

We start by setting up a `Game` class. This will consist of the following six steps:

1. First of all, the `Game` class needs an ID. This is used by the server to keep track of which game messages to relate to (since it supports many games at the same time), and will also be used as a reference for other things.

2. The `Game` class needs the two `Player` objects, `player1` and `player2`, as well as the ID of the player whose turn it currently is. We can call that `currentPlayerId`.

3. The `Game` class needs two boards; one for each player. The boards will be made of 2D `Ship` arrays. Each tile where there is a segment of a ship has a reference to the `Ship` object; the others are null.

4. An integer `status` field lets us know what state the game currently is in, which is useful for message filtering. We can also add constants for the different statuses and set a default status, as follows:

```
public final static int GAME_WAITING = 0;
public final static int GAME_STARTED = 1;
public final static int GAME_ENDED = 2;
private int status = GAME_WAITING;
```

5. Now, we add a `placeShip` method. The method in this implementation is simplified and only contains verification that the ship is inside the board, as follows:

```
public void placeShip(int playerId, int shipId, int x, int y,
boolean horizontal){
  Ship s = GameUtil.getShip(shipId);
  Ship[][] board;
  if(playerId == playerOne.getId()){
    board = boardOne;
    playerOne.increaseShips();
  } else {
    board = boardTwo;
    playerTwo.increaseShips();
  }
  for(int i = 0;i < s.getSegments(); i++){
    [verify segment is inside board bounds]
  }
}
```

6. The other method that does some work in the `Game` class is `applyMove`. This takes `FireActionMessage` as input, checking the supplied tile to see whether there is a ship in that spot. It then checks whether the supposed ship is sunk, and whether the player has any ships left. If a ship is hit, it returns the `Ship` object to the calling method, as follows:

```
public Ship applyMove(FireActionMessage action){
  int x = action.getX();
  int y = action.getY();
  Ship ship = null;
  if(action.getPlayerId() == playerOne.getId()){
    ship = boardTwo[x][y];
    if(ship != null){
      ship.hit();
      if(ship.isSunk()){
        playerTwo.decreaseShips();
      }
    }
  } else {
```

```
            [replicate for playerTwo]
    }
    if(playerTwo.getShips() < 1 || playerOne.getShips() < 1){
      status = GAME_ENDED;
    }
    if(action.getPlayerId() == playerTwo.getId()){
      turn++;
    }
    return ship;
  }
```

Now, let's have a look at the server side of things. In the previous chapters, we had a look at connecting the clients, but a full game requires a bit more communication to set things up as we will see. This section will have the following eight steps:

1. Since the server is meant to handle several instances of a game at once, we'll define a couple of HashMaps to keep a track of the game objects. For each game we create, we put the Game object in the games map with the ID as a key:

   ```
   private HashMap<Integer, Game> games = new HashMap<Integer,
   Game>();
   ```

2. We'll also use Filters to only send messages to players in a related game. To do this, we store a list of HostedConnections, with each being an address to a client, with the game ID as a key:

   ```
   private HashMap<Integer, List<HostedConnection>> connectionFilters
   = new HashMap<Integer, List<HostedConnection>>();
   ```

3. Since we're continuously giving out a new player ID and increasing the value of the game ID, we'll have two fields for that as well: nextGameId and nextPlayerId.

4. Everything starts with a connecting client. Like in the *Setting up a server and client* recipe, we use ConnectionListener to handle this. The method either adds the player to an existing game, or creates a new one if none are available. Regardless of whether a new game is created or not, the addPlayer method is called afterwards, as shown in the following code snippet:

   ```
   public void connectionAdded(Server server, HostedConnection conn)
   {
     Game game = null;
     if(games.isEmpty() || games.get(nextGameId - 1).getPlayerTwo()
   != null){
       game = createGame();
     } else {
       game = games.get(nextGameId - 1);
     }
     addPlayer(game, conn);
   }
   ```

5. The `createGame` method creates a new `game` object and sets the correct ID. After placing it in the `games` map, it creates a new `List<HostedConnection>` called `connsForGame` and adds it to the `connectionFilters` map. The `connsForGame` list is empty for now, but will be populated as players connect:

```
private Game createGame(){
  Game game = new Game();
  game.setId(nextGameId++);
  games.put(game.getId(), game);
  List<HostedConnection> connsForGame = new
ArrayList<HostedConnection>();
  connectionFilters.put(game.getId(), connsForGame);
  return game;
}
```

6. The first thing the `addPlayer` method does is create a new `Player` object and then set the ID of it. We use `WelcomeMessage` to send the ID back to the player:

```
private void addPlayer(Game game, HostedConnection conn){
  Player player = new Player();
  player.setId(nextPlayerId++);
```

7. The server broadcasts this message using the client's connection as a filter, ensuring it's the only recipient of the message, as follows:

```
WelcomeMessage welcomeMessage = new WelcomeMessage();
welcomeMessage.setMyPlayerId(player.getId());
server.broadcast(Filters.in(conn), welcomeMessage);
```

8. It then decides whether the player is the first or second to connect to the game, and adds the player's `HostedConnection` instance to the list of connections associated with this game, as shown in the following code snippet:

```
if(game.getPlayerOne() == null){
  game.setPlayerOne(player);
} else {
  game.setPlayerTwo(player);
}
List<HostedConnection> connsForGame = connectionFilters.get(game.
getId());
connsForGame.add(conn);
```

9. It then creates a `GameStatusMessage` object, letting all players in the game know the current status (which is `WAITING`) and any player information it might have, as shown in the following code snippet:

```
GameStatusMessage waitMessage = new GameStatusMessage();
waitMessage.setGameId(game.getId());
waitMessage.setGameStatus(Game.GAME_WAITING);
```

```
    waitMessage.setPlayerOneId(game.getPlayerOne() != null ? game.
getPlayerOne().getId() : 0);
    waitMessage.setPlayerTwoId(game.getPlayerTwo() != null ? game.
getPlayerTwo().getId() : 0);
    server.broadcast(Filters.in(connsForGame), waitMessage);
}
```

We're going to take a look at message handling on the client side and see how its `MessageListener` interface will handle incoming `WelcomeMessages` and game updates:

1. We create a class called `ClientMessageHandler`, which implements `MessageListener`. First, we will walk through the part handling the start of a game.

2. The `thisPlayer` object has already been instanced in the client, so all we need to do when receiving `WelcomeMessage` is set the player's ID. Additionally, we can display something to the player letting it know the connection is set up:

```
public void messageReceived(Client source, Message m) {
    if(m instanceof WelcomeMessage){
        WelcomeMessage welcomeMess = ((WelcomeMessage)m);
        Player p = gameClient.getThisPlayer();
        p.setId(welcomeMessage.getMyPlayerId());
    }
}
```

3. When a `GameStatusMessage` is received, we need to accomplish three things. First, set the ID of the game. Knowing the ID of the game is not necessary for the client in this implementation, but can be useful for communication with the server:

```
else if(m instanceof GameStatusMessage){
    int status = ((GameStatusMessage)m).getGameStatus();
    switch(status){
    case Game.GAME_WAITING:
        if(game.getId() == 0 &&
          ((GameStatusMessage)m).getGameId() > 0){
            game.setId(((GameStatusMessage)m).getGameId());
        }
```

4. Then, we set the `playerOne` and `playerTwo` fields by simply checking whether they have been set before or not. We also need to identify the player by comparing the IDs of the players in the message with the ID associated with this client. Once found, we let him or her start placing ships, as follows:

```
if(game.getPlayerOne() == null && ((GameStatusMessage)
m).getPlayerOneId() > 0){
    int playerOneId = ((GameStatusMessage)m).getPlayerOneId();
    if(gameClient.getThisPlayer().getId() == playerOneId){
        game.setPlayerOne(gameClient.getThisPlayer());
        gameClient.placeShips();
```

```
        } else {
          Player otherPlayer = new Player();
              otherPlayer.setId(playerOneId);
        game.setPlayerOne(otherPlayer);
      }


    }
    game.setStatus(status);
```

5. When `TurnMessage` is received, we should extract `activePlayer` from it and set it on the game. If `activePlayer` is the same as `thisPlayer` of `gameClient`, set `myTurn` to `true` on `gameClient`.

6. The last message to be handled by the class is the `FiringResult` message. This calls `applyMove` on the `game` object. Some kind of output should be tied to this message telling the player what happened. This example game uses `System.out.println` to convey this.

7. Finally, initialize our `ClientMessageHandler` object in the constructor of the client class, as follows:

```
ClientMessageHandler messageHandler = new
ClientMessageHandler(this, game);
client.addMessageListener(messageHandler);
```

With the received messages handled, we can look at the logic on the client side and the messages it sends. This is very limited as most of the game functionality is handled by the server.

The following steps show how to implement the client-side game logic:

1. The `placeShip` method can be written in many different ways. Normally, you will have a graphical interface. For this recipe though, we use a command prompt, which breaks down the input to *x* and *y* coordinates and whether the ship is placed horizontally or vertically. At the end, it should send five instances of `PlaceShipMessages` to the server. For each added ship, we also call `thisPlayer.increaseShips()`.

2. We also need a method called `setMyTurn`. This uses the command prompt to receive *x* and *y* coordinates to shoot at. After this, it populates `FireActionMessage`, which is sent to the server.

3. For `PlaceShipMessage`, create a new class and have it extend `GameMessage`.

4. The class needs to contain the ID of the player placing the ship, coordinates, and orientation of the ship. The ID of the ship refers to the position in the following array:

```
private static Ship[] ships = new Ship[]{new Ship("PatrolBoat",
2), new Ship("Destroyer", 3), new Ship("Submarine", 3), new
Ship("Battleship", 4), new Ship("Carrier", 5)};
```

5. We create another class called `FireActionMessage`, which also extends `GameMessage`.

6. This has a reference to the player firing and an *x* and *y* coordinate.

Message handling on the server is similar to the one on the client. We have a `ServerMessageHandler` class implementing the `MessageListener` interface. This has to handle receiving messages from the player placing ships, and firing.

1. Inside the `messageReceived` method, catch all `PlaceShipMessages`. Using the supplied `gameId`, we get the game instance from the server's `getGame` method and call the `placeShip` method. Once this is done, we check to see whether both players have placed all their ships. If that is the case, it's time to start the game:

```
public void messageReceived(HostedConnection conn, Message m) {
    if (m instanceof PlaceShipMessage){
        PlaceShipMessage shipMessage = (PlaceShipMessage) m;
        int gameId = shipMessage.getGameId();
        Game game = gameServer.getGame(gameId);
        game.placeShip( … );
        if(game.getPlayerOne().getShips() == 5 && game.getPlayerTwo()
!= null&& game.getPlayerTwo().getShips() == 5){
            gameServer.startGame(gameId);
        }
```

2. In the `startGame` method, the first thing we need to do is send a message to let the players know the game is now started. We know what clients to send the message to by getting the list of connections from the `connectionFilters` map as follows:

```
public Game startGame(int gameId){
    Game game = games.get(gameId);
    List<HostedConnection> connsForGame = connectionFilters.
get(gameId);
    GameStatusMessage startMessage = new GameStatusMessage();
    startMessage.setGameId(game.getId());
    startMessage.setGameStatus(Game.GAME_STARTED);
    server.broadcast(Filters.in(connsForGame), startMessage);
```

3. After this, we decide which player will have the first move and send `TurnMessage` to the players, as follows:

```
    int startingPlayer = FastMath.nextRandomInt(1, 2);
    TurnMessage turnMessage = new TurnMessage();

    server.broadcast(Filters.in(connsForGame), turnMessage);
    return game;
}
```

4. Now, we need to define `TurnMessage`. It is another simple message, only containing the ID of the player whose turn it currently is and extending `GameMessage`.

5. Back in `ServerMessageListener`, we make it ready to receive `FireActionMessage` from a player. We begin by verifying that the `playerId` of the incoming message matches with the current player on the server side. It can be implemented as follows:

```
if(m instanceof FireActionMessage){
   FireActionMessage fireAction = (FireActionMessage) m;
   int gameId = fireAction.getGameId();
   Game game = gameServer.getGame(gameId);
   if(game.getCurrentPlayerId() ==
      fireAction.getPlayerId()){
```

6. Then, we call `applyMove` on the game, letting it decide whether it's a hit or not. If it's a hit, the ship will be returned. It can be implemented by typing the following code:

```
Ship hitShip = game.applyMove(fireAction);
```

7. We go on and create a `FiringResult` message. This is an extension of `FireActionMessage` with additional fields for the (possible) ship being hit. It should be broadcasted to both the players letting them know whether the action was a hit or not.

8. Finally, we switch the active player and send another `TurnMessage` to both the players as follows:

```
TurnMessage turnMessage = new TurnMessage();
turnMessage.setGameId(game.getId());
game.setCurrentPlayerId(game.getCurrentPlayerId()
== 1 ? 2 : 1);
turnMessage.setActivePlayer(game.
getCurrentPlayerId());
gameServer.sendMessage(turnMessage);
}
```

9. This flow will continue until one of the players has run out of ships. Then, we should simply send `GameStatusMessage` with the `END` status to the players and disconnect them.

How it works...

When a player launches the client, it will automatically connect to the server defined in the properties file.

The server will acknowledge this, assign a user ID to the player, and send back `WelcomeMessage` containing the ID. The job of `WelcomeMessage` is to confirm the connection to the client, and let the client know its given ID. In this implementation, it is used for future communication from the client. Another way of filtering incoming messages would be possible using the `HostedConnection` instance, as it holds a unique address to the client.

When the first player connects, a new game will be created. The game is put in the WAITING status until two players have connected, and both have placed their ships. For each player connecting, it creates a GameStatusMessage letting all players in the game know the current status (which is WAITING) and any player information it might have. The first player, PlayerOne, will receive the message twice (again when PlayerTwo connects), but it doesn't matter as the game will be in the WAITING status until both players have placed their ships.

The placeShip method is simplified and doesn't contain all the verification that you will normally have in a full game. Make sure that the the server checks whether a ship is outside the board, or overlapping, and make sure it's of the right type, length, and so on and send a message back if it is wrong. This method simply checks that the ship is inside bounds and skips it if it isn't. Verification can also be done on the client, but to limit exploitation, it has to be done on the server as well.

The starting player will be selected randomly and sent in a TurnMessage to both players stating who begins. The player is asked to enter a set of coordinates to fire at and FireActionMessage is sent to the server.

The server verifies the player and applies it to the board. It then broadcasts a FireResult message to all players with information about the action, and whether any ships are hit. If the attacked player still has ships left, it becomes his or her turn to fire.

Once a player has run out of ships, the game ends. The server broadcasts a message to all the clients and disconnects them.

The clients have very little information about the other player. The benefit of this is that it makes cheating much more difficult.

Implementing a network code for FPS

Networked FPS games are a genre of games that never seem to lose popularity. In this recipe, we'll look at the basics to get a server and multiple clients up and running. We will emulate a server with a persistent environment, where players can connect and disconnect at any time.

We have the benefit of using some of the code generated in earlier chapters. The code we'll use requires some changes to be adapted to a networked game, but it will again show the benefit of using jMonkeyEngine's Control and AppState classes.

Getting ready

Good recipes to read up on before this are the previous recipes in this chapter (especially *Making a networked game – Battleships*, on which the architecture relies heavily) and also the *Creating a reusable character control* recipe from *Chapter 2, Cameras and Game Controls*, as we will use a similar pattern here for our NetworkedPlayerControl implementations. To avoid repetition, this recipe will not show or explain all of the regular gameplay code.

How to do it...

We begin by defining a few classes that will be used commonly across both server and client:

1. First off, we define a class called `NetworkedPlayerControl` extending `AbstractControl`. We will use this both as an identifier for a player object and as a control for the spatial representation of the player.

2. The class will be extended in further recipes, but for now it should keep track of an integer called `ID`.

3. It also needs an abstract method called `onMessageReceived`, taking `PlayerMessage` as input. This is the method that our message handlers will call to apply changes. In `ServerPlayerControl`, the message will contain the actual input from the player, whereas `ClientPlayerControl` simply replicates what has happened on the server.

4. Now, we define a class called `Game`, which will be shared by both the client and server.

5. We add a `HashMap` object called `players`, where `playerId` is the key and `NetworkedPlayerControl` is the value. It keeps track of the players.

We will need a couple of new messages for this example. All messages are assumed to be in a bean pattern with getters and setters. We define the messages with the following steps:

1. We create a base message to be used for player-related information and call it `PlayerMessage`, extending `AbstractMessage`. This only needs an integer called `playerId`.

2. We create the first message that extends `PlayerMessage`. It is called `PlayerActionMessage` and handles player input. This should be set to be reliable as we don't want to ever miss a player's input.

3. Since player input can either be a key press or mouse click, it needs to have both a Boolean value called `pressed` and a float value called `floatValue`.

4. In addition, we also have to add a String value called `action`.

5. We extend `PlayerMessage` in another class called `PlayerUpdateMessage`. This will be used to distribute player location information from the server to the clients. This should not be reliable to avoid unnecessary delays.

6. It has a `Vector3f` field called `position` and a `Quaternion` field called `lookDirection`.

With the messages defined, let's see what the server code looks like:

1. We define a new class called FPSServer, which extends SimpleApplication.

2. It needs to keep track of the following fields. Apart from the Server field, it also keeps track of the next ID to give to a connecting player, a Game, and a Map of all the currently connected players, with their connection as the key:

```
private Server server;
private int nextPlayerId = 1;
private Game game;
private HashMap<HostedConnection, ServerPlayerControl> playerMap =
new HashMap<HostedConnection, ServerPlayerControl>();
```

3. Like in the previous recipe, we use a class called GameUtil to register all our message classes. We also set frameRate to 30 fps. This might be different depending on the game type. Finally, we start the application in the headless mode, to save resources as follows:

```
public static void main(String[] args ) throws Exception{
  GameUtil.initialize();
  FPSServer gameServer = new FPSServer();
  AppSettings settings = new AppSettings(true);
  settings.setFrameRate(30);
  gameServer.setSettings(settings);
  gameServer.start(JmeContext.Type.Headless);
}
```

4. We initialize the server as in the *Making a networked game - Battleships* recipe and create a ConnectionListener instance to look for connecting and disconnecting players. This will call addPlayer and removePlayer respectively, when players connect or disconnect.

5. In the addPlayer method, we create a new ServerPlayerControl instance, which is the server-side implementation of NetworkedPlayerControl, and assign an ID to it for easier reference, as follows:

```
private void addPlayer(Game game, HostedConnection conn){
  ServerPlayerControl player = new ServerPlayerControl();
  player.setId(nextPlayerId++);
  playerMap.put(conn, player);
  game.addPlayer(player);
```

6. Then, we create a spatial for it so that it has a reference in the scene graph (and thus, it will be automatically updated). This is not only for visual representation, but we are dependent on it to update our method, as follows:

```
Node s = new Node("");
s.addControl(player);
rootNode.attachChild(s);
```

7. For any future communication with the server, the client will supply its `playerId` in all messages, so the server sends the assigned ID back to the client in `WelcomeMessage`. It broadcasts the message using the client's connection as a filter, as follows:

```
WelcomeMessage welcomeMessage = new WelcomeMessage();
welcomeMessage.setMyPlayerId(player.getId());
server.broadcast(Filters.in(conn), welcomeMessage);
```

8. Then, we send information about all the other players to the player that joins, as follows:

```
Collection<NetworkedPlayerControl> players = game.getPlayers().
values();
for(NetworkedPlayerControl p: players){
  PlayerJoinMessage joinMessage = new PlayerJoinMessage();
  joinMessage.setPlayerId(p.getId());
  server.broadcast(Filters.in(conn), joinMessage);
}
```

9. Lastly, the server sends a message to all the other players about the new player, as follows:

```
PlayerJoinMessage joinMessage = new PlayerJoinMessage();
joinMessage.setPlayerId(player.getId());
server.broadcast(joinMessage);
}
```

10. The `removePlayer` method works similarly, but it only has to send a message to each player currently connected about the disconnected player. It also uses `PlayerJoinMessage` but it sets the `leaving` Boolean to `true` to indicate the player is leaving, not joining the game.

11. Then, the server will continuously send location and rotation (direction) updates to all players. Since we set `fps` to `30`, it will try to do this every 33 ms as follows:

```
public void simpleUpdate(float tpf) {
  super.simpleUpdate(tpf);
  Collection<NetworkedPlayerControl> players = game.getPlayers().
values();
  for(NetworkedPlayerControl p: players){
    p.update(tpf);
    PlayerUpdateMessage updateMessage = new PlayerUpdateMessage();
    updateMessage.setPlayerId(p.getId());
updateMessage.setLookDirection(p.getSpatial().getLocalRotation());
updateMessage.setPosition(p.getSpatial().getLocalTranslation());
    updateMessage.setYaw(p.getYaw());
    server.broadcast(updateMessage);
  }
}
```

12. We also create a `ServerMessageHandler` class that implements `MessageListener`. It's a short class in this case, which will only listen to messages extending `PlayerMessage` and pass it on to the correct `NetworkedPlayerControl` class to update it. In this recipe, this will mean the input coming from the player, as follows:

```
public void messageReceived(HostedConnection source, Message m) {
  if(m instanceof PlayerMessage){
    PlayerMessage message = (PlayerMessage)m;
    NetworkedPlayerControl p = game.getPlayer(message.
getPlayerId());
    p.onMessageReceived(message);
  }
}
```

13. For the server-side implementation of the `NetworkedPlayerControl` class, we extend it to a new class called `ServerPlayerControl`.

14. Similar to the `GameCharacterControl` class from *Chapter 2, Cameras and Game Controls*, we will use a set of Booleans to keep track of the input, as follows:

```
boolean forward = false, backward = false, leftRotate = false,
rightRotate = false, leftStrafe = false, rightStrafe = false;
```

15. In the implemented `onMessageReceived` method, listen for `PlayerMessages`. We don't know if it will contain Boolean or float values, so we look for both, as follows:

```
public void onMessageReceived(PlayerMessage message) {
  if(message instanceof PlayerActionMessage){
    String action = ((PlayerActionMessage) message).getAction();
    boolean value = ((PlayerActionMessage) message).isPressed();
    float floatValue = ((PlayerActionMessage) message).
getFloatValue();
```

16. Then, we apply the values as shown in the following code snippet:

```
if (action.equals("StrafeLeft")) {
  leftStrafe = value;
} else if (action.equals("StrafeRight")) {
  rightStrafe = value;
}
...
else if (action.equals("RotateLeft")) {
  rotate(floatValue);
} else if (action.equals("RotateRight")) {
  rotate(-floatValue);
}
```

17. In the overridden `controlUpdate` method, we then modify the position and rotation of the spatial based on the input, just like we did in the *Creating a reusable character control* recipe of *Chapter 2, Cameras and Game Controls*.

The client is simple in many ways, since it basically only does two things. It takes a player's input, sends it to the server, receives updates from the server, and applies them as follows:

1. We begin by creating a new class called `FPSClient` extending `SimpleApplication`.

2. In the constructor, we read the network properties file and connect to the server, as follows:

```
Properties prop = new Properties();    prop.load(getClass().
getClassLoader().getResourceAsStream("network/resources/network.
properties"));
        client = Network.connectToServer(prop.getProperty("server.
name"), Integer.parseInt(prop.getProperty("server.version")),
prop.getProperty("server.address"), Integer.parseInt(prop.
getProperty("server.port")));
```

3. Just as with the server, we register all the message classes before launching the application.

4. The application should have a reference to a `Node` class called `playerModel`, which will be the visual representation of the players in the game. There should also be a `ClientPlayerControl` class called `thisPlayer`.

5. In the `simpleInitApp` method, we attach `InputAppState`. This has the same functionality as the one in the *Creating an input AppState object* recipe of *Chapter 2, Cameras and Game Controls*. The only difference is it will benefit from having a direct way of reaching the client to send messages:

```
public void simpleInitApp() {
   InputAppState inputAppState = new InputAppState();
   inputAppState.setClient(this);
   stateManager.attach(inputAppState);
```

6. Next, we create `playerGeometry` to be used for all the players in this example, as follows:

```
   Material playerMaterial   = new Material(assetManager, "Common/
MatDefs/Misc/Unshaded.j3md");
   playerGeometry = new Geometry("Player", new Box(1f,1f,1f));
   playerGeometry.setMaterial(playerMaterial);
```

7. We also turn off the application's `flyByCamera` instance and create a new `game` object, which we will populate when we receive information from the server, as follows:

```
getFlyByCamera().setEnabled(false);
game = new Game();
```

8. Lastly, we create a new `ClientMessageListener` object and add it to the client, as shown in the following code snippet:

```
ClientMessageHandler messageHandler = new
ClientMessageHandler(this, game);
client.addMessageListener(messageHandler);
```

9. In the `createPlayer` method, we create a new `ClientPlayerControl` instance and also a `Node` instance, which we attach to the scene graph, as follows:

```
ClientPlayerControl player = new ClientPlayerControl();
player.setId(id);
final Node playerNode = new Node("Player Node");
        playerNode.attachChild(assetManager.loadModel("Models/
Jaime/Jaime.j3o"));//
playerNode.addControl(player);
```

10. Since we don't know when this method will be called, we make sure that we attach the spatial in a thread-safe way. This can be implemented as follows:

```
enqueue(new Callable(){
  public Object call() throws Exception {
    rootNode.attachChild(playerNode);
    return null;
  }
});
```

11. Finally, we return the created `ClientPlayerControl` instance to the calling method.

12. We add a new method called `setThisPlayer`. This method will be called when the player's `WelcomeMessage` is received. Inside this, we create `CameraNode`, which will be attached to the player, as follows:

```
public void setThisPlayer(ClientPlayerControl player){
  this.thisPlayer = player;
  CameraNode camNode = new CameraNode("CamNode", cam);
  camNode.setControlDir(CameraControl.ControlDirection.
SpatialToCamera);
  ((Node)player.getSpatial()).attachChild(camNode);
}
```

13. We also have to override the `destroy` method to make sure we close the connection to the server when the client is shutdown. This can be implemented as follows:

```
public void destroy() {
   super.destroy();
   client.close();
}
```

14. Now, we need to create the client representation of `NetworkedPlayerControl` and extend it in a class called `ClientPlayerControl`.

15. It has a `Vector3f` field called `tempLocation` and a `Quaternion` field called `tempRotation`. These are used to hold received updates from the server. It can also have a `float` field called `yaw` for head movement.

16. In the `onMessageReceived` method, we only look for `PlayerUpdateMessages` and set `tempLocation` and `tempRotation` with the values received in the message, as follows:

```
public void onMessageReceived(PlayerMessage message) {
   if (message instanceof PlayerUpdateMessage) {
     PlayerUpdateMessage updateMessage = (PlayerUpdateMessage)
message;
     tempRotation.set(updateMessage.getLookDirection());
     tempLocation.set(updateMessage.getPosition());
tempYaw = updateMessage.getYaw();
   }
}
```

17. We will then apply the `temp` variable values in the `controlUpdate` method:

```
spatial.setLocalTranslation(tempLocation);
spatial.setLocalRotation(tempRotation);
yaw = tempYaw;
```

Just like on the server side, we need a message handler listening for incoming messages. To do this, perform the following steps:

1. We create a new class called `ClientMessageHandler`, which implements `MessageListener<Client>`.

2. The `ClientMessageHandler` class should have a reference to `FPSClient` in a field called `gameClient` and `Game` itself in another field called `game`.

3. In the `messageReceived` method, we need to handle a number of messages. The `WelcomeMessage` is most likely to arrive first. When this happens, we create a player object and spatial and assign it to be this client's player, as follows:

```
public void messageReceived(Client source, Message m) {
   if (m instanceof WelcomeMessage) {
```

```
      ClientPlayerControl p = gameClient.
createPlayer(((WelcomeMessage)m).getMyPlayerId());
      gameClient.setThisPlayer(p);
      game.addPlayer(gameClient.getThisPlayer());
```

4. The `PlayerJoinMessage` is received both when player joins and leaves a game. What sets it apart is the `leaving` Boolean. We call both the `game` and `gameClient` methods based on whether the player is joining or leaving, as shown in the following code snippet:

```
PlayerJoinMessage joinMessage = (PlayerJoinMessage) m;
int playerId = joinMessage.getPlayerId();
if(joinMessage.isLeaving()){
   gameClient.removePlayer((ClientPlayerControl)    game.
getPlayer(playerId));
   game.removePlayer(playerId);
} else if(game.getPlayer(playerId) == null){
   ClientPlayerControl p = gameClient.createPlayer(joinMessage.
getPlayerId());
   game.addPlayer(p);
}
```

5. When the `PlayerUpdateMessage` is received, we first find the corresponding `ClientPlayerControl` class and pass on the message to it, as follows:

```
} else if (m instanceof PlayerUpdateMessage){
   PlayerUpdateMessage updateMessage = (PlayerUpdateMessage) m;
   int playerId = updateMessage.getPlayerId();
   ClientPlayerControl p = (ClientPlayerControl) game.
getPlayer(playerId);
   if(p != null){
     p.onMessageReceived(updateMessage);
   }
```

How it works...

The server is running in the headless mode, which means it won't do any rendering and there will be no graphical output, but we still have access to the full jMonkeyEngine application. In this recipe, one server instance will only have one game active at a time.

We instantiate all network messages inside a class called `GameUtil`, since they have to be the same (and serialized in the same order) on the client and server.

The client will try to connect to the server as soon as it launches. Once connected, it will receive `playerId` from the server via `WelcomeMessage`, as well as `PlayerJoinMessages` for all other players that are already connected. Likewise, all other players will receive `PlayerJoinMessage` with the new player's ID.

The client sends any actions the players perform to the server using `PlayerActionMessage`, which applies them to its instance of the game. The server, which runs at 30 fps, will send positions and directions of each player to all the other players, using `PlayerUpdateMessages`.

The `InputAppState` class on the client is very similar to the one in *Chapter 2, Cameras and Game Controls*. The only difference is that instead of directly updating a `Control` instance, it creates a message and sends it to the server. In the `onAction` class, we set the Boolean value of the message, whereas in `onAnalog` (to look and rotate), `floatValue` will be used instead, as shown in the following code snippet:

```
public void onAction(String name, boolean isPressed, float tpf) {
    InputMapping input = InputMapping.valueOf(name);
    PlayerActionMessage action = new PlayerActionMessage();
    action.setAction(name);
    action.setPressed(isPressed);
    action.setPlayerId(client.getThisPlayer().getId());
    client.send(action);
}
```

In the event of a player leaving the game, `PlayerJoinMessages` will be sent to the other players, with `leaving` set to `true`.

The `NetworkedPlayerControl` class is an abstract class, and doesn't do much on its own. You might recognize the implementation of `ServerPlayerControl` from `GameCharacterControl`, and they function similarly, but rather than receiving the input directly from the user, `ServerPlayerControl` gets it via a networked message instead.

Both the client and server implementation of `NetworkedPlayerControl` use the `tempRotation` and `tempLocation` fields to which they apply any incoming changes. This is so we don't modify the actual spatial transforms outside the main loop.

We shouldn't be fooled by the relative simplicity of this recipe. It merely shows the basics of a real-time networked environment. Making a full game creates much more complexity.

See also

> ► If you'd like to see an example of a full real-time game, have a look at the full source of MonkeyZone at `http://hub.jmonkeyengine.org/wiki/doku.php/jme3:advanced:monkey_zone`. It features not only human players, but also networked AI.

Loading a level

No matter if it's an FPS, RTS, or driving game we're making, we'll want to be able to load different kinds of environments for the players to roam around in. How can we do that easily?

In this recipe, we'll add functionalities to the networked FPS game we outlined previously in this chapter. The principle will work for any kind of already networked game, although it might differ depending on how the game implements the level. Here, we'll assume it uses jMonkeyEngine scenes or `.j3o` scenes.

How to do it...

Perform the following set of steps to load a level:

1. We start by defining a new message class: `LoadLevelMessage`. It extends `GameMessage` since it might be useful to know the `gameId`. Apart from that, it has one field `levelName`.

2. We'll add the same field to our `Game` class so that it can keep track of which level it's running.

3. Next, let's create a `levelNode` field on our server, which we can load our level into, as follows:

```
private Node loadLevel(String levelName){
    return (Node) assetManager.loadModel("Scenes/"+levelName +
".j3o");
}
```

4. Then, we create a small method that will load the level from a predefined path, as follows:

```
levelNode = loadLevel("TestScene");
rootNode.attachChild(levelNode);
game.setLevelName("TestScene");
```

5. Inside the `simpleInitApp` method, we'll tell the application to load `TestScene` from *Chapter 1, SDK Game Development Hub*:

```
LoadLevelMessage levelMessage = new LoadLevelMessage();
levelMessage.setLevelName(game.getLevelName());
server.broadcast(Filters.in(conn), levelMessage);
```

6. Finally, inside the `addPlayer` method, we need to create and send the message to the connecting client. That's all for the server side of things.

7. In the client, we create a `levelNode` field and a `loadLevel` method, but it's a little bit different:

```
public void loadLevel(final String levelName){
  enqueue(new Callable(){
    public Object call() throws Exception {
      if(rootNode.hasChild(levelNode)){
        rootNode.detachChild(levelNode);
      }
      levelNode = (Node)
        assetManager.loadModel("Scenes/"+levelName +
        ".j3o");
      rootNode.attachChild(levelNode);
      return null;
    }
  });
}
```

8. We need to make sure we manipulate the scene graph at the correct moment in time so that we can detach and attach the node inside an `enqueue` block.

9. Finally, we make sure `MessageListener` picks up `LoadLevelMessage` as follows:

```
else if (m instanceof LoadLevelMessage){
  gameClient.loadLevel(((LoadLevelMessage)m).getLevelName());
  game.setLevelName(((LoadLevelMessage)m).getLevelName());
}
```

10. That's it! When we connect to the server again, we should see a familiar scene.

How it works...

When a client joins, the server creates a `LoadLevelMessage` class and populates it with the name of the level currently loaded. The server doesn't supply the level itself, but the client must have the levels supplied previously. The `LoadLevelMessage` class only provides a name in this case, which is probably enough in many cases. For some games, it's a good idea to support a custom path when loading levels, since it allows for greater customization options.

Interpolating between player positions

If we were to only run our game in a LAN environment, we would probably never expect low latency or any significant packet loss. While many are blessed even with good Internet connections nowadays, from time to time, problems still happen. One of the tricks to try to mitigate these problems is to use interpolation for entities on the client side.

This means that rather than just applying the position and rotation the client gets from the server, the client will move towards the target position and rotation in steps.

How to do it...

Perform the following steps to interpolate between the player positions:

1. To simulate some network problems, set `framerate` on the server to `10`.

2. If you connect to the server now, the movement will be noticeably jerky.

3. We replace the contents of the `controlUpdate` method of `ClientPlayerControl` with the following lines to apply the interpolation:

   ```
   float factor = tpf / 0.03f; spatial.setLocalTranslation(spatial.
   getLocalTranslation().interpolateLocal(tempLocation, factor));
   spatial.setLocalRotation(spatial.getLocalRotation().slerp(spatial.
   getLocalRotation(), tempRotation, factor));
   ```

4. When we connect again and compare the experience, it will be much smoother.

How it works...

To simulate an environment with problems such as packet loss, we changed the FPS on the server to 10. Instead of sending out the 30 updates per second it did before, it will only send one every tenth of a second. This is not the same as 100 ms of latency, since it says nothing about the turnaround time. It's more as if two out of three updates were lost on the way, a 66 percent packet loss.

Previously, the client simply took the values it got from the server and applied them to the local players. Using interpolation, the player's position and rotation will move towards the latest actual position and rotation in steps every update.

We implemented the interpolation by first determining the interpolation factor. This was done by dividing `tpf` by the amount of time (roughly, in seconds) we would like the interpolation to take. The actual time will be longer since the steps become shorter with each update.

We then input this value and use the interpolation method of `Vector3f` and the `slerp` method of `Quaternion` to move them towards the actual values.

This is done by using a factor based on the `tpf` value provided in the `update` method. By doing so, the interpolation time will be roughly the same regardless of the frame rate. We should be aware that this in reality becomes latency, a delay between the action and appearance, as we have added a slight delay to when the player reaches the actual position.

Firing over a network

An FPS wouldn't be a shooter unless there's actually some shooting possible. We'll look at an example with visible, non-instant bullets. For this, we'll be able to reuse some code from *Chapter 2, Cameras and Game Controls*. The recipe won't describe the actual collision as this is already described in that chapter.

How to do it...

Perform the following steps to fire over a network:

1. To start off, we create a new message, called `BulletUpdateMessage` to send updates on bullet positions. It only needs two fields: a `Vector3f` field for position and a Boolean field for whether it's alive or not.

2. We'll add a check in the `messageReceived` method of `ServerMessageHandler` to see whether a player is firing. Any action verification we want to do should happen prior to this:

```
if(message.getAction().equals("Fire") && message.isPressed()){
    server.onFire(p);
}
```

3. We find out the direction the player is facing and create a new `ServerBullet` instance. It's assigned the next available object ID and added to the `bullets` list, as follows:

```
public void onFire(NetworkedPlayerControl player){
    Vector3f direction = player.getSpatial().getWorldRotation().
getRotationColumn(2);
    direction.setY(-player.getYaw());
    ServerBullet bullet = new ServerBullet(player.getSpatial().
getWorldTranslation().add(0, 1, 0), direction);
    bullet.setId(nextObjectId++);
    bullets.add(bullet);
}
```

4. Now, we need to add another code block to the `simpleUpdate` method to maintain the bullets and send out messages, as follows:

```
int nrOfBullets = bullets.size();
for(int i = 0; i < nrOfBullets; i++){
    ServerBullet bullet = bullets.get(i);
    bullet.update(tpf);
    BulletUpdateMessage update = new BulletUpdateMessage();
    update.setId(bullet.getId());
```

```
update.setPosition(bullet.getWorldPosition());
update.setAlive(bullet.isAlive());
server.broadcast(update);
if(!bullet.isAlive()){
  bullets.remove(bullet);
  nrOfBullets--;
  i--;
}
}
```

5. In a `for` loop, we first update the bullet, and then create a new `BulletUpdateMessage`, which is sent to all players. If the bullet is out of range, it is removed from the list. This is implemented as follows:

```
if (m instanceof BulletUpdateMessage){
  BulletUpdateMessage update = (BulletUpdateMessage) m;
  ClientBullet bullet = gameClient.getBullet(update.getId());
  if(bullet == null){
    bullet = gameClient.createBullet(update.getId());
  }
  bullet.setPosition(update.getPosition());
  if(!update.isAlive()){
    gameClient.removeBullet(update.getId(), bullet.getSpatial());
  }
}
```

6. On the client side, we write a new method that creates a new bullet, once it receives information from the server:

```
public ClientBullet createBullet(int id){
  final ClientBullet bulletControl = new ClientBullet();
  final Spatial g = assetManager.loadModel("Models/Banana/banana.j3o");
  g.rotate(FastMath.nextRandomFloat(), FastMath.nextRandomFloat(), FastMath.nextRandomFloat());
  g.addControl(bulletControl);
  bullets.put(id, bulletControl);
  rootNode.attachChild(g);
  return bulletControl;
}
```

7. Then, we need a `removeBullet` method once we receive the information from the server.

How it works...

Like in the previous recipes, it's the server that is in control of things. The client merely says it wants to fire and any checks happen on the server side (although it's fine to mimick verification on the client side to save bandwidth). The recipe doesn't contain any specific verifications (a player can fire at any time), but this is explained more in *Chapter 2, Cameras and Game Controls*.

Unlike in *Chapter 2, Cameras and Game Controls*, we can't use the camera as input; instead, we use the direction of the firing player and apply the yaw for up and down tilt.

Bullets are different on the server and client side. On the server, they are merely logical objects. Like the non-instant bullets from the *Firing non-instant bullets* recipe of *Chapter 2, Cameras and Game Controls*, they work like slow rays, moving through the world until they hit something or move out of range.

On the client, the bullet is a bit different from the server side, and is based on the contol pattern. The client finds out about the bullet in `ClientMessageHandler`, as the first update is received. It sees if `ClientBullet` exists already, and if not, it will create a new one. All `ClientBullet` does then is update the position in the `controlUpdate` method.

It's not the actual fire message that creates the bullets, but the first time a `BulletUpdateMessage` is received on the client. The client will keep updating the Bullet's position, much like the player positions, until a message says it's no longer alive. At this point, it will be removed.

The recipe currently sends all bullets to all players. As with players, this could (and probably should) be based on a need-to-know basis to avoid cheating (and excessive bandwidth usage).

Optimizing the bandwidth and avoiding cheating

It can be summarized as follows: the less information a client has, the less opportunity there is of exploiting said information for cheating. Also, the less information a client needs, the less bandwidth is required.

Previously, we've generously sent information about every player, every update cycle. In this recipe, we'll change that so that the server checks what players can be seen by others, and only send that information.

We'll build this on top of the *Implementing a network code for FPS* recipe.

We need to add some complexity to the `simpleUpdate` method of the server application. So, instead of sending information about all players to everybody, we need to check who should receive what.

How to do it...

Perform the following steps to optimize a bandwidth:

1. First of all, we'll add a visible field to our `PlayerUpdateMessage`. This is so that a client knows when a player has disappeared from the view.

2. On the server side, we need to change two classes. First, our `ServerPlayerControl` needs to maintain a list of player IDs it currently sees.

3. Before we do our checks, we need to make sure all the players are updated:

```
Collection<NetworkedPlayerControl> players = game.getPlayers().
values();
    for(NetworkedPlayerControl p: players){
        p.update(tpf);
    }
```

4. Next, we iterate through our `playerMap` object. Here, we add a simple range check to see whether a player is visible or not, and lastly broadcast the information to the relevant players, as follows:

```
Iterator<HostedConnection> it = playerMap.keySet().iterator();
while(it.hasNext()){
    HostedConnection conn = it.next();
    ServerPlayerControl player = playerMap.get(conn);
    for(NetworkedPlayerControl otherPlayer: players){
        float distance = player.getSpatial().getWorldTranslation().
distance(otherPlayer.getSpatial().getWorldTranslation());
    PlayerUpdateMessage updateMessage = null;
    if(distance < 50){
        updateMessage = createUpdateMessage(otherPlayer);
        player.addVisiblePlayer(otherPlayer.getId());
    } else if (player.removeVisiblePlayer(otherPlayer.getId())){
        updateMessage = createUpdateMessage(otherPlayer);
        updateMessage.setVisible(false);
    }
    if(updateMessage != null){
        server.broadcast(Filters.in(conn), updateMessage);
    }
}
```

5. That's all for the server side. On the client side, we need to add a visible field to `ClientPlayerControl`.

6. The second change we make is in `ClientMessageHandler`. We check whether the player is supposed to be visible, and whether it's attached to the scene graph or not:

```
if(p.isVisible() && p.getSpatial().getParent() == null){
   gameClient.getRootNode().attachChild(p.getSpatial());
} else if (!p.isVisible() && p.getSpatial().getParent() != null){
   gameClient.getRootNode().detachChild(p.getSpatial());
}
```

How it works...

By using this principle, each client will only receive updates on other relevant players. We can't, however, just stop sending updates about certain players without also letting the client know why, or they would just freeze in their last known position. That's why the last message the server sends about a player is with `visible` set to `false`. However, to do so, the server must keep track of when a player has disappeared, and not just when it's not visible. That's why each `ServerPlayerControl` class needs to keep track of which players it saw the last update in its `visibleList`.

This recipe focused on the networking aspects of visibility and how and when to send updates. A proper game (at least an FPS) will need to keep track of obscured players as well, not only how far away they are.

Optimization can be done in different ways, and it all comes down to the application. An MMO may for example not be as dependent on frequent updates. In a game like that, network updates can be done with less frequency, if a player is further away, and instead rely on good interpolation to avoid jerkiness.

If we're using interpolation, and not absolute updates, we should also turn off interpolation when visible switches from false to true, to avoid players possibly gliding to the new position. We can also turn off updates when visible is false.

See also

▶ The *Sensing vision* recipe in *Chapter 5, Artificial Intelligence*, which provides an idea on how to implement sight on the server

8

Physics with Bullet

This chapter contains the following recipes:

- ▶ Creating a pushable door
- ▶ Building a rocket engine
- ▶ Ballistic projectiles and arrows
- ▶ Handling multiple gravity sources
- ▶ Self-balancing using RotationalLimitMotors
- ▶ The principles of a bridge-building game
- ▶ Networked physics

Introduction

Using physics in games has become very common and accessible, thanks to open source physics engines, such as Bullet. jMonkeyEngine supports both the Java-based jBullet and native Bullet in a seamless manner.

 jBullet is a Java-based library with JNI bindings to the original Bullet based on C++. jMonkeyEngine is supplied with both of these, and they can be used interchangeably by replacing the libraries in the classpath. No coding change is required. Use `jme3-libraries-physics` for the implementation of jBullet and `jme3-libraries-physics-native` for Bullet. In general, Bullet is considered to be faster and is full featured.

Physics can be used for almost anything in games, from tin cans that can be kicked around to character animation systems. In this chapter, we'll try to reflect the diversity of these implementations.

All the recipes in this chapter will require you to have a `BulletAppState` class in the application. To avoid repetition, the process of doing this is described in the *Adding Bullet physics to the application* section in *Appendix, Information Fragments*.

Creating a pushable door

Doors are useful in games. Visually, it is more appealing to not have holes in the walls but doors for the players to pass through. Doors can be used to obscure the view and hide what's behind them for a surprise later. In extension, they can also be used to dynamically hide geometries and increase the performance. There is also a gameplay aspect where doors are used to open new areas to the player and give a sense of progression.

In this recipe, we will create a door that can be opened by pushing it, using a `HingeJoint` class.

This door consists of the following three elements:

- **Door object**: This is a visible object
- **Attachment**: This is the fixed end of the joint around which the hinge swings
- **Hinge**: This defines how the door should move

Getting ready

Simply following the steps in this recipe won't give us anything testable. Since the camera has no physics, the door will just sit there and we will have no way to push it. If you have made any of the recipes that use the `BetterCharacterControl` class, many of them in *Chapter 2, Cameras and Game Controls*, we will already have a suitable test bed for the door. If not, jMonkeyEngine's `TestBetterCharacter` example can also be used.

How to do it...

This recipe consists of two sections. The first will deal with the actual creation of the door and the functionality to open it. This will be made in the following six steps:

1. Create a new `RigidBodyControl` object called `attachment` with a small `BoxCollisionShape`. The `CollisionShape` should normally be placed inside the wall where the player can't run into it. It should have a mass of 0, to prevent it from being affected by gravity.

2. We move it some distance away and add it to the `physicsSpace` instance, as shown in the following code snippet:

```
attachment.setPhysicsLocation(new Vector3f(-5f, 1.52f,
   0f));
bulletAppState.getPhysicsSpace().add(attachment);
```

3. Now, create a `Geometry` class called `doorGeometry` with a `Box` shape with dimensions that are suitable for a door, as follows:

```
Geometry doorGeometry = new Geometry("Door", new
    Box(0.6f, 1.5f, 0.1f));
```

4. Similarly, create a `RigidBodyControl` instance with the same dimensions, that is, 1 in `mass`; add it as a control to the `doorGeometry` class first and then add it to `physicsSpace` of `bulletAppState`. The following code snippet shows you how to do this:

```
RigidBodyControl doorPhysicsBody = new RigidBodyControl(new
    BoxCollisionShape(new Vector3f(.6f, 1.5f, .1f)), 1);
bulletAppState.getPhysicsSpace().add(doorPhysicsBody);
doorGeometry.addControl(doorPhysicsBody);
```

5. Now, we're going to connect the two with `HingeJoint`. Create a new `HingeJoint` instance called `joint`, as follows:

```
new HingeJoint(attachment, doorPhysicsBody, new
    Vector3f(0f, 0f, 0f), new Vector3f(-1f, 0f, 0f),
    Vector3f.UNIT_Y, Vector3f.UNIT_Y);
```

6. Then, we set the limit for the rotation of the door and add it to `physicsSpace` as follows:

```
joint.setLimit(-FastMath.HALF_PI - 0.1f, FastMath.HALF_PI +
    0.1f);
bulletAppState.getPhysicsSpace().add(joint);
```

Now, we have a door that can be opened by walking into it. It is primitive but effective. Normally, you want doors in games to close after a while. However, here, once it is opened, it remains opened. In order to implement an automatic closing mechanism, perform the following steps:

1. Create a new class called `DoorCloseControl` extending `AbstractControl`.

2. Add a `HingeJoint` field called `joint` along with a setter for it and a float variable called `timeOpen`.

3. In the `controlUpdate` method, we get `hingeAngle` from `HingeJoint` and store it in a float variable called `angle`, as follows:

```
float angle = joint.getHingeAngle();
```

4. If the angle deviates a bit more from zero, we should increase `timeOpen` using `tpf`. Otherwise, `timeOpen` should be reset to 0, as shown in the following code snippet:

```
if(angle > 0.1f || angle < -0.1f) timeOpen += tpf;
else timeOpen = 0f;
```

5. If `timeOpen` is more than `5`, we begin by checking whether the door is still open. If it is, we define a speed to be the inverse of the angle and enable the door's motor to make it move in the opposite direction of its angle, as follows:

```
if(timeOpen > 5) {
    float speed = angle > 0 ? -0.9f : 0.9f;
    joint.enableMotor(true, speed, 0.1f);
    spatial.getControl(RigidBodyControl.class).activate();
}
```

6. If `timeOpen` is less than `5`, we should set the speed of the motor to `0`:

```
joint.enableMotor(true, 0, 1);
```

7. Now, we can create a new `DoorCloseControl` instance in the main class, attach it to the `doorGeometry` class, and give it the same joint we used previously in the recipe, as follows:

```
DoorCloseControl doorControl = new DoorCloseControl();
doorControl.setHingeJoint(joint);
doorGeometry.addControl(doorControl);
```

How it works...

The attachment `RigidBodyControl` has no mass and will thus not be affected by external forces such as gravity. This means it will stick to its place in the world. The door, however, has mass and would fall to the ground if the attachment didn't keep it up with it.

The `HingeJoint` class connects the two and defines how they should move in relation to each other. Using `Vector3f.UNIT_Y` means the rotation will be around the y axis. We set the limit of the joint to be a little more than half PI in each direction. This means it will open almost 100 degrees to either side, allowing the player to step through.

When we try this out, there may be some flickering as the camera passes through the door. To get around this, there are some tweaks that can be applied. We can change the collision shape of the player. Making the collision shape bigger will result in the player hitting the wall before the camera gets close enough to clip through. This has to be done considering other constraints in the physics world.

You can consider changing the near clip distance of the camera. Decreasing it will allow things to get closer to the camera before they are clipped through. This might have implications on the camera's projection.

One thing that will not work is making the door thicker, since the triangles on the side closest to the player are the ones that are clipped through. Making the door thicker will move them even closer to the player.

In `DoorCloseControl`, we consider the door to be open if `hingeAngle` deviates a bit more from 0. We don't use 0 because we can't control the exact rotation of the joint. Instead we use a rotational force to move it. This is what we do with `joint.enableMotor`. Once the door is open for more than five seconds, we tell it to move in the opposite direction. When it's close to 0, we set the desired movement speed to 0. Simply turning off the motor, in this case, will cause the door to keep moving until it is stopped by an external force.

Once we enable the motor, we also need to call `activate()` on `RigidBodyControl` or it will not move.

Building a rocket engine

A rocket engine is crucial for most space-based games and many 2D games as well. In this recipe, we'll cover the minimum that is required to create a thruster that can be used in many different contexts. The following figure shows a thruster with `ParticleEmitter`:

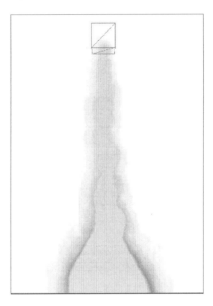

Getting ready

For this recipe, we need to make sure that we see the debug shapes of physics. To do this, we need to call the `bulletAppState.setDebugEnabled(true);` statement.

How to do it...

We will begin by setting up some things that are not strictly needed for the rocket engine but will aid the testing. Perform the following steps to build a rocket engine:

1. First of all we add a floor mesh. For this, we create a new `Node` class called `ground`.

2. To do this, we add `RigidBodyControl` with `PlaneCollisionShape`. The plane should face upwards like floors normally do, as follows:

```
RigidBodyControl floorControl = new RigidBodyControl(new
    PlaneCollisionShape(new Plane(new Vector3f(0, 1, 0), 0)),
    0);
ground.addControl(floorControl);
floorControl.setPhysicsLocation(new Vector3f(0f, -10, 0f));
```

3. We then attach them both to `rootNode` of the application and `physicsSpace` of `bulletAppState`.

4. Finally, we need to add a key to control the booster. For this, we implement an `AnalogListener` interface in our application.

5. Then, add the application to `inputManager` along with a mapping object called boost that is bound to the Space bar:

```
inputManager.addListener(this, "boost");
inputManager.addMapping("boost", new
    KeyTrigger(KeyInput.KEY_SPACE));
```

6. Most of this recipe will be implemented in a class that extends `SimpleApplication`.

7. We begin by defining a `Node` class called `spaceShip` that will be our spaceship's representation.

8. We then create a `RigidBodyControl` instance with `BoxCollisionShape` and add it to the `spaceShip` node as follows:

```
RigidBodyControl control = new RigidBodyControl(new
    BoxCollisionShape(new Vector3f(1, 1, 1)), 1);
spaceShip.addControl(control);
```

9. Now, we create another `Node`, which will be our thruster. Give it the name `Thruster` to be able to identify it more easily later, as follows:

```
Node thruster = new Node("Thruster");
```

10. We set `localTranslation` of this so that it will end up at the bottom of the spaceship, as shown in the following line of code:

```
thruster.setLocalTranslation(0, -1, 0);
```

11. Then, we attach it to the `spaceShip` node.

12. Now, we have to attach the `spaceShip` node to both the `rootNode` and `physicsSpace` of `bulletAppState`.

13. To control the thruster and make it more reusable, we will create a class called `ThrusterControl`, extending `AbstractControl`.

14. It'll have one field, a `Spatial` field called `thruster`, that will store the `thruster` node.

15. We will override the `setSpatial` method and set it by calling `getChild("Thruster")` on the supplied spatial.

16. Lastly, we define a new method called `fireBooster()`.

17. Inside this, we subtract the thruster's location from the spaceship's location and store it in a new `Vector3f` field called `direction` as follows:

```
Vector3f direction =
    spatial.getWorldTranslation().subtract(thruster.getWorldTra
    nslation());
```

18. Then, we find the `RigidBodyControl` class in the spatial and call `applyImpulse` with the direction vector. We use the inverted direction as the relative position that the impulse should originate from. This can be implemented as follows:

```
spatial.getControl(RigidBodyControl.class).applyImpulse(dir
    ection, direction.negate());
```

19. In the application class, we have to make it call the `fireBooster` method. We do this in the `onAnalog` method that was added when we implemented the `AnalogListener` interface:

```
if(name.equals("boost") && value > 0){
    spaceShip.getControl(ThrusterControl.class).fireBooster();
}
```

How it works...

The graphics in this recipe are very minimalistic and mostly rely on the debug mode of `BulletAppState` to draw them. The physics shapes don't normally have a visual representation since they're not part of the scene graph. Using the debug mode can be very useful during early prototypes.

The `RigidBodyControl` instance of the spaceship makes sure it's affected by gravity and other forces.

The sole purpose of a thruster is to be able to easily retrieve the position that is relative to the spaceship from where the boosting force needs to be applied. This is why we place it at the bottom of the spaceship. The benefit of using the `Control` pattern to control a `Thruster` is that we can apply it to other geometries easily (and even use it in `SceneComposer`).

The `fireBooster` method of `ThrusterControl` takes the position of `spaceShip` and subtracts the position of the thruster node to get the direction of the force to apply. The relative position of the force is the direct opposite of this direction.

Ballistic projectiles and arrows

Applying physics to arrows can greatly improve the appearance and gameplay of a medieval or fantasy game. Setting up arrows that are affected by gravity is fairly simple; this recipe, however, will also set the arrows up in a way that they always face the direction they're traveling in, making them more realistic. The following figure shows one of the arrows in flight:

Getting ready

For this recipe, we need to make sure that we see the debug shapes of physics. To do this, we need to call the `bulletAppState.setDebugEnabled(true);` statement.

How to do it...

In this recipe, we'll create three classes. Let's begin by looking at the `Arrow` class, which contains most of the new functionalities. This will be done in the following eight steps:

1. We create a new class called `Arrow`, extending `Node`.

2. Its constructor takes two `Vector3f` variables as parameters. One of these is for the starting location of the arrow and one for the initial velocity, as shown in the following line of code:

   ```
   public Arrow(Vector3f location, Vector3f velocity)
   ```

3. Inside the constructor, we define a `Geometry` instance for the body of the arrow with a `box` mesh as follows:

   ```
   Box arrowBody = new Box(0.3f, 4f, 0.3f);
   Geometry geometry = new Geometry("bullet", arrowBody);
   ```

4. Then, we set `localTranslation` of `Geometry` so that one of its ends touches the center point of the node as follows:

```
geometry.setLocalTranslation(0f, -4f, 0f);
```

5. We set `localTranslation` of this `Arrow` as the supplied location.

6. Next, we create `CollisionShape`. This will represent the head of the arrow and can be `SphereCollisionShape`, as follows:

```
SphereCollisionShape arrowHeadCollision = new
    SphereCollisionShape(0.5f);
```

7. Now, we define `RigidBodyControl` based on `CollisionShape`, as follows:

```
RigidBodyControl rigidBody = new
    RigidBodyControl(arrowHeadCollision, 1f);
```

8. We set `LinearVelocity` of `RigidBodyControl` to be the supplied velocity and add it as a Control to Arrow, as follows:

```
rigidBody.setLinearVelocity(velocity);
addControl(rigidBody);
```

This would be enough for the arrow to follow the laws of physics; however, it will always face the forward direction. By adding another control, we can make it face the direction of the velocity. To do this, perform the following steps:

1. Create another class called `ArrowFacingControl`, extending `AbstractControl`.

2. We add a `Vector3f` field called `direction`.

3. In the `controlUpdate` method, we get `linearVelocity` from `RigidBodyControl` of the spatial and normalize it. We then store it in `direction` as follows:

```
direction =
    spatial.getControl(RigidBodyControl.class).getLinearVelocit
    y().normalize();
```

4. Then, call the spatial and tell it to rotate to the supplied `direction` vector as follows:

```
spatial.rotateUpTo(direction);
```

5. In the constructor of the `Arrow` class, we add an instance of this control, as follows:

```
addControl(new ArrowFacingControl());
```

The last section handles the firing of the arrow from `SimpleApplication`. This can be done with the following steps:

1. First of all, we need to implement `ActionListener` in the application.

2. Add the `ActionListener` class to `inputManager` as a listener, together with a key for firing arrows, as follows:

```
inputManager.addListener(this, "fire");
inputManager.addMapping("fire", new
  KeyTrigger(KeyInput.KEY_SPACE));
```

3. In the `onAction` method, call a new method called `fireArrow` when the `fire` button is released. This can be implemented as follows:

```
if (action.equals("fire") && !isPressed) fireArrow();
```

4. The `fireArrow` method should begin by instancing a new `Arrow` instance and applying a (preloaded) material to it, as follows:

```
Arrow arrow = new Arrow(new Vector3f(0f, 6f, -10f), new
  Vector3f(0.5f, 0.5f, 0.0f).mult(50));
arrow.setMaterial(matBullet);
```

5. We attach it to `rootNode` as well as to `physicsSpace`, as shown in the following code snippet:

```
rootNode.attachChild(arrow);
getPhysicsSpace().add(arrow);
```

How it works...

The `Arrow` object has two major components. One is `Geometry`, which is a simple elongated box. The other is `CollisionShape` for the head of the arrow, which is the only thing that will look for collisions. The geometry is conveniently moved so that its tip will be at the (0,0,0) position of the `Arrow` node. It is convenient since it means we don't have to do any conversions in `ArrowFacingControl` but can use `rotateUpTo` with the actual velocity (direction) of the arrow.

Handling multiple gravity sources

Some games require handling gravity from multiple variable sources. In this recipe, we'll handle this and create a simple miniature solar system to demonstrate it using `ThrusterControl` from the *Building a rocket engine* recipe. To (greatly) simplify the relation between the planets, they won't affect each other with their gravity, but only the ship. It will also be made in a 2D-asteroids-like fashion, although the gravity would still apply for a 3D game.

We'll add some basic controls to rotate the ship to the left and right, and you can use the thruster to make the ship move forward.

How to do it...

Apart from `ThrusterControl`, we'll create two more small classes and an application class that joins everything together. Let's start with a class that represents the player's ship. This will consist of the following six steps:

1. Create a new class called `SpaceShip`, which has a `Node` field called `shipNode` in it.

2. In the constructor, we set up the physics for it by creating a new `RigidBodyControl` instance with `BoxCollisionShape`. To create it in a way that it is affected by gravity, we also give it a mass of 1 that will be supplied in the constructor as follows:

   ```
   RigidBodyControl control = new RigidBodyControl(new
      BoxCollisionShape(new Vector3f(1, 1, 1)), 1);
   shipNode.addControl(control);
   ```

3. Now, we create a `Node` instance called `thruster`. We also set the name of `Node` to `Thruster` for the control to find it automatically, as shown in the following line of code:

   ```
   Node thruster = new Node("Thruster");
   ```

4. We set `localTranslation` to be at one of the sides of the spaceship and attach it to `shipNode`, as follows:

   ```
   thruster.setLocalTranslation(-1, 0, 0);
   shipNode.attachChild(thruster);
   ```

5. Then, we rotate the ship's spatial so that it's facing sideways:

   ```
   shipNode.rotate(0, FastMath.PI, 0);
   ```

6. Finally, we add a new `ThrusterControl` instance to the spaceship's spatial.

That's it for the `SpaceShip` class. Now, we create a class for our planets, as follows:

1. We start off by defining a class called `StellarBody`, which extends `AbstractControl`. The `StellarBody` class has four float fields: `size`, `speed`, `orbit`, and `cycle`.

2. The constructor takes three of these (`size`, `speed`, and `orbit`) as the input, as shown in the following code:

   ```
   public StellarBody(float orbit, float speed, float size)
   ```

3. We override the `setSpatial` method and add `RigidBodyControl` to the supplied spatial with `SphereCollisionShape`, using `size` as the radius and 0 for mass:

   ```
   RigidBodyControl rigidBody = new RigidBodyControl(new
      SphereCollisionShape(size), 0f);
   rigidBody.setGravity(Vector3f.ZERO);
   spatial.addControl(rigidBody);
   ```

4. In the `controlUpdate` method, we make it move along its orbit by increasing the speed of the cycle by multiplying it by `tpf`, as follows:

```
cycle += (speed * tpf)  % FastMath.TWO_PI;
```

5. Then, we set the actual position of the planet along the orbit using the `sin` and `cos` methods of the `FastMath` class:

```
float x = FastMath.sin(cycle);
float z = FastMath.cos(cycle);
```

6. We multiply the result by the orbit and set `localTranslation` of the spatial to the new location as follows:

```
spatial.setLocalTranslation(x * orbit, 0, z * orbit);
```

7. Then, we also need to set `physicsLocation` of `RigidBodyControl` to the same location.

8. We need a new method, `getGravity`, that will take the position of the ship as an input `Vector3f`.

9. The method begins by subtracting the input position by `worldTranslation`, to get the position of the ship relative to the `StellarBody` class, as follows:

```
Vector3f relativePosition = spatial.getWorldTranslation().
subtract(position);
```

10. The result is normalized and then modified by a formula to get a suitable gravity. This value is returned to the calling method, as follows:

```
relativePosition.normalizeLocal();
return relativePosition.multLocal(size * 1000 /
  relativePosition.lengthSquared());
```

To test all of this, we need to add a few things to `SimpleApplication`. To do this, perform the following set of steps:

1. First of all, we implement `AnalogListener`.

2. We add an `ArrayList<StellarBody>` list called `gravitationalBodies`.

3. In the `simpleInitApp` method, we should begin by initializing `bulletAppState` and set up some controls for the spaceship. We add actions to rotate the spaceship to the left and right as well as fire the ship's thruster, as follows:

```
String[] mappings = new String[]{"rotateLeft",
  "rotateRight", "boost"};
inputManager.addListener(this, mappings);
inputManager.addMapping("boost", new
  KeyTrigger(KeyInput.KEY_SPACE));
```

```
inputManager.addMapping("rotateLeft", new
    KeyTrigger(KeyInput.KEY_LEFT));
inputManager.addMapping("rotateRight", new
    KeyTrigger(KeyInput.KEY_RIGHT));
```

4. Since it's a 2D representation, we move the camera some distance up and make it look as if it is at the center of the world. This can be implemented as follows:

```
cam.setLocation(new Vector3f(0, 300f, 0));
cam.lookAt(Vector3f.ZERO, Vector3f.UNIT_Y);
```

5. We create an instance called `ship` of `SpaceShip` and attach its geometry to `rootNode` and `physicsSpace` of `bulletAppState`.

6. Now we can create a number of `StellarBody` instances using the following steps:

    1. For each instance, we should create a `Geometry` class with a `Sphere` shape that will have the same radius as the size we will supply to the `StellarBody` control.

    2. The `Geometry` class should both be attached to `rootNode` and `physicsSpace` of `bulletAppState`.

    3. We add `StellarBody` as a control to the `Geometry` class and the `gravitationalBodies` list.

7. Inside the `update` method, we have to take into account the gravity of the `StellarBody` instances.

8. First, we define a new `Vector3f` instance called `combinedGravity`.

9. Then, we loop through our `gravitationalBodies` list and apply the following line of code to apply the gravity to `combinedGravity`:

```
combinedGravity.addLocal(body.getGravity(ship.getSpatial().
    getWorldTranslation()));
```

10. Finally, we call the `ship.setGravity(combinedGravity);` statement.

How it works...

Due to the extreme difficulty in creating a stable solar system with more than three bodies, `StellarBody` controls the need to have a static orbit around the center of the system. Using 0 as mass ensures that they aren't affected by gravity. The orbit field represents the orbit's distance from the center of the system, and it will rotate around the center using speed as a factor. The cycle field stores information on how far along its orbit it has come, and will reset once it reaches two PI (a full circle).

The `getGravity` method returns the gravity relative to the position that is supplied, which in this case is the location of the ship. It first determines the direction and then applies the gravity based on the distance between the two.

By using the `gravitationalBodies` list, we have a dynamic way to simply add up all the gravitational forces in the system to a single `Vector3f` object, which we then apply to the spaceship in the `update` method of the application.

Self-balancing using RotationalLimitMotors

Many games today use a blend of animations and physics to create realistic movement. For animated characters, this revolves around balance. It could take the shape of a runner who leans inwards through a curve to counter the centrifugal force. Creating a system like this is not easy and requires a lot of tweaking. In this recipe, we'll look into some of the fundamentals of this, and we'll create a new `Control` class that will try to balance itself using the rotational motors of `SixDofJoint`.

 Six Degrees of Freedom (SixDof) relates to the six ways the joint can rotate: +x, -x, +y, -y, +z, and -z. One way it differs from a `point2point` joint is that in addition, it also has motors for each axis, which makes it possible for it to also apply force.

How to do it...

To simulate balancing, we will begin by creating the upper body of a stickman-shape figure with a torso and two rigid arms. To do this, perform the following set of steps:

1. First of all, we should set up an application with `BulletAppState`.

2. In the `simpleInitApp` method, we create a small square `Box Geometry` to be the waist of the character. It can be `0.25f` in all the axes.

3. We add `RigidBodyControl` to it with `0` in mass since it shouldn't move.

4. Then, we create an oblong box to be the torso and place it above the waist. It should have `RigidBodyControl` with `1` in mass and `BoxCollisionShape` should be of the same size as the geometry:

   ```
   torso = new Geometry("Torso", new Box(0.25f, 2f, 0.25f);
   RigidBodyControl torsoRigidBody = new RigidBodyControl(new
     BoxCollisionShape(...), 1f);
   ...
   torsoRigidBody.setPhysicsLocation(new Vector3f(0, 4.25f,
     0));
   ```

5. Next, we create `SixDofJoint` between the waist and torso and afterwards add it to `physicsSpace` as follows:

```
SixDofJoint waistJoint =  new SixDofJoint(waistRigidBody,
    torsoRigidBody, new Vector3f(0, 0.25f, 0), new
    Vector3f(0, -2.25f, 0f), true);
```

6. We should limit the joint so that it can't rotate on any axes other than the *x* axis, and it shouldn't be able to rotate too much. We can use the following `setAngularLowerLimit` and `setAngularUpperLimit` methods for this:

```
waistJoint.setAngularLowerLimit(new Vector3f(-
    FastMath.QUARTER_PI * 0.3f, 0, 0));
waistJoint.setAngularUpperLimit(new
    Vector3f(FastMath.QUARTER_PI * 0.3f, 0, 0));
```

7. Next, we create one of the arms.

8. We create one of the arms by placing it at the same location as that of the torso and giving it a size of `Vector3f(0.25f, 0.25f, 2f)`, making it stretch out sideways, as shown in the following code snippet:

```
leftArm = new Geometry("Left Arm", new Box(0.25f, 0.25f,
    2f);
RigidBodyControl leftArmRigidBody = new
    RigidBodyControl(new BoxCollisionShape(...), 1f);
...
leftArmRigidBody.setPhysicsLocation(new Vector3f(0, 4.25f,
    0));
```

9. We create another `SixDofJoint` for it using the pivot points of `Vector3f(0, 2.5f, 0.25f)` and `Vector3f(0, 0, -2.5f)`, offsetting it some distance to the side of the torso's spatial.

10. Then, we set the angular limits of the joint to `Vector3f(0, 0, 0)` and `Vector3f(FastMath.QUARTER_PI, 0, 0)`.

11. We repeat the previous three steps to create the opposite arm, but we'll reverse the offset values to make the arm protrude in the opposite direction of the torso.

We now have the basics done for our recipe. Running it should show the character slumping to one side with the arms stretched out to the sides. Now, we can begin with balancing by performing the following steps:

1. We create a new class called `BalanceControl`, extending `AbstractControl`.

2. It should have a `SixDofJoint` field called `joint` and a `RotationalLimitMotor` field called `motorX`.

3. Create a `setJoint` method.

4. Inside this method, after setting the joint, we also populate `motorX` with one of the `RotationalLimitMotor` instances, as follows:

```
motorX = joint.getRotationalLimitMotor(0);
```

5. Inside the `controlUpdate` method, we get `bodyA` from the joint and store it in `PhysicsRigidBody`. This is the torso:

```
PhysicsRigidBody bodyA = joint.getBodyA();
```

6. We get the current rotation of `bodyA` to see how much it pivots. We then convert the rotation to angles and store them as follows:

```
float[] anglesA = new float[3];
bodyA.getPhysicsRotation().toAngles(anglesA);
```

7. We then store `angles[0]` in a float variable called `x`.

8. If `x` is more than 0.01f or less than -0.01, we should start `motorX` and rotate it to compensate for the pivot, as follows:

```
motorX.setEnableMotor(true);
motorX.setTargetVelocity(x*1.1f);
motorX.setMaxMotorForce(13.5f);
```

9. Otherwise, we turn off the motor as follows:

```
motorX.setTargetVelocity(0);
motorX.setMaxMotorForce(0);
```

How it works...

Running the result, we should see the stickman desperately trying to stay upright while flailing his arms up and down. The reason is that getting the forces right when balancing can be very difficult. With values that are too high, the stickman will constantly overshoot the target and instead rotate in the other direction. With values that are too low, it won't have the strength to get upright. With some further tweaking to `targetVelocity` and `maxMotorForce`, we might be able make him stable.

We started by creating the basic shape of a figure that would try to keep the balance. The waist was made to not be affected by the physics, so it could be a solid point. We then added a torso and two arms, resulting in a center of mass somewhere in the upper part of the torso. By placing each of the body parts at some distance from each other with the joints, we give them more freedom of movement.

The `BalanceControl` class we created has one simple strategy. It looks for the torso (bodyA)'s rotation along the x axis, and tries to keep it as close to 0 as possible. If it notices that it's anything but near 0, it will try to move the arms, shifting the center of the mass to the opposite direction.

Despite the low number of components, getting it all to balance out is really difficult! Having more components, such as a whole human skeleton, requires a much more advanced strategy, with body parts moving in a synchronized fashion, rather than they trying to do so individually.

The principles of a bridge-building game

Variants of bridge-building games have been around for a long time. The classical *Bridge Builder* is a 2D physics game where the player is required connect beams to create a bridge strong enough for a train (or some other moving object) to pass.

This recipe will describe most of the core functionalities needed to create such a game, including making the objects stay 2D and not wander off on the *z* axis.

We'll have some basic controls for the game:

 ▸ Left-click will select a previously built node in the bridge

 ▸ Right-click will add a new node or connect two previously built ones

 ▸ The Space bar will turn on the physics

The following figure shows a bridge:

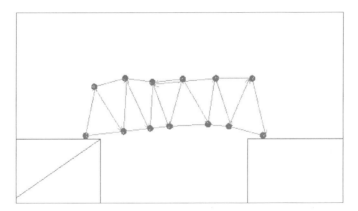

Getting ready

Before we begin with more physics-related functions, we should set up the basic application.

First of all, we create a new class that extends `SimpleApplication`.

Later on, we're going to use the following two lists:

```
private List<Geometry> segments;
private List<Point2PointJoint> joints;
```

We also need some strings as input mappings: `LEFT_CLICK`, `RIGHT_CLICK`, and `TOGGLE_PHYSICS`.

We add a `RigidBodyControl` field called `selectedSegment` that will contain the last selected segment in the game.

Since we're strictly making a 2D game, we should change the camera to be orthographic. This can be done by performing the following steps:

1. Disable `flyCam`.

2. Find out the aspect ratio by dividing the `cam` width by its height and storing it.

3. Set `cam.parallelProjection` to `true`.

4. Then, change `frustrum` of the camera to suit and orthographic view as follows:

   ```
   cam.setFrustum(1, 1000, -100 * aspect, 100 * aspect, 100, -
       100);
   ```

5. We move it some way along the *z* axis and rotate it back towards the center, as follows:

   ```
   cam.setLocation(new Vector3f(0, 0, 20));
   cam.setRotation(new Quaternion().fromAngles(new float[]{0,-
       FastMath.PI,0}));
   ```

Now, we can initialize `bulletAppState` as we usually do. Turn on the debug mode, and most importantly, set `speed` to `0`. We don't want any physics on while we build the bridge.

The world needs a gap to be bridged. So, for this, we'll use `RigidBodyControl` to represent two cliffs, one on either side, as follows:

1. Create one `RigidBodyControl` instance for each side and give it `BoxCollisionShape` with a size of `Vector3f(75f, 50f, 5f)` and 0 mass.

2. Place one of them at `Vector3f(-100f, -50f, 0)` and the other one at `Vector3f(100f, -50f, 0)`.

3. Then, add them to `physicsSpace`.

How to do it...

We're going to start by creating two methods that will help us add new bridge segments to the game:

1. We define a method called `createSegment` that takes a `Vector3f` parameter called `location` as the input.

2. The first thing we do is set the z value of `location` to 0. This is because we're making a 2D game.

3. Then, we create a new `RigidBodyControl` instance called `newSegment`. We add `SphereCollisionShape` to it and then add `newSegment` to `physicsSpace`. It's important that it has some mass. This can be implemented as follows:

```
RigidBodyControl newSegment = new RigidBodyControl(new
    SphereCollisionShape(1f), 5);
bulletAppState.getPhysicsSpace().add(newSegment);
```

4. Now, we create a `Geometry` instance based on a `Sphere` shape with the same radius as `RigidBodyControl`. We will use this as a target for mouse clicks.

5. The `Geometry` object needs `modelBound` for which we'll use `BoundingSphere`. The radius may be bigger than `RigidBodyControl`.

6. The `RigidBodyControl` object is added to `Geometry` as a control and we use the `setPhysicsLocation` method to move it to the to the supplied location, as follows:

```
geometry.addControl(newSegment);
newSegment.setPhysicsLocation(location);
```

7. The `Geometry` object is then added to the segments list we defined earlier and then it is attached to `rootNode`.

8. If `selectedSegment` is not null, we will call a method we will define next:

```
createJoint(selectedJoint, newSegment);
```

9. Lastly, in the `createJoint` method, we set `selectedSegment` to be `newSegment`.

10. Now, we can define the `createJoint` method. It takes two `RigidBodyControl` parameters as the input, as shown in the following code:

```
createJoint(RigidBodyControl body1, RigidBodyControl body2)
```

11. First, we find out the location that should be the pivot point of `body2`. This is the same as `physicsLocation` of `body2` subtracted from `physicsLocation` of `body1`, as follows:

```
Vector3f pivotPointB = body1.getPhysicsLocation().subtract(body2.
getPhysicsLocatio
    n());
```

12. Then, we define `Point2PointJoint` by joining the two segments. The vectors supplied mean that `body2` will pivot in a way that is relative to `body1`; we do this using the following code:

```
Point2PointJoint joint = new Point2PointJoint(body1, body2,
    Vector3f.ZERO, pivotPointB);
```

13. We then add the newly created joint to the `joints` list and to `physicsSpace`.

We're now getting to the controls of the application and need another method to help us. The method will check whether a mouse click has hit any segment and return it. To do this, perform the following steps:

1. We define a new method called `checkSelection`, which returns `RigidBodyControl`.

2. Inside this method, we create a new `Ray` instance, which will have the current mouse cursor's location as the origin; the following code tells you how to do this:

```
Ray ray = new Ray();
ray.setOrigin(cam.getWorldCoordinates(inputManager.getCurso
   rPosition(), 0f));
```

3. Since the view is orthographic, we let the direction be `Vector3f(0, 0, -1f)`.

4. Now, we define a new `CollisionResults` instance to store any segments that `Ray` collides with.

5. The next thing we do is parse through the segment's list and check whether the ray hits any of them.

6. If it does, we're done, and then return `RigidBodyControl` of segment to the calling method.

We defined a couple of input mappings earlier. Now, we can all implement the functionality for them in the `onAction` method by performing the following steps:

1. If the left mouse button is clicked, we should call `checkSelection`. If the returned value is not null, we should set `selectedSegment` to that value, as follows:

```
if (name.equals(LEFT_CLICK) && !isPressed) {
  RigidBodyControl newSelection = checkSelection();
  if (newSelection != null) {
    selectedSegment = newSelection;
  }
}
```

2. If the right mouse button is clicked, we should also call `checkSelection`. If the returned value is not null and it's not `selectedSegment`, we call `createJoint` with `selectedSegment` and the value of `checkSelection` to create a link between `selectedSegment` and the segment returned from the method, as shown in the following code snippet:

```
else if (name.equals(RIGHT_CLICK) && !isPressed) {
  RigidBodyControl hitSegment = checkSelection();
  if (hitSegment != null && hitSegment != selectedSegment) {
    createJoint(selectedSegment, hitSegment);
  }
```

3. Otherwise, if we didn't hit anything, we call `createSegment` with the position of the mouse cursor to create a new segment at that location as follows:

```
createSegment(cam.getWorldCoordinates(inputManager.getCurso
    rPosition(), 10f));
```

4. If the Space bar has been pressed, all we need to do is set the speed of `bulletAppState` to 1 to start the physics.

We're almost done with our simulation now, but we need to do a few more things. This last section will handle the `update` method and what happens when the physics is running and the bridge is being tested:

1. In the `update` method, we parse through all the items in the segment list and set the z value of `linearVelocity` to 0, as follows:

```
Vector3f velocity =
    segment.getControl(RigidBodyControl.class).getLinearVelocit
    y();
velocity.setZ(0);
segment.getControl(RigidBodyControl.class).setLinearVelocit
    y(velocity);
```

2. After this, we parse through all the items in the joint's list. For each, we should check whether the joint's `appliedImpulse` value is higher than a value, let's say `10`. If it is, the joint should be removed from the list as well as from `physicsSpace`, as follows:

```
Point2PointJoint p = joints.get(i);
    if (p.getAppliedImpulse() > maxImpulse) {
        bulletAppState.getPhysicsSpace().remove(p);
        joints.remove(p);

    }
```

How it works...

The `createSegment` method creates a new bridge segment that is sphere shaped, both in `physicsSpace` and the visible world. This is the part that has a mass and can be selected by clicking on it, since `Ray` only collides with spatials.

The `createJoint` method creates the visible connection between the newly created segment, and the currently selected one. It does this using `Point2PointJoint`. This is different from, for example, `HingeJoint`, since it's not fixed in space, when several `Point2Pointjoints` are connected and you have something that resembles a bridge.

The mouse selection is covered more in depth in other chapters, but it works by shooting `Ray` from the mouse's position on the screen, inwards into the game world. Once `Ray` hits `Geometry` (which has `BoundingSphere` that is slightly larger than the visible mesh for increased selectability), the corresponding `RigidBodyControl` will be selected.

There's no challenge in a bridge-building game if the segments don't have a maximum force they can handle before they break. This is what we take care of in the `update` method where we check `appliedImpulse` on each segment. If it goes above a certain threshold, it can be considered to be overloaded and removed, often with disastrous results. We also set `linearVelocity` along the z axis on each segment to 0 since it's a 2D game and we don't want anything to move to the depth layer.

We start the game with the physics simulation off by setting the speed of `bulletAppState` to 0. Without doing so, building the game will get tricky pretty fast as everything will fall down. Pressing the Space bar will start the physics, and let the player know whether their engineering skills are up to par.

There's more...

There are a couple of things missing from the recipe to make it a full-blown bridge builder. First of all, there is usually a limit to the length the segments can have. There might also be a grid structure along which they have to be placed.

It's also quite easy since the bridge currently only has to support its own weight. In a full game, the difficulty is usually increased by adding a heavier object that needs to pass the bridge to complete the level.

Add some monetary constraints to this or a varied terrain and you have a challenging game.

Networked physics

This recipe will go into something of a final frontier in game development. The topic is extremely application-dependent, and it is difficult to get right. Hopefully, after going through this recipe, you will have a basic framework in place that can be adapted to specific projects.

Getting ready

This recipe is for those who have a fundamental understanding of both *Chapter 7, Networking with SpiderMonkey*, and *Chapter 8, Physics with Bullet*. This recipe will describe how to implement networked physics in the networked fps that was discussed previously in the book. Since this is built on top of the existing framework, an `AppState` pattern has been chosen to isolate as much of the physics code as possible. There will be some overlapping, though.

Physics can be expensive as it is and has its own problems and requirements. Sending translations and rotations for objects over the network with every tick will seriously affect the bandwidth load. The ground rule is this: send only what you must.

Divide physics objects into those that you're interested in sharing and those that you don't. In most games, this means separating those that affect the gameplay and those that don't.

For example, a meter-sized crate that can be climbed upon will definitely affect the gameplay. It has to be networked.

A bucket that can be kicked or small debris from an explosion do not affect the gameplay and should only have local physics. It doesn't matter if they show up in different places for different players.

The second part of the rule is this: send only when you must. There's no point in sending an update for an object that is not moving.

How to do it...

Based on the first rule, we'll start by defining a new `Control` class for our networked physics objects:

1. We create a new class called `PhysicsObjectControl` that extends `AbstractControl`.

2. It should have two fields: a Boolean field called `serverControlled` and an integer field called `id`.

We now define a network message to handle updates to objects with physics:

1. Let's call it `PhysicsObjectMessage` and have it extend `AbstractMessage`.

2. There are three mandatory fields for it; they are as follows:

   ❏ The first is an integer field called `objectId`

   ❏ It also needs a `Vector3f` field called `translation`

   ❏ Finally, we add a `Quaternion` field called `rotation`

3. Don't forget to add the `@Serializable` annotation, and add it to the list of messages in the `GameUtil` class!

4. The last common implementation we do is for the `Game` class where we add a list of `Spatials` called `physicsObjects`; the following code tells us how to do this:

```
private Map<Integer, Spatial> physicsObjects = new
  HashMap<Integer, Spatial>();
```

Now, we can dig into the server-side implementation by performing the following steps:

1. We contain most of the code in a new `AppState` class called `ServerPhysicsAppState`. This `AppState` class will contain the reference to the `BulletAppState` class, and it will handle the initialization.

2. Inside its `initialize` method, it should add the loaded level to `physicsSpace` as follows:

   ```
   bulletAppState.getPhysicsSpace().add(server.getLevelNode().
     getChild("terrain-
     TestScene").getControl(PhysicsControl.class));
   ```

3. A strategy is needed to collect all the objects that should be affected by server physics and assign them to `PhysicsObjectControl` (unless this has been done in **SceneComposer** already). Objects that should have server physics should also have `serverControlled` set to `true` and a unique ID, which is known by both the client and the server. The resulting spatials should be stored in the `physicsObject` class map, as follows:

   ```
   bigBox.addControl(new PhysicsObjectControl(uniqueId));
   bigBox.getControl(PhysicsObjectControl.class).setServerCont
     rollled(true);
   physicsObjects.put(uniqueId, bigBox);
   ```

4. In the `update` method of `ServerPhysicsAppState`, we parse through the values of the `physicsObject` map. If any of the item in `physicsObjects` has `PhysicsObjectControl` that `isServerControlled()` and their `isActive()` is `true`, a new `PhysicsObjectMessage` should be created as follows:

   ```
   PhysicsObjectMessage message = new PhysicsObjectMessage();
   ```

5. It should have the ID of `PhysicsObjectControl` as `objectId` and `physicsLocation` and `physicsRotation` of `RigidBodyControl`; refer to the following code:

   ```
   message.setObjectId(physicsObject.getControl(PhysicsObjectC
     ontrol.class).getId());
   message.setTranslation(physicsObject.getControl(RigidBodyCo
     ntrol.class).getPhysicsLocation());
   message.setRotation(physicsObject.getControl(RigidBodyContr
     ol.class).getPhysicsRotation());
   ```

6. The message is then broadcasted to the clients.

We'll revisit the server code in a bit, but first let's look at what is needed for the client to receive messages.

1. First of all, the client has to have `BulletAppState` set up.

2. Next, it needs to have knowledge of the objects to be handled by the server physics. If the objects are gathered from the scene, a strategy is needed to make sure the IDs are the same, or they're read in the same order.

3. They should then be stored in the `Game` class as on the server.

4. The second thing is a change to `ClientMessageHandler`. If the message is an instance of `PhysicsObjectMessage`, it should get the `physicsObject` Map from the `Game` class as follows:

```
Map<Integer, Spatial> physicsObjects =
  game.getPhysicsObjects();
```

5. A spatial should then be selected based on the `objectId` in the message as follows:

```
int objectId = physicsMessage.getObjectId();
Spatial s = physicsObjects.get(objectId);
```

6. The rotation and translation should be applied as `physicsLocation` and `physicsRotation` respectively on the spatial's `RigidBodyControl`:

```
PhysicsObjectControl physicsControl = s.getControl(PhysicsObjectCo
ntrol.class);
if(physicsControl.getId() == objectId){
   s.getControl(RigidBodyControl.class).setPhysicsLocation(phy
   sicsMessage.getTranslation()); s.getControl(RigidBodyControl.
class).setPhysicsRotation(phy
   sicsMessage.getRotation());
}
```

7. Now, the pipeline for transmitting physics updates from the server to the clients should work. If we run it, not much is happening. This is because the players in the implementation in *Chapter 7, Networking with SpiderMonkey*, weren't using physics. They were simply coded to stick to the surface of the terrain. We can change the player's representation to handle this.

8. In `ServerPlayerControl`, we add a `BetterCharacterControl` field called `physicsCharacter` and a Boolean field called `usePhysics`.

9. Next, we override the `setSpatial` method, and perform a check to see whether the spatial supplied has `BetterCharacterControl`. If it does, `usePhysics` should be set to `true` and the local `physicsCharacter` field should be set to `spatial` as follows:

```
if(spatial.getControl(BetterCharacterControl.class) !=
   null){
   usePhysics = true;
```

```
physicsCharacter =
    spatial.getControl(BetterCharacterControl.class);
}
```

10. Finally, in the `controlUpdate` method, we check whether `usePhysics` is `true`. If it is, rather than updating the spatial like we normally do in the method, we should instead set `walkDirection` of `physicsCharacter` to the local one and set `viewDirection` to the forward vector of its rotation as follows:

```
if(usePhysics){
physicsCharacter.setWalkDirection(walkDirection.multLocal(5
    0));
physicsCharacter.setViewDirection(tempRotation.getRotationC
    olumn(2));
}
```

11. In our server's main class, inside the `addPlayer` method, we should now add `BetterCharacterControl` to the player's spatial before we add `ServerPlayerControl`, as shown in the following code snippet:

```
Node playerNode = new Node("Player");
playerNode.addControl(new BetterCharacterControl(0.5f, 1.5f,
    1f));
playerNode.addControl(player);
rootNode.attachChild(playerNode);
stateManager.getState(ServerPhysicsAppState.class).addPlaye
    r(player.getPhysicsCharacter());
```

12. There also needs to be some logic to add and remove `BetterCharacterControl` from `physicsSpace` as it joins and leaves the game.

How it works...

The first thing we did in the recipe was to lay some ground work by defining a new control called `PhysicsObjectControl` to be applied to the objects that should be handled by bullet physics. This control can either be added at runtime; alternatively, if **Scene Composer** is used to lay out levels and scenes, it can be added to the objects beforehand. It's recommended that you define which ones should be handled by the server by setting `serverControlled` on the relevant objects before they're being added to the scenes. The ID should then be set in a deterministic way on both the client and the server when they parse the scene for the objects.

The architecture to handle the physics might very well look different in another implementation, but here, the `AppState` pattern was used so that it could be easily added as an extension to the existing framework from *Chapter7, Networking with SpiderMonkey*. In this chapter, we didn't use any physics for the players but simply checked the height of the terrain to find out where the ground was. Hence, we added an optional `BetterCharacterControl` instance to the player—again, a change that would still make it compatible with the previous implementation. However, this was only added on the server side. For client-side physics, a similar change would have to be made there.

The server will check every update and see whether any of the objects with `serverControlled` enabled is active and will send any updates to the clients. Actually, you could leave out the physics all together on the client and simply update the spatial's rotation and translation, if you wanted. This would lower the requirements on the client's hardware, but this will only work if all of the physics are handled by the server of course.

There's more...

There is an opportunity here to introduce a third state on `PhysicsObjectControl`; a state in which the object is affected but not controlled by the server. This could be used for objects that are important in their initial state; however, once they've been moved, it's no longer important that all the clients have the same information, for example, a door that at some points get blown off its hinges. In this case, a new message type can be introduced that will apply an impulse or force to an object from the server side. Once the object has been activated, the client can take care of the calculations, lowering the network load.

9
Taking Our Game to the Next Level

In this chapter, we'll cover the following topics:

- ▶ Creating a muzzle flash using ParticleEmitter
- ▶ Creating a trigger system
- ▶ Creating a timer trigger
- ▶ Adding an interaction trigger
- ▶ Controlling AI with triggers
- ▶ Creating a dynamic skybox with a moving sun
- ▶ Improving a scene with postprocessing filters
- ▶ Performing complex movements with MotionPaths
- ▶ Cutscenes using cinematics
- ▶ Using a positional audio and environmental effects

Introduction

So the core mechanics are in and the game is playable, yet it still feels like the game lacks something. In this chapter, we will explore different methods to enhance games and fuse together some of the recipes from other chapters.

Creating a muzzle flash using ParticleEmitter

Weapons of some sort are a common feature of many games and muzzle flashes greatly enhance the appearance and feeling when you fire. This recipe will show a way to create good-looking muzzle flashes by tweaking a ParticleEmitter's properties. The following screenshot shows a texture with four muzzle flashes:

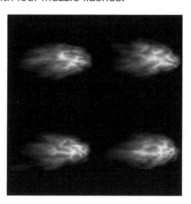

Getting ready

There are two things needed before we can begin work on the ParticleEmitter:

▶ First of all we need a texture for the muzzle flash. This can have anything from one to several images of muzzle flashes. The texture should be gray scaled. We'll add color using `ParticleEmitter`.

▶ Secondly, we need to create a `Material` using the texture by performing the following steps:

1. Right-click on your project's material folder and select **New.../Empty Material file**.

2. Select **Particle.j3md** as **Material Definition**.

3. Then select the muzzle flash texture as **Texture**.

How to do it...

Now, we can begin creating the muzzle flash emitter:

1. Navigate to the **Emitters** folder in the project and select **New.../Empty jme3 Scene**. We should now have a fresh scene.

2. Right-click on the main node in the **SceneExplorer** window and select **Add Spatial/Particle Emitter**.

3. Select the emitter instance and open the **Properties** window.

4. Make sure the **Shadow Mode** option is **Off** and **Queue Bucket** is **Transparent**.

5. Then, select the muzzle flash material we created in the **Geometry/Material** section.

6. Make the **Emitter** shape really small, for example, something like [Sphere, 0.0, 0.0, 0.0, 0.05].

7. **Num Particles** should be 1, and **Particles Per Sec** should be 0.0.

8. Set **Start Color** to something like [1.0, 1.0, 0.4, 1.0] and **End Color** to [1.0, 0.6, 0.2, 0.7].

9. Both **Start Size** and **End Size** should be 1.0.

10. **High Life** and **Low Life** should be 0.15.

11. **Gravity** and **Face Normal** should be [0.0, 0.0, 0.0].

12. Check the **Facing Velocity** box and set the **Initial Velocity** to [0.0, 0.0, 1.0].

13. **Images X** and **Images Y** should reflect the number of frames in the texture we created.

14. We can now test the emitter by clicking on the **Emit!** button.

All these values can be seen in the following screenshot:

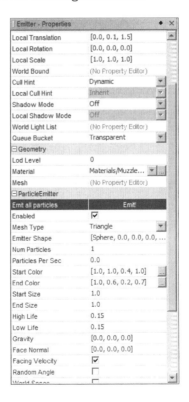

How it works...

The muzzle flash works pretty much like a normal ParticleEmitter with a couple of exceptions. Instead of outputting a constant stream of particles, it will only emit one. This is because **Num Particles** is set to 1, meaning only one particle can be alive at any given time. **Particles Per Sec** is 0.0 so it won't continuously emit anything.

The colors are set to be yellowish, turning a bit orange and fading slightly at the end of the lifetime; the lifetime being very short in this case, only 0.15 seconds.

A muzzle flash is emitted in one direction only. This is why we set **Facing Velocity** to true so that the particle will point in the direction of the velocity.

Getting it to appear in the correct position in relation to the weapon can require a bit of tweaking. Using **Local Translation** can help us in this.

To use the muzzle flash on a weapon, open the target in **Scene Composer** and then choose **Link in Scene** on the muzzle flash. This way the original file can be modified and the changes will automatically appear in the places its being used.

There's more...

Now that we have the muzzle flash and added it to a weapon, we can create a control in order to use it within the game by performing the following steps:

1. Create a new class called `WeaponControl` extending `AbstractControl`.

2. Add a `ParticleEmitter` field called `muzzleFlash`.

3. In the `setSpatial` method, check whether the supplied spatial has a suitable child, either by type or name (requires that the muzzle flash has a fixed name), and set the `muzzleFlash` field:

   ```
   muzzleFlash = (ParticleEmitter) ((Node)spatial).
   getChild("MuzzleFlash");
   ```

4. Now, we create a publicly available `onFire` method and add the following:

   ```
   if(muzzleFlash != null){
     muzzleFlash.emitAllParticles();
   }
   ```

This control should then be added to the weapon spatial inside the game and `onFire` should be called whenever the weapon fires. The class is suitable to play sounds and keeps track of ammunition as well.

Creating a trigger system

Almost all story-driven games require some kind of system to trigger some sort of event for example, dialogs, enemies, or doors opening. Unless the game is very small, you generally don't want to hardcode these. The following recipe will describe a trigger system, which can be used for almost any type of game from FPSs to RTSs and RPGs.

We'll start out by laying the ground work with an AppState controlling all the script objects and the basic functionality of a `Trigger` class. Then, we'll look into how to actually activate the trigger and use it for something.

Getting ready

Before we start with the actual implementation, we create a small interface that we will use for various scripting scenarios. We call it `ScriptObject` and it should have the following three methods:

```
void update(float tpf);
void trigger();
voidonTrigger();
```

How to do it...

Now, we can implement the `ScriptObject` in a class called `Trigger`. This will have six steps:

1. Add the following fields to the `Trigger` class:

    ```
    private boolean enabled;
    private float delay;
    private boolean triggered;
    private float timer;
    private HashMap<String, ScriptObject> targets;
    ```

2. The `enabled` and `delay` fields should have getters and setters and `targets` should have a `addTarget` and `removeTarget` method publically available.

3. In the `trigger` method, we add the following functionality:

    ```
    If enabled is false it shouldn't do anything.
    Otherwise timer should be set to 0 and triggered to true.
    ```

4. If the script is enabled in the `update` method, we should perform the following steps:

    1. If `triggered` is `true` and delay is more than 0, the timer should be increased by tpf.
    2. Then if the timer is more than or equal to delay, it should call `onTrigger()`.

5. If delay is 0 and `triggered` is `true`, the timer should also call `onTrigger()`.

6. In the `onTrigger` method, we should parse through all the values of `targetsMap` and call the trigger on them. Then `triggered` should be set to `false`.

Now, perform the following set of steps to control the `Trigger` class.

1. We define a new class called `ScriptAppState`, which extends `AbstractAppState`.

2. It should have a `List<ScriptObject>` called `scriptObjects`, together with methods to add and remove ScriptObjects from `List`.

3. In the `update` method, if `isEnabled()` is `true`, it should parse `scriptObjects` and call an update on all of the ScriptObjects.

Now, we have a flexible system where one `ScriptObject` can trigger another. We're still lacking input and output effects though. One common way to trigger events is when a player enters an area. So let's go ahead and add that functionality by performing the following steps:

1. Create a new class called `EnterableTrigger`, which extends `Trigger`.

2. This trigger needs a `Vector3f` field called `position` to define its place in the physical world along with a getter and setter.

3. Add a `BoundingVolume` field called `volume`. In the `setter` method for this, we should call `volume.setCenter(position)`.

4. Also, it needs a `List<Spatial>` called `actors` along with `add` and `remove` methods.

5. Now, we should override the `update` method and then call the trigger if any item in the `actors` list is inside `volume`:

```
if(isEnabled() && volume != null && actors != null){
  for(int i = 0; i<actors.size(); i++ ){
    Spatial n = actors.get(i);
    if(volume.contains(n.getWorldTranslation())){
      trigger();
    }
  }
}
```

6. We've taken care of the triggering now. Let's actually do something with that trigger by creating a new class called `SpawnTarget`, implementing `ScriptObject`.

7. Like the `EnterableTrigger` class, the `SpawnTarget` class needs a `position` field and also a `Quaternion` field called `rotation`.

8. The `SpawnTarget` class also requires a `Spatial` field called `target` and a Boolean field called `triggered` to know whether it's been triggered yet or not.

9. We should also add a `Node` field called `sceneNode` to attach the target to.

10. In the `trigger` method, we should check whether it has been triggered already. If not, we should set `triggered` to `true` and call `onTrigger`.

11. The `onTrigger` method should apply the position and rotation to the target and attach it to the `sceneNode`. Depending on the implementation, we might want to subtract the `worldTranslation` and `worldRotation` values from the values we apply:

```
target.setLocalTranslation(position);
target.setLocalRotation(rotation);
sceneNode.attachChild(target);
```

Let's have a look at another common game object that can be picked up. In many games, characters can pick up various power-up weapons or other items simply by walking over them. This section will have the following eight steps:

1. We create a new class called `Pickup` extending `Trigger`.

2. Like `EnterableTrigger`, the `Pickup` class needs a position and a `List<Spatial>` called `actors`. We also need to add a `Spatial` field called `triggeringActor` and a float called `triggeringDistance`.

3. For this class, we also need something to pick up, represented here by an interface called `Pickupable`. In addition, we need to keep track of whether it's been picked up by a Boolean called `pickedUp`.

4. The difference between the previous ScriptObjects we've worked with and the current ScriptObjects is that the one in this recipe should be visible in the world, represented by a `Spatial` called `model`.

5. In the `update` method, we should check whether the `Pickup` object is enabled and not `pickedUp`.

6. To make it stand out a bit in the game world, we rotate the model a little bit by applying the `model.rotate(0, 0.05f, 0)` value.

7. Still inside the `if` clause, we check that `actors` is not null and parse through the list. If any of the actors is inside the radius of the `triggerDistance`, we set it to be `triggeringActor` and call the `trigger` method:

```
for(int i = 0; i<actors.size(); i++ ){

  Spatial actor = actors.get(i);
  if((actor.getWorldTranslation().distance(position)
<triggerDistance)){
    triggeringActor = actor;
    trigger();
  }
}
```

8. Finally, in the `onTrigger` method, we should set `pickedUp` to `true`, detach `model` from scene graph and call `pickupObject.apply(triggeringActor)` to have it apply whatever the `Pickupable` object is supposed to do.

How it works...

The `Trigger` class has a fairly simple functionality. It will wait for something to call its `trigger` method.

When this happens, it will either trigger all the connected ScriptObjects immediately or if a delay is set, it will start counting until the time has passed and then execute the trigger. Once this is done, it will be set up so it can be triggered again.

The `ScriptAppState` state is a convenient way to control the scripts. Since the `AppState` is either disabled or not attached to the `stateManager`, no call to `update` in `ScripObjects` is made. This way, we can easily disable all the scripting if we want to.

To create a working example with `Trigger`, we extended it into a class called `EnterableTrigger`. The idea with the `EnterableTrigger` class was that if any of the supplied actor spatials enter its `BoundingVolume` instance, then it should trigger whatever is connected to it.

The basic `Trigger` method doesn't have the need for a position as it is a purely logical object. The `EnterableTrigger` object, however, has to have a relation to the physical space as it needs to know when one of the actors has entered its `BoundingVolume` instance.

This is true for `SpawnTarget` as well, which in addition to a location should have a rotation, to rotate a potential enemy in a certain direction. Spawning characters or items in games is commonly used to control the gameplay flow and save some performance. The `SpawnTarget` option allows this kind of control by adding new spatials only when triggered.

The strategy for how to perform spawning might differ depending on the implementation but the way described here assumes it involves attaching the target `Spatial` to the main node tree, which would generally activate its update method and controls.

Likewise, the `rootNode` of the scene graph is not necessarily the best choice to attach the target to and depends a lot on the game architecture. It could be any `Spatial`.

Lastly, in this recipe, we created a `Pickup` object, which is very common in many games. These can be anything from items that increase health instantly or weapons or other equipment that are added to an inventory. In many cases, it's similar to the `EnterableTrigger` except it only requires a radius to see whether someone is within the pickup range or not. We keep track of the actor that enters it so that we know who to apply the pickup to. In this recipe, the pickup is represented by an object called `Pickupable`.

Once it's picked up, we set `pickedUp` to `true` so that it can't be picked up again and detach the model from the node tree to make it disappear. If it is a recurring power up, a delay can be used here to make it available again after some time.

Pickups in games usually stand out from other objects in the game world to draw attention to them. How this is done depends on the game style, but here we apply a small rotation to it in each call to the `update` method.

Since `Pickup` also extends `Trigger`, it's possible to use it to trigger other things as well!

Creating a timer trigger

In the *Creating a trigger system* recipe, we laid the foundation for a `Trigger` system as well as created some basic implementations. A timer can be very useful when creating complex scripts that rely on timing or sequenced events. Not only does it do the obvious (trigger the blast of the door and then the soldiers running through) but it can also work as a relay trigger in case many things should be triggered at the same time. In this recipe, we'll create this `Timer` object as well as an actual implementation of it where it triggers an explosion with several components. To save some time, we'll use the `TestExplosion` test from jMonkeyEngine to get `ParticleEmitters` set up and the timing for free. We'll also create a new `ScriptObject` called `PlayEffect`, which controls the particle emitters.

How to do it...

To be able to control a `ParticleEmitter` object from our script system, we need a new class to handle the `ParticleEmitter` object:

1. Start by creating a new class called `PlayEffect`, which implements `ScriptObject`.
2. The `PlayEffect` class needs a Boolean called `emitAllParticles`, a `ParticleEmitter` field called `effect`, and a Boolean to control whether it's enabled or not (default it to `true`).
3. The `trigger` method should call `onTrigger` if the object is enabled.
4. The `onTrigger` method should enable `effect` and if `emitAllParticles` is true, it should call `emitter.emitAllParticles()`.

Apart from the setter methods, this is all that's needed for the `PlayEffect` class. Now, we can look at the `Timer` class by performing the following steps:

1. We create a new class called `Timer`, which implements `ScriptObject`.
2. It will use a simple callback interface to keep track of events:

```
public interface TimerEvent{
  public Object[] call();
}
```

3. It needs two Boolean fields. One called `enabled` and another called `running`. It also needs to keep track of time with three floats called `time`, `lastTime`, and `maxTime`.

4. Finally, we will store the events in `HashMap<Float, TimerEvent>`.

5. We need a method to add events to the timer. Call it `addTimerEvent` and add inputs for `time` in seconds to execute the event, as well as a `TimerEvent` object with the code to execute it. After `TimerEvent` is placed in the `timerEvents` map, we check whether the supplied `time` value is higher than the current `maxTime` and set `maxTime` to `time` if true, as shown in the following code:

```
public void addTimerEvent(float time, TimerEvent callback){
   timerEvents.put(time, callback);
   if(time >maxTime ){
      maxTime = time;
   }
}
```

6. The `trigger` method should call `onTrigger`, if it is enabled.

7. The `onTrigger` method should set time to `0` and set `running` to `true`.

8. The `update` method should first check whether the `Timer` is `enabled` and `running`.

9. If it is, tpf should be added to the time.

10. Inside the `same` statement, we then create an iterator based on `keySet` of `timerEvents` and parse through it. If the key (a float) is more than `lastTime` and less or equal to the current time, we should get the corresponding value from the `timerEvents` map and execute it. Otherwise, if the key is less than `lastTime`, we should just continue using the following code:

```
Iterator<Float> it = timerEvents.keySet().iterator();
while(it.hasNext()){
   float t = it.next();
   if(t >lastTime&& t <= time){
      TimerEvent event = timerEvents.get(t);
      if(event != null){
         event.call();
      }
   } else if(t <lastTime){
      continue;
   }
}
```

11. Outside of the previous loop, we check if `time` is more than `maxTime`, in which case, we should set `running` to `false`.

12. Finally in the `update` method, we set `lastTime` to be equal to `time`.

With the basic logic done, let's take a look at how we can use the timer for something real and use it to trigger an explosion by performing the following steps:

1. Copy the `TestExplosion` class from jMonkeyEngine's test package and strip it from everything except the methods that create `ParticleEmitters` and the lines in `simpleInitApp`, which uses them and sets up the camera.

2. Then, create a `PlayEffect` instance for each of `ParticleEmitters` and set the effect accordingly with `emitAllParticles` set to `true`.

3. Create a new `Timer` instance called `explosionTimer`.

4. Add a new `TimerEvent` at time 0 where it triggers the `flash`, `spark`, `smoke`, `debris`, and `shockwave` effects, by calling `trigger()` on each of the `PlayEffects`, as shown in the following code:

```
explosionTimer.addTimerEvent(0, new Timer.TimerEvent() {

    public Object[] call() {
        flashEffect.trigger();
        sparkEffect.trigger();
        ...
        return null;
    }
});
```

5. Then, add another `TimerEvent` at time `0.05f`, which triggers the `flame` and `roundSpark` effects.

6. The last `TimerEvent` should happen at time `5f` and should call `stop()` on all of the effects.

7. Finally, we create a `ScriptAppState` instance to which we add `explosionTimer` and then add it to `stateManager` using the following code:

```
ScriptAppStateappState = new ScriptAppState();
stateManager.attach(appState);
appState.addScriptObject(explosionTimer);
```

8. Now, we can trigger `explosionTimer`. It should perform the explosion in the same way as `TestExplosion` does.

How it works...

Once triggered, `Timer` works by checking the time that has passed since it was started (`time`). It then checks each of the events in the `timerEvents` map to see whether their execution time is anywhere between the current time and the last time (`lastTime`). The `maxTime` option is used by the `Timer` to know when it has executed the last of its events and can switch itself off. If the `Timer` was only meant to be used once, the events can simply be removed from the `timerEvent` map. This way it can be reused.

The `PlayEffect` instance has a fairly simple functionality to turn it on and off. Since `ParticleEmitters` can be used in two ways, fire all their particles at once, or emit a continuous stream of particles, it needs to know which way to fire it.

In the example application, we create `ScriptAppState` since it's needed to update the `Timer` with the passed time. We don't need to add the `PlayEffect` instances since they don't use the `update` method.

Adding an interaction trigger

Another common trigger is the one where an action from the player is required. For example, you can use it to open a door, or access an in-game store system or dialog.

How to do it...

1. We begin by creating a new class called `InteractionTrigger`, which extends `Trigger` and also implements `ActionListener`.

2. The `InteractionTrigger` class needs a `Vector3f` field called position, a `BoundingVolume` field called `volume`, a `Spatial` field called `player`, and a `boolean` field called `inside`.

3. Furthermore, the `InteractionTrigger` class needs access to the application's `guiNode`, which we store in a `Node` field with the same name and a `BitmapText` field called `interactionPrompt`. The text will be displayed when interaction is possible.

4. We also have to define a static string called `INTERACTION_KEY = "Interact"` either in this class or the `input manager` class

5. The `update` method will check whether the player is inside `BoundingVolume`. If it is and `inside` is `false`, it will show `interactionPrompt`. On the other hand, if `inside` is `true` and the player is not inside `BoundingVolume`, it will remove it, as shown in the following code:

```
Boolean contains = volume.contains(player.getWorldTranslation());
if(!inside && contains){
  guiNode.attachChild(interactionPrompt);
} else if (inside && !contains){
  guiNode.detachChild(interactionPrompt);
}
inside = contains;
```

6. In the implemented `onAction` method, we check for when the key corresponding to `INTERACTION_KEY` is released. Then, we see whether the trigger is enabled and whether `inside` is `true` or not. If both are `true`, we call `trigger()`.

7. Some logic outside the class is required to get the trigger to work. Apart from supplying `guiNode` and `BitmapText` to the trigger, the `INTERACTION_KEY` needs to be bound to `inputManager`. This can be done with the following line:

    ```
    inputManager.addMapping(INTERACTION_KEY, new KeyTrigger(KeyInput.
    KEY_SPACE));
    ```

8. The `InteractionTrigger` instance also needs to be added as a listener to `inputManager`:

    ```
    inputManager.addListener(interactionTrigger, mappingNames);
    ```

How it works...

The `InteractionTrigger` instance has several things in common with `EnterableTrigger`, which we created in the *Creating a trigger system* recipe, and it also has a new functionality. Rather than firing the trigger as soon as the player enters it, it sets the `inside` flag, which defines whether it's possible to interact with it or not. It also displays a text on the GUI for the player.

Once the `InteractionTrigger` receives a call to its `onAction` method from `InputManager`, it checks whether `inside` is `true` and calls `trigger`. To brush up your knowledge on how input is handled, check out *Chapter 2, Cameras and Game Control*.

Controlling AI with triggers

Chapter 5, Artificial Intelligence, deals with several methods to control AI in games. As we learned in that chapter, control and predictability are very important. Even if we have the smartest AI in the world, as programmers, we want to be able to know that the AI will perform a certain action at a certain time. This is where triggers can be extremely useful. In fact, with a good trigger system there might not be need for much AI at all.

One example of trigger usage might be a warehouse where guards are in a patrolling state. Once the player reaches a certain area (maybe where they should not go), an alarm is triggered. At this point, we also want the guards to switch to a more aggressive state.

Getting ready

This recipe will link the trigger system we created previously in the chapter with the StateMachine-based `AIControl` class from the *Decision making – Finite State Machine* recipe in *Chapter 5, Artificial Intelligence*. Even if you haven't followed the recipes in *Chapter 5, Artificial Intelligence*, but have a different class controlling AI, it should be quite easy to adapt this recipe to accommodate that class.

How to do it...

As with the previous examples, we begin by creating a new class that extends the `ScriptObject` interface. We can call it `AIScriptControl`.

1. It needs to have an `AIControl` field called `aiControl` and a `Class<AIState>` field called `targetState`.

2. It might also have a `Spatial` called `target`.

3. Finally, we add a Boolean called `enabled`.

4. In its `trigger` method, we should call `onTrigger` if `enabled` is true.

5. In the `onTrigger` method, we apply `targetState` to `aiControl`:

   ```
   aiControl.setState(targetState);
   ```

6. If `target` is not null, we call `aiControl.setTarget(target)`.

7. The `StateMachine` for the `AIControl` we created was a closed system and it didn't need any external input to change the states. Now, we need to be able to trigger it externally so let's add a setter method in the `AIControl`. Create a new method called `setState`, which takes a `Class<AIState>` called `state` as an input parameter.

8. Inside, we check whether `spatial` has the supplied state, and enable it if possible:

   ```
   if(spatial.getControl(state) != null){
   spatial.getControl(state).setEnabled(true);
   }
   ```

How it works...

This recipe follows the pattern we established in the *Creating a trigger system* recipe. In the `onTrigger` method, we apply `targetState`, which will change the behavior and actions of the AI. For example, it can change from `PatrolState` to `AttackState`. We only supply the class type and not a whole instance of the class since the AI should already have the state and it might be configured already. In this way, we tell the AI to simply change the state if it is available. We also have a `target` field, in case the new state requires that.

There's more...

It doesn't have to end with that. We can, for example, with some modification trigger the AI to start walking a path, turn in a certain direction, or take cover and other things. This functionality can either be built into this class or be made as separate classes.

To explore an example in detail, let's have a look at what will be needed to have the AI move to a specific location once `AIScriptControl` is triggered.

1. We will need an `AIState`, which handles moving to a set location. *Chapter 5, Artificial Intellegence*, explains this. The `SeekCoverState` can easily be modified to only have a `target` field rather than a list to choose from.

2. We will need something to function as a waypoint or target. Again, the `CoverPoint` control from the same recipe can function as a waypoint too. It can also be extended so that using cover at `WayPoint` is an option within the class.

3. Finally, we will need to pass `WayPoint` to the state. Since we're not supplying a whole class, we can't set it in `AIState` itself. One way would be to pass it through the `setTarget` method of `AIControl`.

Creating a dynamic skybox with a moving sun

We covered how to create static skyboxes in *Chapter 1, SDK Game Development Hub*. While they are fine for many implementations, some games require day and night cycles.

Getting ready

This recipe will show us how to create a moving sun, which can be superimposed on a regular skybox. In this case, a neutral skybox without any protruding features such as mountains will work best. We'll also learn how to make a sky that changes color during the day. In this case, no skybox is required.

We will also need a texture that should have a transparent background with a filled, white circle in it, as shown in the following figure:

A colorful sunset by the sea

How to do it...

1. We begin by creating a new application class extending `SimpleApplication`.

2. In the `simpleInitApp` method, we first need to create `Geometry` for the sun:

   ```
   Geometry sun = new Geometry("Sun", new Quad(1.5f, 1.5f));
   ```

3. We need to set some rendering hints on it, as shown in the following code:

   ```
   sun.setQueueBucket(RenderQueue.Bucket.Sky);
   sun.setCullHint(Spatial.CullHint.Never);
   sun.setShadowMode(RenderQueue.ShadowMode.Off);
   ```

4. Now, we can load a `Material` instance based on the unshaded material definition.

5. For `ColorMap`, we load the texture with the white circle in it and apply the texture. Then, for `Color` we can set an almost white color with a tint of yellow in it. We also have to enable alpha in the material:

   ```
   sunMat.getAdditionalRenderState().setBlendMode(RenderState.
   BlendMode.Alpha);
   sunMat.setTexture("ColorMap", assetManager.loadTexture("Textures/
   sun.png"));
   sunMat.setColor("Color", new ColorRGBA(1f, 1f, 0.9f, 1f));
   ```

So, the basic `Geometry` is set up and we can create a `Control` class to move the sun across the sky by performing the following steps:

1. Create a class called `SunControl`, which extends `AbstractControl`.

2. It should have a `float` field called `time`, a reference to the application camera called `cam`, a `Vector3f` field called `position`, and a `DirectionalLight` field called `directionalLight`.

3. In the `controlUpdate` method, we start by finding the x and z positions based on the time and multiply the result to move it some distance away. We can also make the sun move up and down by doing the same for the y value:

   ```
   float x = FastMath.cos(time) * 10f;
   float z = FastMath.sin(time) * 10f;
   float y = FastMath.sin(time ) * 5f;
   position.set(x, y, z);
   ```

4. Then, we should set `localTranslation` of the sun. Since we want it to appear to be very far away, we add the camera's location. This way it will always appear to be the same distance from the camera:

   ```
   spatial.setLocalTranslation((cam.getLocation().add(position)));
   ```

5. We also want the sun to always face the camera. This is easily done by calling the following code:

```
spatial.lookAt(cam.getLocation(), Vector3f.UNIT_Y);
```

6. If the `directionalLight` field is set, we should also set its direction. We get the direction by inverting `position`, as shown in the following code:

```
directionalLight.setDirection(position.negate());
```

7. Finally, we increase the `time` value by a factor of `tpf` (depending on how fast we want the sun to move). Since two PI in radians make up a circle, we start over once `time` exceeds that value, using the following code:

```
time += tpf * timeFactor;
time = time % FastMath.TWO_PI;
```

8. Going back to the `application` class, we add the control to the `Geometry` sun and `Geometry` to the scene graph:

```
sun.addControl(sunControl);
rootNode.attachChild(sun);
```

The previous implementation can be enough for many games but it can be taken much further. Let's explore how to make the sun color dynamic based on its height above the horizon and how to also have a dynamic sky color by performing the following steps:

1. First of all, let's introduce two static `ColorRGBA` fields in the `SunControl` class called `dayColor` and `eveningColor`. We also add another `ColorRGBA` field called `sunColor`.

2. In the `controlUpdate` method, we take the `y` value of the sun and divide it so that we get a value between `-1` and `1`, and store this as the height.

3. `ColorRGBA` has a method to interpolate two colors that we can use to get a smooth transition during the day:

```
sunColor.interpolate(eveningColor, dayColor, FastMath.
sqr(height));
```

4. After this, we set the color of `directionalLight` to the same as `sunColor` and also set the material's `Color` parameter to the same:

```
directionalLight.setColor(sunColor);
((Geometry)spatial).getMaterial().setColor("Color", sunColor);
```

Handling the sky color will take a bit more work. To do this, perform the following steps:

1. We begin by creating a new class called `SkyControl` extending `AbstractControl`.

2. Like `SunControl`, the `SkyControl` class needs a `Camera` field called `cam`. It also needs a `ColorRGBA` field called `color` and three static `ColorRGBA` fields for different times in the day:

    ```
    private static final ColorRGBAdayColor = new ColorRGBA(0.5f, 0.5f,
    1f, 1f);
    private static final ColorRGBAeveningColor = new ColorRGBA(1f,
    0.7f, 0.5f, 1f);
    private static final ColorRGBAnightColor = new ColorRGBA(0.1f,
    0.1f, 0.2f, 1f);
    ```

3. The `SkyControl` class needs to know about the sun's location so we add a `SunControl` field called `sun`.

4. In the `controlUpdate` method, we set the `localTranslation` of the spatial to the location of the `cam`.

5. Next, we get the sun's height and if it is higher than 0, we interpolate the color between `eveningColor` and `dayColor`. Otherwise, we interpolate between the `eveningColor` and `nightColor` instead. Then, we set the resulting color in the sky's material's `Color` parameter, as shown in the following code:

    ```
    if(sunHeight> 0){
      color.interpolate(eveningColor, dayColor, FastMath.
    pow(sunHeight, 4));
    } else {
      color.interpolate(eveningColor, nightColor, FastMath.
    pow(sunHeight, 4));
    }
    ((Geometry)spatial).getMaterial().setColor("Color", color);
    ```

6. Going back to the `application` class, we create a box shaped `Geometry` called `sky`

7. for the control with `10f` sides.

8. Like the sun geometry, sky should have the Sky `QueueBucket`, `ShadowMode.Off` and `CullHint.Never` settings applied to it.

9. In addition, we should call `getAdditionalRenderState` and set `FaceCullMode` to `FaceCullMode.Off`.

How it works...

Always causing the geometries of this recipe follow the camera around is one of the parts that make this recipe work. The other trick is using the Sky `QueueBucket`. The Sky `QueueBucket` can be thought of as lists of items to be rendered. Everything in the Sky bucket is rendered first. Because it's rendered first, other things will be rendered on top of it. This is why it appears to be far away even though it's really close to the camera.

We also use the direction of the sun from the camera for `DirectionalLight` in the scene, making it follow the sun as it moves across the sky.

When updating the control, we handle the movement of the sun using the `time` value, which increases with each update. Using `FastMath.sin` and `FastMath.cos` for the x and z values, we get it to move in a circle around the camera. Using `FastMath.sin` again for the y value will move it in an arc above (and below) the horizon. By multiplying the y value, we can get it to rise higher in the sky.

The resulting position was added to the camera's location to always make the sun centered around the camera. Since the sun is a simple quad, we also had to rotate it to face the camera with every update.

We went on to change the color of the sun based on the height above the horizon. We used the interpolate method of `ColorRGBA` to do this. Interpolation requires a value between `0.0` and `1.0`. That's why we needed to divide the y value by the max y value (or amplitude) in the case where we've multiplied it earlier to get a higher arc in the sky.

The movement of the box simulating the sky is similar. We just keep it centered around the camera so that even if it's a small box, it appears to cover the whole sky. Normally, we wouldn't see the sides of the box when we're inside it so we set `FaceCullMode` to `Off` to always make it render the sides.

`SkyControl` was fitted with three instances of `ColorRGBA`: `dayColor` with a bluish tint, `eveningColor` with orange, and `nightColor` almost black. The `SunControl` was supplied to the control and used to interpolate between the colors based on the height of the sun. Anything above `0.0f` is considered day.

In this implementation, the whole sky changes color with the sun. Any further development of `SkyControl` could include a more complex shape, such as a cylinder or sphere where only the vertices on the same side as the sun change color. Clouds can be implemented and they also use a quad that moves in the xz-plane.

Another improvement would be to have a night-time, star-filled skybox outside of the box we made and fade the alpha value of `nightColor` to let it gradually shine through the night time.

There's more...

If we try the recipe with the unshaded material definition for the sky, it will work well in most cases. However, when it comes to the postprocessor water filter, it will not pick up the sky color properly. To achieve this, we will have to make some modifications to its material. We don't need to actually change any of the `.vert` or `.frag` files, but can create a new `Material Definition (.j3md)` file.

To make things as easy as possible, we can copy the `Unshaded.j3md` file. Refer to the following code within the `Unshaded.j3md` file:

```
VertexShader GLSL100:   Common/MatDefs/Misc/Unshaded.vert
```

Replace the previous line with the following line:

```
VertexShader GLSL100:   Common/MatDefs/Misc/Sky.vert
```

This means we'll be using the vertex shader normally used by the Sky material to handle the positions of the vertices for the renderer.

We also need to change the `WorldParameters` segment to contain the following:

```
ViewMatrix
ProjectionMatrix
WorldMatrix
```

Improving a scene with postprocessing filters

In the *Creating dynamic skybox with moving sun* recipe, we created a dynamic skybox that has many applications. It's possible to improve the appearance of this (and any other) scene significantly with postprocessing filters. They are called postprocessing filters because they are applied after the scene has already been rendered. This also makes them affect everything in the scene.

We also covered how to create an advanced postfilter in *Chapter 1, SDK Game Development Hub*.

How to do it...

The sun we have is now moving across the sky. It has very sharp edges and we can use a bloom filter to smooth it out a bit. Perform the following steps to improve a scene with the help of postprocessing filters:

1. First of all, we need to create a new `FilterPostProcessor` instance called `processor`.

2. Add this to the main view port, by calling `viewPort.addProcessor(processor)` from within the application.

3. Then, we create a new bloom filter called `bloomFilter`. The default settings will produce a decent result, but it might be worth playing around a bit with the settings.

4. Add the `bloomFilter` to `processor.addFilter(bloomFilter)` and try it again.

5. Then, we create a new `LightScatteringFilter` instance called `lightScatteringFilter` and add it again to `processor.addFilter(lightSc atteringFilter)`.

6. This is dependent on a position for the light to scatter, so we need to make it aware of the sun's location. We can achieve this by adding a new field for the filter in the `SunControl` class from the last recipe along with a setter.

7. Then in the `controlUpdate` method, once we have updated `position`, we add the following code:

```
lightScatteringFilter.setLightPosition(position.mult(1000));
```

8. We still have some tweaking to do as it will now also apply the effect when the sun is below the ground. To mitigate this, we can disable the filter during nighttime:

```
if(y > -2f){
  if(!lightScatteringFilter.isEnabled()){
    lightScatteringFilter.setEnabled(true);
  }
  lightScatteringFilter.setLightDensity(1.4f);
} else if(lightScatteringFilter.isEnabled()){
  lightScatteringFilter.setEnabled(false);
}
```

How it works...

The `FilterPostProcessor` acts as a container for the filters and applies them to the rendered result. Several filters can be added to the same processor and the order matters. If we add `LightScatteringFilter` before `bloomFilter`, we will get bloom applied to the light scattering and vice versa.

The `bloomFilter` works by blurring the image slightly and intensifying colors, making the result appear a bit softer. Bloom filters work best with tweaking and shouldn't just be slapped on to the scene. It's easy to be impressed by the initial effect and leave it at that but it should always be adapted to the art style of the game. A fantasy game in an enchanted forest might get away with more bloom than a hard-boiled cyberpunk shooter.

The `LightScatteringFilter` instance does two things. Firstly, it creates a halo of rays emanating from the direction of the light source. Secondly, if the camera is pointing towards the light source, it will whiteout the image increasingly, simulating glare.

In a normal skybox, the sun would be static but in this example the sun keeps moving. By supplying the filter to `SunControl`, we could keep the logic to update the position within that class. We will also get some weird effects as the glare will still show. The easy way out is to simply turn off the effect as the sun gets below the horizon.

Performing complex movements with MotionPaths

Players in games have been obliged to jump on moving platforms since the dawn of gaming. Even with the incredibly advanced games of today, it's not uncommon to encounter this most primitive game mechanic albeit with better graphics. There's also a popular retro genre that calls for the same, not the least for mobile games.

How do we do that in jMonkeyEngine? One way is, of course, to simply use move or `setLocalTranslation` on geometries. This can quickly get complex if we want to make sequenced paths. A better option is to use MotionPaths and MotionEvents.

A `MotionPath` object is basically a set of waypoints through which an object will move in an interpolated way meaning the movement will be smooth. The `MotionEvent` is the control class defining when and how the object should move along the `MotionPath` object. It can define how an object should be rotated along the path and if and how the path should be cycled through.

In this recipe, we'll check out how to use them for a game, which could be a side-scrolling 2D game, but the same principles can be used to create advanced cinematic cutscenes.

How to do it...

Let's begin by creating a platform object to move, by performing the following steps:

1. We define a new `Geometry` called `platform` and apply the `Unshaded` material to it, as shown in the following code:

   ```
   platform = new Geometry("Platform", new Box(1f, 0.1f, 1f));
   platform.setMaterial(new Material(assetManager, "MatDefs/Misc/
   Unshaded.j3md"));
   ```

2. Then, we attach the `platform` object to `rootNode`.

3. Next, we define a new `MotionPath` object called `path`.

4. We add 8 waypoints in a circular pattern, using the following code:

   ```
   for(inti = 0 ; i< 8; i++){
     path.addWayPoint(new Vector3f(0, FastMath.sin(FastMath.QUARTER_
   PI * i) * 10f, FastMath.cos(FastMath.QUARTER_PI * i) * 10f));
   }
   ```

5. Then, we call `path.setCycle(true)` to make it connect the first and last waypoints.

6. Now, we can define a new `MotionEvent` called `event` and supply `platform` and `path` in the constructor.

7. We call `event.setInitialDuration(10f)` and `setSpeed(1f)`.

8. Finally, we call `event.setLoopMode(LoopMode.Loop)`.

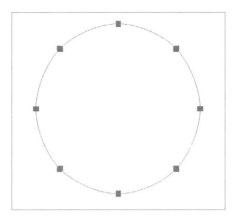

Debug MotionPath with red waypoints

9. Optionally, we can visualize the path by calling the following method:

   `path.enableDebugShape(assetManager, rootNode);`

10. Now, all we need to do is call `event.play()` to start the event!

How it works...

The `for` loop creates eight waypoints along a circle at 45 degrees distance from each other. However, to make a complete circle the first and last waypoints need to be connected or the path will stop at the final one. This is why `setCycle(true)` must be set. This is treated as the ninth waypoint at the same position as the first.

MotionEvent's `initialDuration` is the time it should take to complete the path. The speed defines the factor at which the `initialDuration` should be completed. So, setting the speed to 2f will halve the actual time it takes for the object to complete its movement. The `loopMode`, not surprisingly, defines whether the object should stop once it has completed the path, or continue. There's also an option to make it go back the same path again with `LoopMode.Cycle`. This is not related to MotionPath's `setCycle` method.

While this recipe doesn't explore the option, it's possible to have the spatial in `MotionPath` perform various types of rotation. By default, no rotation will be applied. By calling `setDirectionType` it is possible to, for example, let the object follow the path's rotation (face the direction of the path) or rotate by a fixed amount or always face a certain point. Some of the direction types require a rotation to be supplied with the `setRotation` method.

There's more...

Now, the object is moving along its given path and we can add several platforms moving in different patterns. Let's say we want something to happen once a platform reaches the end of its path. Maybe it should start the next one or trigger one of our ScriptObjects from the previous recipes.

In that case, we can use `MotionPathListener`. This is an interface with a callback method called `onWayPointReached`, which will be called every time the path passes a waypoint. It will supply both the `MotionEvent` and the `index` of the waypoint. If we want to trigger something at the end of the path, it might look like the following code snippet:

```
path.addListener(new MotionPathListener() {
   public void onWayPointReach(MotionEvent control,
intwayPointIndex) {
      if (path.getNbWayPoints() == wayPointIndex + 1) {
        nextMotionEvent.play();
      }
   }
});
```

Cutscenes using cinematics

The previous recipe explored the possibilities of using `MotionPaths` to move objects around. One step up from that and a way to organize many events in a sequence is cinematics. It can be used both to create in-game scripted events and advanced cutscenes. The power of a well-scripted in-game event should not be underestimated but neither should the time it takes to get one right.

In this recipe, we'll explore the possibilities of the `Cinematics` system by creating a cutscene using content that we have created before.

Getting ready

Some basic knowledge of `MotionPaths` and `MotionEvents` is required. Checking out the *Performing complex movements with MotionPath* recipe should provide enough information to get started. A new class that is introduced is the `Cinematic` class. This works as a sequencer or manager of many events firing them at set times. The events don't just have to be `MotionEvents` but could be `AnimationEvents` dealing with skeleton-based animations, `SoundEvents`, and even `GuiEvents`. It can also manage several cameras and switch between them.

Before starting the actual implementation of a cinematic scene, it's good to have some kind of script describing what is going to happen. This will help organize the cinematic event and will save time in the end.

This recipe will use the `TestScene` from *Chapter 1, SDK Game Development Hub.* We can also use the animated sky box from earlier in this chapter. It will display Jaime walking from his initial position to stand by the edge of the water looking into the horizon. While he's walking, several switches between panning cameras will occur.

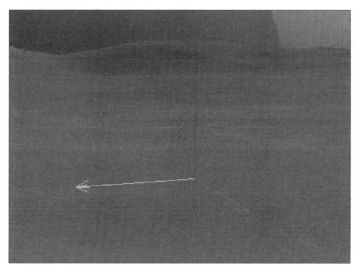

Using an empty node as a waypoint

Finding out good waypoints for characters and cameras can be difficult enough and it's not any easier if you have to do it all in code. A trick is to use the SceneComposer to create markers much like real movie makers use tape to designate where actors should move. Right-clicking on the scene node and selecting **Add Spatial.../New Node** will give us an invisible marker. Give this a recognizable name and drag it into place by using the `Move` function.

How to do it...

So now that we have a scene prepared with some waypoints we can get to work with implementing the cutscene itself by performing the following steps:

1. We start by loading a scene where the `Cinematic` will be played out. The scene reference will be used in several places, so it is a good idea to store it in a field.

2. We'll also create a `Spatial` field called Jaime, the main actor and either load or extract him from the scene (depending on the setup).

3. Now, we can create a `MotionPath` instance called `jaimePath` for Jaime. Since we created `Nodes` for each waypoint in `SceneComposer`, we can get their location from the scene by using:

   ```
   jaimePath.addWayPoint(scene.getChild("WayPoint1").
   getWorldTranslation());
   ```

4. We go on and create a `MotionEvent` called `jaimeMotionEvent` using `jaimePath` and `initialDuration` of 25 seconds:

```
jaimeMotionEvent = new MotionEvent(jaime, jaimePath, 25f);
```

5. It's also preferable if Jaime faces in the direction of the path he travels along, so we also set `directionType` to `MotionEvent.Direction.Path`.

Before we get too far, we want to check out that the path Jaime follows is alright. Therefore, we should go ahead and create a `Cinematic` instance at this point. To do this, perform the following steps:

1. Doing this is as simple as supplying it with a scene, which will affect `rootNode` together with the total duration of the cinematic:

```
cinematic = new Cinematic(scene, 60f);
```

2. After that, we add `MotionEvent` with the following line; 0 being the time it should start at:

```
cinematic.addCinematicEvent(0, jaimeMotionEvent);
```

3. We also need to add cinematic to the `stateManager` of the application with `stateManager.attach(cinematic)`.

4. Calling `cinematic.play()` at this point should display Jaime sliding along the path.

Once we're happy with it, we can go on and do the camera work as follows:

1. The `Cinematic` instance will create a `CameraNode` for us if we call `cinematic.bindCamera("cam1", cam)`, so let's do that for our first camera. The string is the reference that `Cinematic` will know the camera by.

2. It will be a camera that pans so we create a `MotionPath` instance and a `MotionEvent` instance for it. Again, we can get the waypoints of the camera path from the scene. Since the `Node` we added in `SceneComposer` by default snaps to the ground, we need to add between 1.5f and 2.0f to the y axis to get it to a suitable height.

3. The camera should look at a fixed point as it pans, so we set `directionType` of camera's `MotionEvent` to `LookAt` and then also set the direction it should look at with `cam1Event.setLookAt` where the first `Vector3f` is the location to look at and the second is `Vector3f`, which is up in the world:

```
cam1Event = new MotionEvent(camNode, camPath1, 5f);       cam1Event.
setDirectionType(MotionEvent.Direction.LookAt);
cam1Event.setLookAt(Vector3f.UNIT_X.mult(100), Vector3f.UNIT_Y);
```

4. With that done, we can test the first camera pan. We do that by calling the following code:

```
cinematic.activateCamera(0, "cam1");
```

5. The next camera will get its own `MotionPath` and `MotionEvent` instances and can similarly get its own `CameraNode`. It's perfectly fine to use the same physical camera for both of the CameraNodes.

Now, we can start doing something about the lack of animation in the scene.

1. The first thing Jaime does in the scene is walk towards the beach. We can create a new `AnimationEvent` instance that uses the `Walk` animation:

    ```
    AnimationEventwalkEvent = new AnimationEvent(jaime, "Walk",
    LoopMode.Loop);
    ```

2. We then add it to `cinematic` at 0 seconds:

    ```
    cinematic.addCinematicEvent(0, walkEvent);
    ```

3. Jaime should stop when he reaches the last waypoint, which is also when the `jaimeMotionEvent` ends. So we create another `AnimationEvent` with the idle animation and add it at the end of the duration of the `jaimeMotionEvent`.

At the time of writing this, it seems the cinematic doesn't end the animation when it starts a new one, so we have to do something to stop it ourselves. Using a MotionPathListener, we can check when the final waypoint is reached and manually stop the walking animation:

```
jaimePath.addListener(new MotionPathListener() {
   public void onWayPointReach(MotionEventmotionControl,
intwayPointIndex) {
      if(wayPointIndex == 2){
        walkEvent.stop();
      }
   }
});
```

How it works...

The `Cinematic` acts as a sequencer for all the different events and apart from firing events at the defined intervals, we can instead use `cinematic.enqueueCinematicEvent`. Doing so will start the supplied event just after the previous one is done. This can be useful if we want to trigger a series of animations right after each other. Cinematics can also be set to loop or cycle just like `MotionEvents` and you don't need to start them at time 0.

In conclusion, using cinematics is not particularly technical. It's just difficult to get all the positions, angles, and timings right, especially since there's no intelligence or collision involved in the script. Once you get it right, however, the result will be extremely rewarding.

Using a positional audio and environmental effects

Audio is an incredibly powerful mood setter and should not be overlooked in a game. In this recipe, we'll go through how to make the most of your sound assets using runtime effects and settings. If you're simply looking for omnipresent sounds or the basics on how to play them, check out *Chapter 1, SDK Game Development Hub*.

This recipe will do well in an FPS, where you have a number of footstep sounds that are played when the player moves around. However, the principle is true for any short sound that is played often enough to sound repetitive.

We'll approach this recipe in two steps:

1. First, we will learn how to vary a basic, repetitive sound. We can achieve this by varying the sound's pitch and using `LowPassFilter`.

2. In the second step, we'll use reverb to vary it further, depending on the scene.

How to do it...

First of all, we need some basics set up.

1. We create a new application extending `SimpleApplication`, and add an `AudioNode` field called `audioNode`.

2. In addition to this, we need to keep track of passed time with a `float` field called `time` and another `float` field called `pauseTime`, which we set to `0.7f`.

3. In the `simpleInitApp` method, we create a new `audioNode` instance:

    ```
    new AudioNode(assetManager, "Sound/Effects/Foot steps.ogg");
    ```

4. We override the `simpleUpdate` method and begin by checking whether `time` is more than `pauseTime`.

5. If it is, we should set a new float called `pitch`. This should have a value of `1f +- 10%`, which can be achieved with the following code:

    ```
    FastMath.nextRandomFloat() * 0.2f + 0.9f.
    ```

6. Then, we call `audioNode.setPitch(pitch)` to set it.

7. Since this particular sound file plays four footsteps in sequence, we tell the node to not start from the beginning and only play the last of the footsteps by skipping forward in time, using the following code:

    ```
    audioNode.setTimeOffset(2.0f);
    audioNode.playInstance();
    ```

8. Before exiting the `if` statement, we set `time` to `0`.

9. Finally, we shouldn't forget to increase `time` by tpf.

10. Try running the application now. We should hear the same sound over and over again but with a slight variation.

11. We can use `LowPassFilter` to further vary the sound. We instantiate it by supplying a float for the general volume, and another for the high frequency volume. To get the most variation, we can supply two random values between 0f and 1f:

    ```
    LowPassFilter filter = new LowPassFilter(FastMath.
    nextRandomFloat(), FastMath.nextRandomFloat());
    ```

12. Then, we call `audioNode.setDryFilter(filter)` before `audioNode.playInstance()`.

13. When we play it again, we should hear a slightly more varied sound that from time to time gets more muffled.

Reverb is another parameter we can use for our sounds. But unlike the previous examples, this should not be randomized each time we play it (or randomized at all!). We can add reverb using the following steps:

1. Create a new instance of `Environment` in the `simpleInitApp` method using one of the premade static ones in the `Environment` class and telling the application's `audioRenderer` to use it:

   ```
   Environment env = Environment.Cavern;
   audioRenderer.setEnvironment(env);
   ```

2. Running the application again with this environment should give each footstep a huge echo.

How it works...

In the first part of the recipe, we varied a single sound by changing its pitch slightly every time it was played. This will still sound repetitive and it is recommended to have several premade variants of a sound and use it in combination with this technique to get more out of them.

At the time of writing this, filters are not developed past `LowPassFilter` and have a limited use. It can still be used to cut the dryness of the sound and make it more muffled, as if heard through a wall, for example.

Having a sound file with a sequence of footsteps, like the one in the test-data library is fine for some types of games. They work best when you know how far a character will move each time, such as in an RTS or turn-based game. In an FPS, however, where we don't know how fast or far a player decides to move, it's better to have footstep sounds split up and played individually based on movement speed.

Using an `Environment` class is a great way to add immersion to sounds without having to bake the effect into the sound file. Controlling the effect unless it's level-wide can be a bit trickier. For example, you may want more reverb outside than in a furnished room. One way could be to use the trigger system from earlier in the chapter and big bounding volumes triggering a change in environment as the player enters their area.

In this example, we used the `setDryFilter` method of the `audioNode`. This will not modify any reverb coming from the environment. To do that, we have to use `setReverbFilter`.

There's more

The recipe has covered playing audio originating from the player. It is almost as easy doing this for other entities in the scene. Since `AudioNode` extends `Node`, it has a position in the scene graph. Attaching an `AudioNode` instance to the scene graph will play the sound using its `worldTranslation` field, just like how a model will be shown at that location.

Apart from setting `localTranslation`, we also need to make sure that the positional Boolean in `AudioNode` is `true` (which it is by default). We're also only allowed to use mono channel sounds when using positional audio.

Information Fragments

Introduction

This appendix contains various bits of code and procedures that are too generic to appear in regular chapters. They are used across several chapters but are presented here to avoid repetition.

This appendix covers the following topics:

- Downloading the plugins
- Enabling nightly builds
- Adding Bullet physics to the application
- Jaime animation frames for phonemes
- The `AnimationEvent` patch
- The `ImageGenerator` class
- The `CellUtil` class

Downloading the plugins

Go to the **Tools** menu and select **Plugins**. In the **Available Plugins** tab, look for the plugin you would like to install, check the box next to it, and select **Install**.

Enabling nightly builds

Nightly builds will give you the latest updates from the jMonkeyEngine repository, but it should be mentioned that these are unstable. From time to time, functions may be broken, and there is no guarantee at all that they can be built. To enable nightly builds, perform the following steps:

1. In the SDK, go to the **Tools** menu and select **Plugins**.
2. Go to the **Settings** tab and check the **jMonkeyEngine SDK Nightly (Breaks!)** checkbox.
3. To look for updates, go to the **Help** menu and select **Check for updates**.

Adding Bullet physics to the application

This section provides a description of the basic steps to add bullet physics to an application.

In the `simple InitApp` method of the application, add the following lines of code:

```
BulletAppState bulletAppState = new BulletAppState();
stateManager.attach(bulletAppState);
```

To get a basic ground and some items to play with, add the following code:

```
PhysicsTestHelper.createPhysicsTestWorldSoccer(rootNode, assetManager,
bulletAppState.getPhysicsSpace());
```

Objects that require physics should both be attached to the scene graph and have a `RigidBodyControl` object, which is added to `physicsSpace` of `bulletAppState`.

Jaime animation frames for phonemes

The following list provides a number of frames found among Jaime's animations that are suitable for use as phonemes. They can be useful for those who wish to build up a library:

- To find the AAAH phoneme, use frame 30 of the Punches animation
- To find the EEH phoneme, use frame 4 of the Wave animation
- To find the I phoneme, use frame 9 of the Wave animation
- To find the OH phoneme, use frame 22 of the Taunt animation
- To find the OOOH phoneme, use frame 15 of the Wave animation
- To find the FUH phoneme, use frame 7 of the Taunt animation

- To find the MMM phoneme, use frame 1 of the Wave animation
- To find the LUH phoneme, use frame 21 of the Punches animation
- To find the EES phoneme, use frame 22 of the Wave animation
- To find the RESET phoneme, use frame 0 of the Wave animation

The AnimationEvent patch

The following code snippet shows the patch needed for the *Lip syncing and facial expressions* recipe of *Chapter 4, Mastering Character Animations*. Apply this to the file in your project. If you're applying it manually, the constructor must be added to `AnimationEvent`, and the following lines of code have to go into the `initEvent` method just after `cinematic.putEventData(MODEL_CHANNELS, model, s);`:

```
int numChannels = model.getControl(AnimControl.class).
getNumChannels();
for(int i = 0; i < numChannels; i++){
  ((HashMap<Integer, AnimChannel>)s).put(i, model.
    getControl(AnimControl.class).getChannel(i));
}
```

The full patch is:

```
Index: AnimationEvent.java
===================================================================
— AnimationEvent.java      (revision 11001)
+++ AnimationEvent.java      (working copy)
@@ -221,6 +221,24 @@
  initialDuration = model.getControl(AnimControl.class).getAnimationLen
    gth(animationName);
  this.channelIndex = channelIndex;
}
+
+/**
+ * creates an animation event
+ *
+ * @param model the model on which the animation will be played
+ * @param animationName the name of the animation to play
+ * @param channelIndex the index of the channel default is 0. Events
on the
+ * @param blendTime the time during the animation are going to be
blended
+ * same channelIndex will use the same channel.
+ */
```

```
+public AnimationEvent(Spatial model, String animationName, LoopMode
loopMode, int channelIndex, float blendTime) {
+this.model = model;
+this.animationName = animationName;
+this.loopMode = loopMode;
+initialDuration = model.getControl(AnimControl.class).getAnimationLen
gth(animationName);
+this.channelIndex = channelIndex;
+this.blendTime = blendTime;
+}

/**
* creates an animation event
@@ -264,11 +282,16 @@
Object s = cinematic.getEventData(MODEL_CHANNELS, model);
if (s == null) {
s = new HashMap<integer , AnimChannel>();
+int numChannels = model.getControl(AnimControl.class).
getNumChannels();
+for(int i = 0; i < numChannels; i++){
+ ((HashMap<Integer, AnimChannel>)s).put(i, model.
getControl(AnimControl.class).getChannel(i));
+}
cinematic.putEventData(MODEL_CHANNELS, model, s);
 }

Map</integer><integer , AnimChannel> map = (Map</integer><integer ,
AnimChannel>) s;
this.channel = map.get(channelIndex);
+
if (this.channel == null) {
if (model == null) {
                    //the model is null we try to find it according
to the name
```

The ImageGenerator class

The ImageGenerator class is used in the *Using noise to generate a terrain* recipe of *Chapter 3, World Building*. The code to create this class is as follows:

```
public class ImageGenerator {

  public static void generateImage(float[][] terrain){
    int size = terrain.length;
```

```
    int grey;

    BufferedImage img = new BufferedImage(size, size, BufferedImage.
    TYPE_INT_RGB);
    for(int y = 0; y < size; y++){
      for(int x = 0; x < size; x++){
        double result = terrain[x][y];

        grey = (int) (result * 255);
        int color = (grey << 16) | (grey << 8) | grey;
        img.setRGB(x, y, color);

      }
    }

    try {
      ImageIO.write(img, "png", new File("assets/Textures/heightmap.
    png"));
    } catch (IOException ex) {
        Logger.getLogger(NoiseMapGenerator.class.getName()).
    log(Level.SEVERE, null, ex);
      }
    }
}
```

The CellUtil class

The `CellUtil` class is used in the *Flowing water with cellular automata* recipe of *Chapter 3, World Building*. The code to create this class is as follows:

```
public class CellUtil {

  private static int[][] directions = new int[][]{{0,-1},{1,-
    1},{1,0},{1,1},{0,1},{-1,1},{-1,0},{-1,-1}};
  public static int getDirection(int x, int y){
    witch(x){
      case 1:
      switch(y){
        case -1:
        return 1;
        case 0:
        return 2;
        case 1:
        return 3;
```

```
        }
        break;
        case -1:
        switch(y){
          case -1:
          return 7;
          case 0:
          return 6;
          case 1:
          return 5;
        }
        break;
        case 0:
        switch(y){
          case -1:
          return 0;
          case 0:
          return -1;
          case 1:
          return 4;
        }
        break;
      }
      return -1;
    }

  public static int[] getDirection(int dir){
   return directions[dir];
   }
  }
```

Index

L

lean around corners feature
  using 60-63
leanValue field 62
level
  loading 204, 205
light
  adding 14-16
LightControl class 74
lightmap 73
LightScatteringFilter 261
light types
  about 72
  ambient light 72
  directional light 72
  point light 72
  spot light 72
LimbDampening 121
linking
  versus adding 10
lip syncing 111-114
lowCollisions field 65
low cover 64
lowHeight variable 64

M

managing options menu
  initializing 154-158
Material parameter 81
maxImages property 26
maxLean field 62
maxTime option 251
mini map
  offscreen rendering, used for 175-179
model
  importing 9
modelspace 115
modifyTerrain method 94
MonkeyZone
  URL 203
MotionEvent 262
MotionPaths
  complex movements, performing
    with 262, 263

movement of lights
  controlling 72-74
moveSpeed 32
moveTiles method 82
multiple gravity sources
  handling 222-225
muzzle flash emitter
  creating 242
muzzle flashes
  creating, ParticleEmitter used 242-244

N

NavMesh
  using 140-143
NavMesh generation
  in SDK 138, 139
network
  firing over 207-209
network code
  implementing, for FPS 194-203
networked physics
  implementing 234-239
network message
  defining 235
Nifty GUI
  about 153
  initializing 154-158
nightly builds
  enabling 272
node 148
node object
  defining 149
noise
  used, to generate terrain 70-72
non-instant bullets
  firing 42-45

O

offscreen rendering
  about 178
  used, for mini map 175-179
onAction method 81
onAnalog method 34
onAnimCycleDone method 105
outputToConsole method 165

P

ParticleEmitter
  used, for creating muzzle flashes 242-244
  using 22-25
ParticleEmitter class
  configuring 24
ParticleInfluencer class 28
ParticleInfluencer instance
  creating 26
Pathfinding 140
PatrolState 132
Phoneme 111
phonemes
  Jaime animation frames, used for 272
player positions
  interpolating between 205, 206
plugins
  downloading 271
point light 72
postprocessing filters
  scene, improving with 260, 261
project
  setting up 8
pushable door
  creating 214-217

R

RANGE field 43
real-time strategy. *See* **RTS**
RetreatState 132
reusable AI control class
  creating 124-127
reusable character control
  creating 32-37
rocket engine
  building 217-220
role playing game (RPG) 31
rotate method 48
RotationalLimitMotors
  used, for self-balancing 226-229
RotationSpeed method 57
Roughness slider 72
RPG dialog screen
  creating 161-164

RTS

  about 31
  units, selecting 50-54
RTS camera AppState
  creating 45-50

S

scene
  improving, with postprocessing
      filters 260, 261
Scene Composer
  using 9-11
screen
  about 153
  loading 158-160
SDK
  advanced ParticleEmitter 25-29
  ambient audio, adding 18, 19
  animations, previewing 98
  attachment node, obtaining 21, 22
  bitmap fonts, creating with
      Font Creator 20, 21
  filter used, for adding water 16, 17
  heightmaps, modifying with Terrain
      Editor 12-14
  light, adding 14-16
  model, importing 9
  NavMesh generation, using 138, 139
  ParticleEmitter, using 22-25
  project, setting up 8
  Scene Composer, using 9-11
  sky box, adding 14-16
  URL 8
SelectAppState 51
self-balancing
  creating, RotationalLimitMotors
      used 226-229
server
  setting up 182, 183
ServerMessage 185
server-side implementation 236
setSpatial method 83
settings page
  customizing 172-175

simpleInitApp method 19
simpleUpdate method 44
Six Degrees of Freedom (SixDof) 226
SkeletonControl class 22
sky box
  adding 14-16
SpawnTarget option 248
SpiderMonkey 182
spotInnerAngle parameter 73
spot light 72
spotOuterAngle parameter 73
stateAttached method 39
stateDetached method 39
status field 187
subanimation
  creating 110
  extracting 110, 111

T

targetLocation variable 54
TCP
  versus UDP 182
terrain
  deforming 75-77
  generating, noise used 70-72
Terrain Editor
  heightmaps, modifying with 12-14
TestJoystick 60
Texture field 13
Timer object
  creating 249-251
toggleConsole() method 165
tree distribution
  automating 77-79
treeLimit field 78
treeNode field 78

triggered explosion
  implementing 249-251
triggers
  AI, controlling with 253, 254
trigger system
  creating 245-248

U

UDP
  versus TCP 182
units
  selecting, in RTS 50-54
update method 27, 47, 252
updateParticle method 25
updateTiles method 82
Util class
  creating 176

V

vertex lighting 74
vision 128-130
Volume property 19

W

walkDirection vector 67
water
  adding, filter used 16-18
  flowing, with cellular automata 84-89
WaterFieldControl class 88
while loop 27

Y

yaw field 34

Thank you for buying
jMonkeyEngine 3.0 Cookbook

About Packt Publishing

Packt, pronounced 'packed', published its first book "*Mastering phpMyAdmin for Effective MySQL Management*" in April 2004 and subsequently continued to specialize in publishing highly focused books on specific technologies and solutions.

Our books and publications share the experiences of your fellow IT professionals in adapting and customizing today's systems, applications, and frameworks. Our solution based books give you the knowledge and power to customize the software and technologies you're using to get the job done. Packt books are more specific and less general than the IT books you have seen in the past. Our unique business model allows us to bring you more focused information, giving you more of what you need to know, and less of what you don't.

Packt is a modern, yet unique publishing company, which focuses on producing quality, cutting-edge books for communities of developers, administrators, and newbies alike. For more information, please visit our website: www.packtpub.com.

About Packt Open Source

In 2010, Packt launched two new brands, Packt Open Source and Packt Enterprise, in order to continue its focus on specialization. This book is part of the Packt Open Source brand, home to books published on software built around Open Source licenses, and offering information to anybody from advanced developers to budding web designers. The Open Source brand also runs Packt's Open Source Royalty Scheme, by which Packt gives a royalty to each Open Source project about whose software a book is sold.

Writing for Packt

We welcome all inquiries from people who are interested in authoring. Book proposals should be sent to author@packtpub.com. If your book idea is still at an early stage and you would like to discuss it first before writing a formal book proposal, contact us; one of our commissioning editors will get in touch with you.

We're not just looking for published authors; if you have strong technical skills but no writing experience, our experienced editors can help you develop a writing career, or simply get some additional reward for your expertise.

jMonkeyEngine 3.0 Beginner's Guide

ISBN: 978-1-84951-646-4   Paperback: 352 pages

Develop professional 3D games for desktop, web, and mobile, all in the familiar Java programming language

1. Create 3D games that run on Android devices, Windows, Mac OS, Linux desktop PCs, and in web browsers—for commercial, hobbyists, or educational purposes.

2. Follow end-to-end examples that teach essential concepts and processes of game development, from the basic layout of a scene to interactive game characters.

3. Make your artwork come alive and publish your game to multiple platforms, all from one unified development environment.

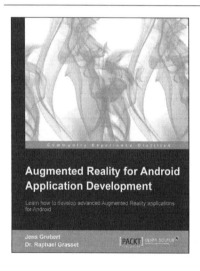

Augmented Reality for Android Application Development

ISBN: 978-1-78216-855-3   Paperback: 130 pages

Learn how to develop advanced Augmented Reality applications for Android

1. Understand the main concepts and architectural components of an AR application.

2. Step-by-step learning through hands-on programming combined with a background of important mathematical concepts.

3. Efficiently and robustly implement some of the main functional AR aspects.

Please check **www.PacktPub.com** for information on our titles

Monkey Game Development Beginner's Guide

ISBN: 978-1-84969-203-8   Paperback: 402 pages

Create monetized 2D games deployable to almost any platform

1. Create eight fun 2D games.

2. Understand how to structure your code, your data structures, and how to set up the control flow of a modern 2D game.

3. Learn how to deploy your games to iOS, Android, XNA (Xbox, Windows Phone 7), and desktop platforms (Windows, OS X).

Unity 3.x Game Development by Example Beginner's Guide

ISBN: 978-1-84969-184-0   Paperback: 408 pages

A seat-of-your-pants manual for building fun, groovy little games quickly with Unity 3.x

1. Build fun games using the free Unity game engine even if you've never coded before.

2. Learn how to "skin" projects to make totally different games from the same file – more games, less effort!

3. Deploy your games to the Internet so that your friends and family can play them.

4. Packed with ideas, inspiration, and advice for your own game design and development.

Please check **www.PacktPub.com** for information on our titles

Made in the USA
San Bernardino, CA
11 March 2015